The Ends of Critique

New Critical Humanities

Series Editors: Birgit M. Kaiser, Associate Professor of Comparative Literature, Utrecht University, Timothy O'Leary, Professor of Philosophy, UNSW, Sydney, and Kathrin Thiele, Associate Professor of Gender Studies and Critical Theory, Utrecht University

In this time of global crises, from the COVID-19 pandemic and climate change to transnational inequalities and persistent racial injustices, the value of the critical humanities and their intervention into public discourse is once again of central concern. This series publishes books that demonstrate an understanding of critique in action, while also questioning and redefining its inherited methodologies and perspectives. The books in this series contribute to a reimagination of critique; its powers, its strengths, and its transformative potential. Grounded in the core humanities disciplines (including philosophy, literature, gender studies, and cultural studies), the series challenges and sharpens the question of critique itself, thus situating the critical humanities at the center of envisioned collective responses to the fundamental demands of the twenty-first century.

The series is linked to the international research network *Terra Critica: Interdisciplinary Network for the Critical Humanities*, which the editors Birgit M. Kaiser and Kathrin Thiele founded and coordinate since 2012 (www.terracritica.net), and of which Timothy O'Leary is a member.

Untranslating Machines: A Genealogy for the Ends of Global Thought
Jacques Lezra
Naturally Late: Synchronisation in Socially Constructed Times
Will Johncock
Urban Arabesques: Philosophy, Hong Kong, Transversality
Gray Kochhar-Lindgren
Revolts in Cultural Critique
Rosemarie Buikema
Diffractive Reading: New Materialism, Theory, Critique
Edited by Kai Merten
The Ends of Critique: Methods, Institutions, Politics
Edited by Kathrin Thiele, Birgit M. Kaiser, and Timothy O'Leary

The Ends of Critique

Methods, Institutions, Politics

Edited by
Kathrin Thiele, Birgit M. Kaiser, and
Timothy O'Leary

ROWMAN & LITTLEFIELD
Lanham • Boulder • New York • London

Published by Rowman & Littlefield
An imprint of The Rowman & Littlefield Publishing Group, Inc.
4501 Forbes Boulevard, Suite 200, Lanham, Maryland 20706
www.rowman.com

Selection and editorial matter copyright © 2021 by Kathrin Thiele; Birgit M. Kaiser and Timothy O'Leary.

Copyright in individual chapters is held by the respective chapter authors.

All rights reserved. No part of this book may be reproduced in any form or by any electronic or mechanical means, including information storage and retrieval systems, without written permission from the publisher, except by a reviewer who may quote passages in a review.

British Library Cataloguing in Publication Information Available

Library of Congress Cataloging-in-Publication Data

Names: Thiele, Kathrin, 1972– editor. | Kaiser, Birgit Mara, editor. | O'Leary, Timothy, 1966– editor.
Title: The ends of critique : methods, institutions, politics / edited by Kathrin Thiele, Birgit M. Kaiser and Timothy O'Leary.
Description: Lanham : Rowman & Littlefield, 2021. | Series: New critical humanities | Includes bibliographical references and index.
Identifiers: LCCN 2021029531 (print) | LCCN 2021029532 (ebook) |
  ISBN 9781786616463 (cloth) | ISBN 9781538160534 (paperback) |
  ISBN 9781786616470 (epub)
Subjects: LCSH: Critical theory. | Criticism. | Critical thinking. | MESH: Essays. lcgft
Classification: LCC B809.3 .E53 2021 (print) | LCC B809.3 (ebook) | DDC 160—dc23
LC record available at https://lccn.loc.gov/2021029531
LC ebook record available at https://lccn.loc.gov/2021029532

∞™ The paper used in this publication meets the minimum requirements of American National Standard for Information Sciences—Permanence of Paper for Printed Library Materials, ANSI/NISO Z39.48-1992.

Contents

Acknowledgments   vii

Introduction   1
Birgit M. Kaiser, Kathrin Thiele, and Timothy O'Leary

PART I: VISIONS OF CRITIQUE

1   "*After* Humanism?"—Time and Transformation in
Critical Thinking   19
Kathrin Thiele

2   The Most Difficult Task: On the Idea of an Impure Pure
Nonviolence in Derrida   41
Leonard Lawlor

3   The Changeability of the World: Utopia and Critique   57
Sam McAuliffe

4   Seeking Intelligent Life in the Time of COVID-19, or, Thinking
"Epicritically"   77
Jennifer A. Wagner-Lawlor

PART II: CRITICAL READING

5   Suspicious Minds: Critique as Symptomatic Reading   97
Esther Peeren

6   The Ends of Critical Intimacy: Spivak, Fanon, and Appropriative
Reading   117
Birgit M. Kaiser

7	Critical Vivisection: Transforming Ethical Sensibilities *Timothy O'Leary*	139

PART III: INSTITUTIONS AND TECHNOLOGIES

8	Unwinding the Abstraction of Whiteness *Shannon Winnubst*	161
9	How Not to Be Governed Like That by Our Digital Technologies *Mercedes Bunz*	179
10	Defective Institutions: or, Critique *Jacques Lezra*	201
Index		219
About the Contributors		223

Acknowledgments

The editors want to thank all members of the *Terra Critica* collective who participated in the production of this volume, especially through reading and commenting on one another's work. Their shared commitment and expertise has made this volume a truly collective endeavor. We are also thankful to Ella van Driel for her editing support and good spirits during the publication process. Much gratitude also goes to Kader Attia for granting us permission to reproduce his artwork *Traditional Repair, Immaterial Injury, 2014–2018*, on the cover of this volume.

This volume could not have been made available in Open Access without the generous support of Utrecht University and UNSW Sydney.

Introduction

Birgit M. Kaiser, Kathrin Thiele, and Timothy O'Leary

CRITIQUE

The question of the ends of critique is central to this volume. We ask after the ends of critique, after its purposes and how it figures today, at a time when the traditional forms of critique might be said to have reached their end. This problem of ends—implying both *telos* and termination—guides all the contributions gathered here as they explore the methods, institutions, and politics of critique. What is the point of critique today, we might ask—or has it come to an end? This double evocation of ends echoes Jacques Derrida's unfolding of a similar doubling in his early text "The Ends of Man" (1972), in which he deconstructs anthropocentric humanism and does so precisely by unraveling the dynamic of end (purpose) and end (termination).[1] The chapters in this volume are equally committed to a foundational questioning of the end—of the temporality that underlies the notion of having come to an end of critique as well as of the teleology implicit in striving for an end. We are especially also questioning the figure of "Man" as the figure that underpins the very temporality of *telos* and termination and with this the very tradition of critique in Western thought practice.

The question of critique always poses itself anew, for its own moment. It might be said that critique is in essence nothing but an assessment of and an intervention into the present, with a view to an altered future. It is, as Michel Foucault suggests, a "curious activity" with a very long history, yet one which always hones in on its own present, as "a means for a future or a truth that it will not know nor happen to be" (1997, 42). Hence, as the contributors to this volume will also propose, critique always poses itself as a question for, of, and to the present, with a view to transformation. However, at our current historical juncture, at the beginning of the 2020s, it seems as if critique itself is (again) at a particular critical moment. Its terrain is shifting in multiple ways. When listening, for example, to the recent protests in many countries of the Global North, where anti-vaxxers, QAnon shamans, conspiracy theorists, and COVID-19-deniers meet to voice their discontent with the current state of the world—a status quo they identify, in a mix of right-wing populism, anti-intellectualism, racism and anti-Semitism, as upheld by "the deep state" and "elite minorities"—it is striking that they present themselves as concerned citizens, as critical, suspicious minds. Despite the disparate worries about alleged child-trafficking, DNA-altering vaccination or mind-control through 5G technology, what comes together offline at rallies and online under different hashtags is "a strong suspicion of the establishment" (Sardarizadeh 2020). This recalls what Bruno Latour already diagnosed almost twenty years ago:

> Remember the good old days when university professors could look down on unsophisticated folks because those hillbillies naïvely believed in church, motherhood, and apple pie? Things have changed a lot . . . I am now the one who naïvely believes in some facts because I am educated, while the other guys are too *un*sophisticated to be gullible. (2004, 228)

Many participating in these movements today describe their realizations of, for example, #pizzagate or #SaveOurChildren as a moment of "awakening" after which they finally see through the "elites in power" and feel compelled to take their concerns onto the streets. But what becomes of critique if it is called upon here as a means to detect conspiracy and as an affirmation of blatant post-truth proclamations? If suspicion is invoked once more as the key mode of critique and—in a strange morphing of ideology critique—serves the claim to now see through today's (however alleged) charades of "elite" power? If critique is now employed to support calls for the (re-)emergence of authoritarian leaders, by social groups who themselves display traits of what Adorno would have identified as an authoritarian character (2019), what, we wonder, is the function of critique today?

First of all, this volume does not approach critique in the mode of suspicion that is evoked above; that is, as an exposure of alleged conspiracies. Nor is that the *modus operandi* of the research network *Terra Critica*, whose participants have been exploring the changing visions and modalities of critique in the twenty-first century since the network's founding in 2012, and from whose work this volume results (more on *Terra Critica* in the next section). And yet, as a collective holding on to the question of critique, we differ also from Latour's critical diagnosis, in his influential essay "Why Has Critique Run Out of Steam?" (2004). It is perhaps not critique *as such* that has run out of steam, but rather, partly because of the polymorphous claims currently made on it, it is critique *as we used to know it* that has run out of steam.

Critique is currently receiving renewed attention from various sides, including the right-wing populisms touched on above, and it is into this constantly changing landscape of conflicting claims on and assessments of critique that this volume intervenes. By way of introduction, we want to sketch the terrain on which we see critique currently challenged to reinvent itself. *Terra Critica* itself was founded almost a decade ago as one intervention into that shifting terrain. Since then, the question regarding the efficacy of critique in view of "the planetary condition" (Bunz et al. 2017) has only been growing more complex. With this volume—the second *Terra Critica* book publication after the *Critical Vocabulary: Symptoms of the Planetary Condition* (2017)—its editors and authors, who are all part of the collective, aim to intervene again into the current debates around critique.

As already noted above, the proclamation of the end of critique—that critique is over, that it has run its course and is *passé*—is a recurrent claim in the scholarly debates on critique in these last, indeed critical, decades on the planet. Prominently, Latour articulated this in "Why Has Critique Run Out of Steam? From Matters of Fact to Matters of Concern" (2004), but more recently forms of it can also be found in Rita Felski's *The Limits of Critique* (2015) and the terminological suggestion of "postcritique." The proposition of postcritique (or the limits of critique) focuses on critique as an analysis of the (cultural) text that is founded on suspicion, on "what Ricoeur calls a *hermeneutics of suspicion*" (Felski 2015, 1). While Felski endeavors to *specify* the particular mood or method that critique has come to imply (and thus does not discard critique *per se*),[2] she associates critique firmly with suspicion and with critics who speak from seemingly elevated, exceptional positions of insight: "Critics read against the grain and between the lines; their self-appointed task is to draw out what a text fails—or willfully refuses—to see." (1) Postcritique wishes to counter that "suspicious mind-set" (9) by a pragmatism that cuts critique down to size, as one analytic endeavor among many. Felski's attempt to delineate this particular mode of critique as an exceptional methodological sensibility draws mostly on the field of literary critique and it is in that field that such nonsuspicious modes of critique (or noncritical ways of reading) have found resonance.[3] The call for a shift of terrain is evident: the proposition is to move *beyond* critique, which is defined largely as a form of suspicion, a predisposition that must be overcome by moving toward greater pragmatism or objectivity.

Suspicion is indeed a strong legacy of critique, especially when we think back to one of its dominant manifestations in the form of ideology critique. But it is certainly not the only one. Reducing critique to suspicion (or its particular instantiation as *Crrritique*) misses the mark.[4] And declaring critique on that basis as finished and moving on to other terrains repeats the well-known gesture of a critical teleological progress, rather than breaking with it. While this critical endeavor is a necessary and welcome critique of critique itself, it is one that sees a move beyond critique, a move onto other noncritical terrains, as the only way forward. A similar move can be found in works such as Pamela Fraser and Roger Rothman's edited collection *Beyond Critique: Contemporary Art in Theory, Practice, and Instruction* (2017). Next to its quite specific focus on the role of critique in the arts, and despite the plurivocal conversation it offers between the different contributions, Fraser and Rothman also propose that critique has come to an end and that it is time to move beyond it. With their equally strong characterization of critique as operating primarily via suspicion and as tied quite exclusively to the (ideology-)critical legacy of the Frankfurt school, the end of critique that is declared is in fact directed at a very particular mode of Western (Eurocentric) critique.

While propositions such as Felski's postcritique or Fraser and Rothman's "beyond critique" are welcome voices of the recent renewal of attention to critical theory, criticality and critique, the broader revival of critique and critical thinking, which has gained momentum quite pronouncedly in the past five years, nonetheless remains inspired by the critical theories that link it to a hermeneutics of suspicion. In Anglo-American academic debates, for example, a pronounced return to critique became manifest with a sense of urgency in the mid-2010s, with publications such as Dino Franco Felluga's *Critical Theory: The Key Concepts* (2015), the translations into English of Rahel Jaeggi's *Alienation* (2014) and later her *Critique of Forms of Life* (2018), as well as the Mellon-funded "International Consortium of Critical Theory Programs," which is connected to publications such as Penelope Deutscher and Cristina Lafont's *Critical Theory in Critical Times* (2017) and the journal *Critical Times*.[5] The present volume relates its engagement to this renewed interest in critical work, especially also in the necessity to turn to ideas, scholars, and institutions from the Global South. We share the hesitation regarding the legacy of critical practice inherited from the enlightenment and a colonizing Europe, but at the same time we also decisively aim to stay *with* critique. And yet, while as editors of this volume we are enthusiastic about this renewed appraisal of critique, the conceptual frameworks in which critique receives renewed attention does, it seems to us, maintain the well-known critical frameworks of earlier times and this is not entirely sufficient to twenty-first-century realities.

So, our volume makes two gestures at the same time: it argues—as does the wider work of *Terra Critica*—that the shifting parameters of the planetary condition today do not call for (nor permit) an abandonment of critique *tout court*. Such a response to the condition of entangledness of critique with the very problems it aims to address would just, as the saying goes, throw out the baby with the bathwater. At the same time, while we strongly affirm the insistence of the above-referenced works on a return to critique and fully embrace that move, we also aim to question the very framing of critique and its conceptual parameters as they have been understood in Western and specifically European discourse. The significant question that poses itself to us is precisely not only the *what* of critique, but also very much the *how*; how do we re-turn (to) critique today? This approach resonates with Didier Fassin and Bernard E. Harcourt's reexamination of critique in their edited volume *A Time for Critique* (2019), where they argue that "the challenges critique faces today call for a reappraisal of its practice, and simultaneously a deepening and a displacement of our own reflection" (2).

As critical practitioners, we aim to find altered and revised visions of critique. We look for different styles of critique, so that the critical matters of (in)justice can be tackled as entangled matters and with reference to a much broader imaginative and conceptual framework of what is considered to be critical. Rather than striving to leave critique behind in order to inhabit anew the desire for neutral description and objectivity, this volume calls for a questioning of the continued securing of subject and object of critique, and it works for further specifications of the kinds of difference(s) that critical approaches can make in the world. We aim to thoroughly examine the established methods, practices, and dispositions of critique; the institutions in which it is practiced and the politics it might imply and speak for. We do this certainly in order to move past the colonial-rationalist practices of established forms of critique. Yet, we also insist on the necessity to stay *with* criticality as a troubled and troubling force of living, urgently needed in and for today; we insist on staying with the troubles and concerns of the past and present in order to inherit the legacy of critique well; an inheritance that does not demand pious preservation but bold alteration.[6]

Critical methodology itself, along with its underlying onto-epistemological frameworks, needs to be reexamined, we assert, in view of the Eurocentric legacy of the critical tradition on the one hand, and in view of the transforming sociopolitical state of affairs in the twenty-first century on the other. The realities of neoliberalism and globalization, the persistent intersections of systemic racism and sexism, the acceleration of climate change and species extinction all exemplify complex *entanglement* as the disturbing shared condition of our world.[7] One of the ends of critique today, as the contributions to this volume hold, is therefore to think through the implications of entanglement not only regarding the issues under discussion (what Latour calls the "matters of concern" [2004]), but also regarding the very methods of critique itself (what could be called the manners of concern). If entanglement is the onto-epistemological constitution of the world, then also the entanglement of knower and known—established by both contemporary human and natural sciences—must be accounted for in critical articulations. Critical practice can no longer build on the neat distinction between a (knowing) critical subject and a (known) critiqued object, which was the common analytical framework of critical investigations in which the focus remained on *what* is critiqued rather than *how* it is done. Rather, critical analyses—and this seems crucial to us—emerge from within a constellation of multifaceted connectedness and in complex, asymmetrical entanglements.

Therefore, any methodological conception of critique has to acknowledge that critical evaluation and assessment comes about from *within* the constitutive processes of change and differentiation, thus delimiting critique in specific and situated ways. Both the Hegelian tradition of dialectical negativity (overcoming by way of opposition) and the Kantian liberal tradition of critical judgment (always relying on a prefixed set of values) as the operative modes of critical analyses, leave intact the secure differentiation between subject of critique and object of critique. They leave intact the intimate onto-epistemological nexus between liberalism and colonialism, the entangled history of modernity and enslavement. As Lisa Lowe has shown in *The Intimacy of Four Continents* (2015), liberal humanism (with its ideas of freedom, property, and sovereignty) emerged historically and conceptually coterminously with "[r]acial classifications and an international division of labor" (39).[8] Freedom, Lowe writes, was "constituted through a narrative dialectic that rested simultaneously on a spatialization of the 'unfree' as exteriority and a temporal subsuming of that unfreedom as internal difference or contradiction" (39). In light of that history, this volume is based on the premise that critical theory today cannot effectively examine the conditions of global capitalism and the forms of governance in inter- and intraspecies life in the Anthropocene, with the established critical tools that are framed by liberalism and liberal democracy alone. This volume, therefore, develops a different approach to critique than recent considerations of postcritique or those based exclusively on the value of liberal theories of democracy.

Building on the work done to date by the network *Terra Critica*, this volume proposes an approach to critical thinking and planetary enactment which highlights the entangled situatedness from which analyses and interventions arise. The contributions reflect on the necessary revision of critique as method and move towards a situated, perspectival, and entangled critique. Each chapter begins with a short *vignette* that situates the author both in relation to their field of investigation and in relation to the world they inhabit. In this way, they begin to account for their own situatedness and propose a shift away from the hegemonic, traditional critical practices in the Eurocentric, Kantian, and Hegelian traditions.

METHODS, INSTITUTIONS, POLITICS

In light of the terrain sketched above, our shared starting point in this volume is that the ends of critique need to be reexamined in view of the contemporary planetary condition, in the sense of method as much as in the sense of critical disposition. This volume embarks on the endeavor of interrogating critique's methods, institutions, and politics from diverse scholarly perspectives within the humanities; incorporating interventions from decolonial and systemic, aesthetic and literary, deconstructive and (post)human(ist) perspectives. The central questions that drive the interventions in this volume are the following: What visions of critique are required to intervene into the tangle of ecological, economic, cultural, and sociopolitical conditions of today? What are today's institutions of critique; both the institutions formulating critique and the institutions submitted to critique? And also, who performs critical interventions, how and from what position(s)?

Working to revise critique under the contemporary conditions of planetary (political and/as onto-epistemological) entanglement means paying close attention to the asymmetrical relations implicit in the ecological, economic, sociopolitical constitution of today; to the transforming East-West and South-North relations; to the growing digitization of economies and cultures; and to the racialized grammar of modernity. It also means, and this is one of the volume's key propositions, understanding critique as an always situated, generative, and world-making intervention, which can never claim (conceptual) innocence.[9] *Terra Critica*, as a collective of critical combatants (Kaiser and Thiele 2020), aims for practical and theoretical interventions within and outside the academy, where theory *is* a practice and practice *is* also theorizing. This interventionist modus of critique needs to be fleshed out for the complex global situation "we" find ourselves in "today"; with "today" and "we" always examined as pressing questions for further differentiation in order not to fall for any misleading assumption of already known entities. In this way, the subtitle of the book—methods, institutions, politics—indicates the kind of difference that this inquiry into the ends of critique aims to make. It can be argued that all the chapters collected in the volume pay attention to all three of these dimensions of critique: the issue of critical methods or methodologies, the connection to specific institutional settings and the political horizon of critique. Yet, it is in the divergent composition of how these dimensions are addressed in each contribution that plurivocal and partial responses to the concern around the ends of critique are produced.[10] Working together in the *Terra Critica* collective over many years, we have learned to appreciate divergences in conversation as opening up space for a multiplicity of critical inquiries.

In the final part of this introduction, the overview of the chapters will address in more detail the particular focus chosen in each contribution. But it is important to clarify here that our concern with the ends of critique does not look for a final, definitive answer. Instead, this volume hopes to provide opening strategies—on the methodological, institutional, and political level—for engaged critical debates, affirmative critical investigations and ongoing critical conversations. The combination of a common concern—the ends of critique today—with the affirmation of divergent and singularly embedded contributions, has led us also to the decision to mark the "today-ness" of each chapter; that is, to make explicit the specific instance or experiential situation which triggered the interventions for the authors. For that purpose, as mentioned above, each chapter starts with a *vignette*. This attention to situatedness and to critique as perspectival seems to us essential if we are to develop a revisioning of critique that aims to avoid universalizing gestures, presupposed critical values, and a supposedly homogenous canon of critical knowledge. The volume thus reexamines the stakes of critique under conditions of global entanglement and asymmetrical relations. We are convinced that a mere guarding of intellectual territories, or self-preserving architectures of institutional division, are insufficient to the challenges faced today. Critical self-reflexivity in the field of critical studies and critique, in the widest sense, is now overdue.

Before proceeding to an overview of each chapter in the volume, a few words on the *Terra Critica* network. *Terra Critica* brings together scholars from diverse fields, in critical and cultural theory, philosophy, sociology, gender studies, comparative literature, digital cultures, the arts, and posthuman(ist) and postcolonial studies.[11] *Terra Critica* was founded at Utrecht University in 2012, as a response to the increasing pressures on the humanities and critical scholarship—largely by a neoliberalist market logic put on the university, society and, in a broader sense, knowledge production itself—in the wake of the financial crisis of 2008 with its full impact on Dutch universities (and the broader cultural sector) after 2010.

The questions that posed themselves back then were: How do we, as academics, intellectuals, teachers, respond in a politically (and scholarly) viable manner to the increasing pressure of the market logic that since then produces such a problematic shift in higher education? How do we continue critical scholarship in a climate that invests mainly in "applicable" knowledge production and "impact," with deliverables for financial profit? And how to move forward as critical thinkers when the critical methods, inherited from the European Enlightenment, themselves need to be subjected to an analysis of their own onto-epistemological colonial-patriarchal-capitalist (CPC) legacy? In view of the existential pressures of globalized capitalism, "to be on the good side" becomes a nearly impossible task and the space of the university is no longer by default a critical space (if it ever was). So, if critique as a mode of (institutional) knowledge production, as an (ethico-political) attitude, and as a (praxis-based) methodology is a very specific quality of the humanities, how can we who are invested in the humanities *keep* this tool (in light of shrinking institutional space for criticality and an increasing demand of the applicability of scholarship); *and yet*, how must we also transform or rethink our intellectual habitats (in light of their Eurocentric legacy and colonial entanglements)? Convinced that criticality is still one of the humanities' key contributions to our lived realities, this volume affirmatively strives to re-vision and re-turn (to) critique otherwise and to reexamine critical thinking under the ever more complex conditions of the twenty-first century.

Whereas in 2012, at the moment of inaugurating *Terra Critica*, the question of critique was increasingly sidelined in an academic climate that claimed to no longer be in need of critiques of governing structures (the neoliberal fallacy), critique has quickly arisen to new prominence in the second half of the 2010s, when sociopolitical and ecologico-economic catastrophes are proliferating all over the globe. Thus, the questions out of which *Terra Critica* arose a decade ago still pose themselves today, maybe even with more urgency and with the additional twist of the contemporary populist claims on critique noted at the opening, which will not so easily disappear in the future. Whatever the fate of neoliberal governance might be "after" COVID-19, we can already be certain that the methods of critique need to be sharpened and made adequate to the tasks that will have to be faced in that future.

THE ENDS OF CRITIQUE: OVERVIEW

The volume is divided into three sections: Part I, Visions of Critique; Part II, Critical Reading; and Part III, Institutions and Technologies. This division, however, should not be taken to be exclusionary; in fact, each chapter in the volume addresses to varying degrees the three angles of interrogation that we identified above: revisioning critique and its methodologies; reworking modes and methods of critical reading; and engaging with the political, institutional, and technological contexts and subjects of critique. As we explained above, our aim is not to produce a neat delineation of the ends of critique, but rather a diffractive arrangement that produces echoes and interferences between chapters and invites further critical conversations and debates. A diffractive approach across disciplines and perspectives is far more promising for future critical work than blindly maintaining the conventions of critical delimitation and stubbornly remaining within disciplinary borders. As editors, we hope that readers will experience a full range of echoes and resonances between and across these chapters. Part of this resonance is due to the mode of work of the *Terra Critica* network itself. The chapters collected here grew out of intensive discussions in the context of *Terra Critica* workshops over the past five years. Those annual meetings were always based on shared readings, some of which (e.g., Foucault's "What is critique?," Félix Guattari's *The Three Ecologies*, Sylvia Wynter's "Unsettling the Coloniality of Being," Derrida's "The Ends of Man," and most recently Saidiya Hartman's *Wayward Lives*) are recurring references throughout the chapters, thereby increasing the resonances and also the cohesion across this volume.

Part I, Visions of Critique, comprises four chapters, each conveying a vision of the ends of critique that emerges out of an engagement with some of the core methodological approaches in the critical humanities. Kathrin Thiele opens the section with a consideration of the challenge posed by the tenet that, however one might understand critique, it will always be seen as a demand for, and somehow a step towards social, political, and ethical transformation. In one sense, this demand and expectation has not changed since Karl Marx, in 1845, urged philosophy to move beyond interpreting the world and to start changing it.[12] But, in another sense, everything has changed since then; not just the world the critic desires to change, but also the intellectual tools and frameworks of critique itself. Perhaps the biggest change is the rejection of a form of Western humanism that is founded on a racialized, gendered, and exclusionary concept of "Man." Rising to the challenge of practicing and theorizing critique "*after* humanism," Thiele draws on the work of, in particular, Wynter to propose a model of critique as a "thought-practice" that, first of all, rejects the old Marxist dichotomy between interpretation and praxis. And, second, seeks out and mobilizes what Thiele characterizes as "interferences" and "frictional polyvocality" in order to incorporate the perspectives of a wealth of de/anti-colonial (post-)humanisms. Only in this way can critique hope to be effective in our present.

Leonard Lawlor's chapter then gives a detailed reading of Derrida's concept of transcendental violence and his idea of "violence against violence." It does this by examining the structure of the gift as Derrida presents it in *Given Time* (1992), and by examining Derrida's analysis of the giving of counterfeit money. The conclusion Lawlor draws is that the giving of counterfeit money comes closest to the golden mean between exchange and non-exchange (or pure gift-giving), the golden mean between violence and nonviolence. But the open question remains: should we prescribe the giving of counterfeit money for all gift-giving and even for human relations of friendship and love? And how, in particular, can this contribute to arguments for the abolition of the death penalty, which is a form of violence repaid with violence? Lawlor concludes that critique, as an ethical practice, cannot avoid violence, but it might be defined as taking sides for *the least* violence.

From here, the volume moves to Sam McAuliffe's chapter which explores debates about the critical efficacy of utopian discourses, reaching back to discussions between Brecht, Adorno, and Bloch. McAuliffe identifies an often-overlooked element in Brecht's thought—the concept of the critical *pedagogium*, a repository of human gestures, behaviors, and social concretions that individuals could "try out" and test in a form of play. This institution would perform a utopic function because it provides a critical distance from the lived experience of contemporary social structures and processes, allowing participants to see through their social reality and thus open up the possibility of a changed future. Inspired by this utopic institution, McAuliffe argues that critique, like utopic discourse, must take aim at the perceived naturalness of any given state of affairs, thus making it possible to imagine and work toward a future that is different to the one being prepared by today's social order.

In the concluding chapter of Part I, Jennifer Wagner-Lawlor argues that in today's world, in which intelligence seems to be in such short supply, what is needed is a form of critical intelligence that can think "epicritically." That is, a mode of thought that grows out of a recognition of the crucial role of *epigenesis* in human capacities and social structures. Drawing on Catherine Malabou's work, Wagner-Lawlor demonstrates that the plasticity of human thought, underpinned by the phenomenon of epigenesis, opens up realms of the possible that promise new modes of living, feeling, and acting. Critique, on this view, is very far from being past its moment of efficacy; it is, rather, faced now with the task of developing and maintaining the radical, regenerative possibilities of epicritical thought.

Part II, Critical Reading, comprises three chapters that each focus on the question of how to read critically. Whether one is "reading" literature, critical theory, philosophy, or social structures, how does reading contribute to the understanding and achievement of the ends of critique? Esther Peeren makes a forceful case that the current "post-truth" era, in which anti-vaxxers and climate change deniers thrive, calls for a re-intensification of critique through a return to symptomatic reading. Peeren explores Latour's recent return to critique as redescription in *Down to Earth: Politics in the New Climatic Regime* (2018) and situates that approach in the context of earlier deconstructions of the "modern Man" of humanism, in the work of Derrida and Wynter. Wynter's texts undertake a thoroughgoing critique of "Man" in modern Western humanism, while also echoing Derrida's endorsement of close, symptomatic reading (despite barely mentioning reading directly). Ultimately, Peeren rejects recent calls for "surface reading," arguing that the world is never simply made up of facts, it is always imbricated with narrative and the fictive; and, therefore, a symptomatic mode of reading remains essential if critique is to be effective.

Birgit M. Kaiser's chapter then starts from the position that critique must be committed not only to diagnosing social ills, but also to producing emancipatory transformative effects. Such transformations, she argues, do not automatically follow after rational critique has delivered new insights; rather, transformation also requires the unlearning of old habits and privileges. Kaiser follows Spivak in identifying and exploring two modes of reading texts that can provide such critical retuning of habits toward sociality; two mutually complementary models of critical engagement. Her argument draws on Spivak's account of reading as a form of aesthetic education that can either be non-appropriative, for example, in the case of reading literature, or appropriative, for example, in the case of Fanon's reading of Hegel in *Black Skin, White Masks* (1986). Both modes of reading require a kind of "critical intimacy" that provides a model for a critique that works differently from the traditional notion of critique as opposition, or as the detection and correction of shortcomings in the texts of others. Rather, as Kaiser shows, reading in critical intimacy is a kind of dance, an affective-corporeal practice.

In the last chapter of Part II, Timothy O'Leary argues for an understanding of critique as a transformative engagement with contemporary modes of "ethical sensibility"; an engagement that can take many forms, whether in philosophy, critical history, or works of literature. His chapter makes three suggestions. First, that the idea of critique as "vivisection," that runs through Nietzsche's work of the 1880s, maybe a helpful metaphor for conceptualizing critique in the present. Second, that a work of literature, such as the novel *Milkman* (Burns 2018), can be instructively read as engaging in a critical vivisection of a person's ethical subjectivity. Third, that thinkers such as Foucault, Guattari, and Judith Butler give us the theoretical tools to understand both the ways in which ethical sensibility takes shape and the possibilities for its transformation. On this view, one of the ends of critique would be to provide a meticulous, experimental vivisection of contemporary modes of sensibility, thus opening up the possibility of their future reimagination and transformation.

Part III, Institutions and Technologies, offers close analyses of a range of institutions, ranging through democratic and legal structures, social media networks, and the infrastructures of big data and machine learning. Each chapter takes up a specific institutional framing—racialization, digitalization, education—and explores their stakes for contemporary practices of critique. Shannon Winnubst opens her chapter with an account of a dance performance by Miguel Gutierrez and his troupe which resonates with Gutierrez's argument that abstraction—in its many forms—is a racialized practice. Winnubst follows through the implications of this insight for politics, social institutions, and critique itself. Her argument is that the disavowal of race, along with the assumption of a universalizable white experience, is the defining hallmark of whiteness. It is this abstraction that enables white institutions, laws, and technologies to sustain a fundamental violence while blithely disavowing its reality. Winnubst offers a detailed analysis of how this abstraction operates in three domains: the concept of capital, the conceptualization of difference as Other, and the concept of race. Winnubst concludes that if critique is to remain effective in the twenty-first century, its point of departure must be the decentering of white narcissism, affects, and epistemologies.

In the next chapter, Mercedes Bunz poses the question whether twentieth-century concepts of power, resistance, and critique can still provide an adequate basis for a response to the ways in which digital technology has saturated contemporary life. Going back to Foucault's engagement with Kant's concept of Enlightenment, and Foucault's characterization of critique as the will "not to be governed like that," Bunz asks what does the drive to critique mean in a world in which we are, to a growing degree, governed by machine-learning algorithms. Arguing that Foucauldian conceptions of power and resistance are not adequate to critically addressing these phenomena, Bunz draws on Gilles Deleuze and the information studies scholar Philip E. Agre, to sketch out a mode of critical resistance that involves a more active engagement with the technologies themselves. Echoing Kant, Bunz concludes that, in this domain, we can only emerge out of our self-incurred tutelage by accepting a responsibility towards the technologies we use and by engaging actively in their transformation.

Jacques Lezra concludes this section, and the book, with his proposal for both a critique of political institutions and a model of critique itself more generally. Key to his argument is his concept of a "defective institution" and, more particularly, his appeal for the essential, irreducible role of "defects" in political institutions. For Lezra, the task of critique is to put into play defective narratives, defective political concepts, and defective institutions; where "defective" is understood as discontinuous, disorganized, decentered, radically open, and contingent. On this understanding, critique comprises the constantly changing set of practices that arrest, disorganize, denaturalize, and de-hegemonize, in whatever domain. Ultimately, in terms of political institutions, his vision of small-r republican governance is for defective subjectivities to act, not necessarily in concert and not necessarily intentionally, to constitute defective institutions. And, for Lezra, the task of critique today is to contribute to that *constructive* project.

NOTES

1. In "The Ends of Man," Derrida (1972) argues that despite their striving to delimit phenomenology from anthropology, the "Hegelian, Husserlian, and

Heideggerian critiques [...] of metaphysical humanism" (119) in fact sublate the figure of Man. Derrida, thus, notes that "phenomenology is the *relève* of anthropology. It is *no longer*, but it is *still* a science of man" (121). In that sense, the two ends of Man—"as a factual anthropological limit" and "as a determined opening or the infinity of a *telos*" (123)—are inscribed into phenomenology. In view of this, the question Derrida poses is after "an end of man which would not be organized by a dialectics of truth and negativity, an end of man which would not be a teleology in the first person plural" (121). *Terra Critica* explored this question of the end(s) of Man in a workshop in 2017, by bringing Derrida's text in resonance with the work of Wynter, especially her more recent "The Ceremony Found" (2015).

2. Felski follows Helen Small in the observation that although the field of literary studies is often summarily subsumed under the notion of the "critical," in fact much of "the work of the humanities is frequently descriptive, or appreciative, or imaginative, or provocative, or speculative, more than it is critical" (Small in Felski, 1). Yet, striving to specify critical by delimiting it from or even opposing it to appreciation, imagination, and speculation might limit the investigation of critique more than enhance it. For more on postcritique, see also Anker and Felski (2017).

3. In "Surface Reading" (2009), for example, Stephen Best and Sharon Marcus argue in a similar vein against symptomatic reading, which they say is to suspiciously search for unspoken, deeper truths, and ideological machinations in texts, machinations one is said to know or project before starting. Best and Marcus instead want their readers to "simply" expose themselves to "what is evident, perceptible, apprehensible in texts" (9) and, thus, propose the seemingly objective position of "just reading" (12).

4. "Crrritique" is the title of chapter 4 in Felski (2015). Surely, the gesture of a *critique of* social, artistic, or philosophical phenomena has never lost traction in critical discussions. There are innumerous works which perform this continually necessary modus of a *critique of*. See for more recent works in this vein, for example, Boltanski, Esquerre, and Porter's *Enrichment: A Critique of Commodities* (2020), Mbembe's *Critique of Black Reason* (2017), Deutscher's *Foucault's Futures: A Critique of Reproductive Reason* (2017). In the following overview, we only focus on works that make critique itself the object of analysis.

5. The Consortium is connected to the University of California, Berkeley, and Northwestern University, with project leaders Judith Butler and Penelope Deutscher (2016–2020) and Natalia Brizuela and Samera Esmeir, both at UC Berkeley, since 2020. See http://directory.criticaltheoryconsortium.org/about/); for the *Critical Times* journal, see https://ctjournal.org/. Its inaugural volume appeared in 2018.

6. The phrase "staying with the troubles" is borrowed from Donna Haraway's book *Staying with the Trouble* (2016).

7. *Terra Critica*'s work is inspired by a deep understanding of entanglement as critical disposition. In this combination of entanglement and critique, we draw on Karen Barad's notion of entanglement (Barad 2007); in this context, see also Thiele, "Entanglement" in Bunz et al. (2017).

8. Susan Buck-Morss's *Hegel, Haiti and Universal History* (2009) demonstrates a similar nexus or co-emergence of the values of freedom, property, and the dialectic.

9. We draw here on Gloria Wekker's critical analysis in *White Innocence* (2016), where she argues that it is by claiming innocence that truly emancipatory transformations in current societies are prevented; and also on Donna Haraway's seminal claim from "Situated Knowledges" (1988) that there is no pure or innocent knowledge production. Non-innocence also resonates for us with Wynter's emphasis that the "rewriting of knowledge" needs to be pursed within established (educational) institutions (see, for example, 1994).

10. The characterization of "divergent" here should be read in line with Isabelle Stengers who uses this terminology building on Gilles Deleuze. In a conversation with Heather Davis and Etienne Turpin, Stengers says: "I like the term 'divergences,' as used by Deleuze, who wrote that only diverging lines communicate (meaning that communication here is creation, not redundancy). But diverging is not 'from something.' It designates what matters for you, and *how* it matters (in the positive sense), and therefore allows for symbiotic alliances, always lateral, never grounded on a 'same' that would transcend or reconcile them" (2013, 174).

11. See the activities of *Terra Critica*: www.terracritica.net.

12. "The philosophers have only interpreted the world, in various ways; the point is to change it." Thesis XI of *Theses on Feuerbach* (https://www.marxists.org/archive/marx/works/1845/theses/theses.htm).

BIBLIOGRAPHY

Adorno, Theodor, Else Frenkel-Brunswik, Daniel J. Levinson, and R. Nevitt Sanford. 2019 (1950). *The Authoritarian Personality*. London: Verso.

Anker, Elizabeth S., and Rita Felski (eds). 2017. *Critique and Postcritique*. Durham, NC: Duke University Press.

Barad, Karen. 2007. *Meeting the Universe Halfway: Quantum Physics and the Entanglement of Matter and Meaning*. Durham, NC: Duke University Press.

Best, Stephen, and Sharon Marcus. 2009. "Surface Reading: An Introduction." *Representations* 108 (1): 1–21.

Boltanski, Luc, Arnaud Esquerre, and Catherine Porter. 2020. *Enrichment: A Critique of Commodities*. Cambridge: Polity Press.

Buck-Morss, Susan. 2009. *Hegel, Haiti and Universal History*. Pittsburgh: University of Pittsburgh Press.

Bunz, Mercedes, Birgit M. Kaiser, and Kathrin Thiele (eds). 2017. *Symptoms of the Planetary Condition: A Critical Vocabulary*. Lüneburg: Meson Press. http://meson.press/books/symptoms-of-the-planetary-condition/.

Derrida, Jacques. [1968] 1972. "The Ends of Man." In *Margins of Philosophy*, translated by Alan Bass, 111–136. Chicago: University of Chicago Press.

Deutscher, Penelope. 2017. *Foucault's Futures: A Critique of Reproductive Reason*. New York: Columbia University Press.

Deutscher, Penelope, and Cristina Lafont (eds). 2017. *Critical Theory in Critical Times: Transforming the Global Political and Economic Order*. New York: Columbia University Press.

Fassin, Didier, and Bernard E. Harcourt. 2019. *A Time for Critique*. New York: Columbia University Press.

Felluga, Dino Franco. 2015. *Critical Theory: The Key Concepts*. London/New York: Routledge.

Felski, Rita. 2015. *The Limits of Critique*. Chicago: University of Chicago Press.

Foucault, Michel. 1997. "What Is Critique?" In *The Politics of Truth*, edited by Sylvère Lotringer, translated by Lysa Hochroth, 23–82. Cambridge: MIT Press (distributed forSemiotext(e)).

Fraser, Pamela, and Roger Rothman (eds). 2017. *Beyond Critique: Contemporary Art in Theory, Practice, and Instruction*. London: Bloomsbury.

Guattari, Félix. [1989] 2005. *The Three Ecologies*, translated by Ian Pindar and Paul Sutton. London/New York: Continuum.

Haraway, Donna. 1988. "Situated Knowledges: The Science Question in Feminism and the Privilege of Partial Perspective." *Feminist Studies* 14/3: 575–599.

Hartman, Sadiya. 2019. *Wayward Lives, Beautiful Experiments: Intimate Histories of Social Upheaval*. New York/London: Norton & Company.

Jaeggi, Rahel. 2014. *Alienation*. New York: Columbia University Press.

———. 2018. *Critique of Forms of Life*. Boston: Harvard University Press.

Kaiser, Birgit M., and Kathrin Thiele. 2020. "Forms of Critique, Modes of Combat." In *The Stakes of Form*, edited by Sami Khatib, Holger Kuhn, et al., 95–116. Zurich: Diaphanes/Chicago: University of Chicago Press.

Latour, Bruno. 2004. "Why Has Critique Run Out of Steam? From Matters of Fact to Matters of Concern." *Critical Inquiry* 30/2: 225–248.

Lowe, Lisa. 2015. *The Intimacy of Four Continents*. Durham, NC: Duke University Press.

Mbembe, Achille. 2017. *Critique of Black Reason*. Durham, NC: Duke University Press.

Sardarizadeh, Shayan. 2020. "What's Behind the Rise of QAnon in the UK?" *BBC*, 12 October 2020. https://www.bbc.com/news/blogs-trending-54065470 [last accessed 21 February 2021].

Stengers, Isabelle. 2013. "Matters of Cosmopolitics: On the Provocations of Gaïa: Isabelle Stengers in Conversation with Heather Davis and Etienne Turpin." In *Architecture in the Anthropocene: Encounters among Design, Deep Time, Science and Philosophy*, edited by Etienne Turpin, 171–182. London: Open Humanities Press.

Wekker, Gloria. 2016. *White Innocence: Paradoxes of Colonialism and Race*. Durham, NC: Duke University Press.

Wynter, Sylvia. 1994. "'No Humans Involved': An Open Letter to My Colleagues." *Forum N.H.I.: Knowledge for the 21st Century* 1 (1): 42–73.

———. 2003. "Unsettling the Coloniality of Being/Power/Truth/Freedom: Towards the Human, After Man, Its Overrepresentation—An Argument." *CR: The New Centennial Review* 3 (3): 257–337.

———. 2015. "The Ceremony Found: Towards the Autopoietic Turn/Overturn, Its Autonomy of Human Agency and Extraterritoriality of (Self-)Cognition." In *Black Knowledges/Black Struggles*, edited by J. R. Ambroise and S. Broek, 184–252. Liverpool: Liverpool University Press.

Part I

VISIONS OF CRITIQUE

1

"After Humanism?"—Time and Transformation in Critical Thinking

Kathrin Thiele

Preparing for the Terra Critica VIII *meeting that was due to be held in Kolkata, India, in March 2020—preparing for it without then being able to travel due to the COVID-19 pandemic—I sit immersed in Jacques Derrida's seminar on* Theory & Practice *(Derrida 2019), and I am struck by a vivid memory, a flashback: It is 1992, I have just returned from a ten-month social work stay in Santiago de Chile; I am full of texts and ideas from what today I would call activist feminist and decolonial critical thinking; I also have just started my first semester in Sociology, and I visit a friend in the newly "unified" Berlin. This friend, who like me grew up in the western part of Germany in the 1970s and 1980s, has—as so many of our generation—just moved to Berlin a few months before. He lives in the eastern part of the city, which for financially precarious students is so much more affordable, and he also just started his studies at the famous Humboldt University. When on my visit in this autumn of 1992, I accompany him to one of his 1st year study seminars, we enter the university at* Unter den Linden—*via its main entry, opposite the grand* Berliner Staatsoper *with the* Opern- *or* Bebelplatz *right next to it, this infamous square where on May 10, 1933, Nationalist Socialist students and professors of what was then still the* Friedrich-Wilhelm-University *burned the works of hundreds of literary, political, and journalistic writers, philosophers, and scientists. Following myself now into this multilayered scenario written by different temporalities, I look into the entrance hall of the university again as if for the first time. And there it is, right in front of me, in golden letters, on the wall when one walks up the stairs:*

Die Philosophen haben die Welt
nur verschieden *interpretiert*,
es kommt aber darauf an,
sie zu *verändern*.[1]

I think I knew that the author of this statement was Karl Marx. But I doubt that I could have placed it as one of his Theses on Feuerbach *at that time. When I see my friend and myself now walk up these stairs, I feel how again I am hit by a thought, one that—from today's point of view—I can also no longer disentangle from the whole experience I had back then in those transitional times in Germany (and in Berlin in particular): How weird, I think walk-reading, that one could actually see philosophy's task as a form of interpretation, striving to merely* define *"what is." How could one not always have seen this act of "thinking the world" as a transformative move, as* always/already *practical and, therefore, as an "altering" engagement with what is conceptualized? From today's point of view, one might safely say that my choice of studying Sociology fits quite well with how I responded to Marx's* Thesis Eleven *at that moment. Already then—or is it rather because of "back then" that I "now" think this way?—I could not (and cannot) do without a more active assessment of what thinking does.*

Back in March 2020: A very different time when considering a belief in philosophy and the critical question of how to assess and distribute agencies for change. Yet, this recollection, bringing back to me the times of the early 1990s as something much more than just a fleeting moment in view of my critical engagements today, makes me here and now very attentive to the question that Derrida puts forth as a starting point for his seminar on Theory & Practice: *How to actually read Marx's thesis "today"? What to make of the affectively so seductive or terrifying—or terrifyingly seductive?—sense of "ends" in this thesis? The move from interpretation to change as a form of transformation and alteration (Derrida 2019, 11–13)? Or, asked otherwise: How to think ideation as a material (performative) enacting? And is then also the material—matter(s)—ideational? And finally, how does all of this register in a time when pandemic conditions once more infect so substantially what it might mean to think?*

***

Critical Conundrum

I have arranged my remarks in a way that I hope you will find what you call
   "logical."
On Mashupzyx, we have the ability to assimilate information in stratified blocks,
like large helpings of layer cake; but you cannot do that,
limited as you are by your own neural structures,
so we shall have to proceed sequentially.

Margret Atwood, *Greetings, Earthlings!*

Critical thinking, the quest for earthly critical engagements, can hardly avoid the following truth-claim: critique is a transformative move, or it *is* not. That is to say, critical thinking is always interventionist to some degree. A critical position is one that invests in its own power to transform, and it relies on an active engagement with the issues it addresses so that it allows, or even more so, strives for change to happen. Thus, if pressured to name one characteristic of critical thinking and/as critique, I cannot see it otherwise: criticality, the force driving both critical thinking and critique more generally, embodies an *ethos of transformation*, with the goal to un-work what appears as fixed. Yet, of course, herein lies the very trap into which this criticality or its *ethos* might (or will) always fall: the unavoidable slippage into a critical position that occupies a place of knowing better in a "sequential" way, as Atwood has it also in the epigraph (Atwood 2019, 11). A position that also so clearly expresses its incapacity to let go of the vision that another world is possible, that change and alteration are what matters. Critical thinking is all about imagining things differently, and most of the time it projects them into a future, as something to come, to achieve—a hope. What these ends of critique then lead me to conclude here is that no critical movement of thought and practice—no matter how humbly expressed or small in envisioned reach—can fully avoid the dangers of a belief in progress and from there also the production of overgeneralizing truth claims.

What to do with this *critical* evaluation of critical thinking right at the beginning of this chapter? How, as a critical theorist, do I want to handle the challenge that in engaging with critique as a transformative practice, its very logic—linear progress narrative and sequentiality—might actually re-institutionalize itself? That critical thinking carries this weight is in no way a new realization, as many authors in the various critical studies (feminist, queer, Black, de/postcolonial, posthuman(ist) or deconstructive) have long shown. And yet, what if I started from this end rather than end here? Is it possible to continue the ends of critique at the end of critique? As a feminist critical theorist, I affirm and want to hold on to the subversive capitals of critique as intervention in and transformation of relations of power and governance. And yet, in view of systemic global asymmetries and planetary implicatedness, such affirmation cannot describe a push for criticality based on visions of progress, (universalizing) truth claims, and (hegemony-recentering) optimism. A different *affective temporality* than the powerful "forward-looking" is needed; a different critical register is asked for.[2] The question in my title, "*After* humanism?," tries to express what is at stake when, on the one hand, the critical project I pursue aims to attack critique's hegemonic legacy in the Western humanist-colonial order; and yet, on the other hand, it also tries to circumnavigate the characteristically modern defense mechanism to simply move away and move on (either dialectically or progressively, as in postcritique). Inspired by the critical decolonial work of Sylvia Wynter, who in an interview once stated that her analyses of the West are written from what she calls an "occidentalist" position—"A place outside, although I am in it as well" (Wynter and Thomas 2009, 50, emphasis in original), in this chapter I want to wonder about and wander with different modalities of *after* as critical temporality.

AFTER HUMAN(ISM)

Sylvia Wynter's intellectual project, which engages in the painstaking work of moving "towards the human, after Man" (Wynter 2003), might be a good place to start my inquiry into how temporality and/as transformative potential is written in critical endeavors.[3] The specific question that I am asking here is how to read Wynter's critical (de-/anti-colonial) project as think-practicing (i.e., "altering") the world. Two moves, happening at the same time, seem to be at stake in this project when read through the above statement: a push "after" that is also a move "toward," yet without at the same time repeating an evolutionary progress narrative, since what literally stays on both sides of these directional propositions remains entangled: hu/man. But how to envision this move without reducing it to a linear understanding in which the statement appears when read straightforwardly? How, that is, not to stuff Wynter's thought-practice into the modern progress narratives in which "toward" and "after" are well-known points or directions on the linear arrow of time? That such a conclusion would be all too hasty is utterly clear to me. But then, how (else) does her critical work *move*?

If we look more closely into Wynter's guiding motto ("toward the human, after Man"), three modalities of "after" (implicating the move "toward") can perhaps be made out. First, Wynter's analyses of the coloniality of Being and/as the anti-Black order can be read as critically *being after* the genre of the human in terms of Man. Since her seminal text "The Ceremony Must Be Found: After Humanism" (Wynter 1984), Wynter comes after and radically exposes modern Western hegemonic humanism in all its naturalization and normalization as a (dys)selective white-phallic-bourgeois-colonial history

"After *Humanism?*"—Time and Transformation in Critical Thinking

that counts in an exclusivist manner what it means to be hu/man. More recently, Wynter once more explicates this constitutive violence that should be put at the center of critical interventions today: "The larger issue is [. . .] the incorporation of all forms of human being into a single homogenized descriptive statement that is based on the figure of the West's liberal monohumanist *Man*" (Wynter and McKittrick 2015, 23). It is the foundational one-dimensionality in hegemonic thought traditions—Western liberal monohumanism—that spark her tireless and meticulous rewriting of the *systemic ongoingness* of Western colonial history, which she has also come to conceptualize in terms of the figures of Man1 (*homo politicus*) and Man2 (*homo oeconomicus*).[4] As many scholars engaged with Wynter's work have shown, it is crucial for her own critical project to "recuperate what remains illegible in Foucault's critique of Man: 'the idea of race' " (Ferreira da Silva 2015, 91) and to pursue a "cognitive shift" by radically rethinking "the system through which knowledge and knowing are constituted" (Mignolo 2015, 106). Taking these two things together—recuperating what remains illegible and pursuing a cognitive shift—Wynter's critical *being after* is a *move towards*. And yet, in her radical (in the sense of "to the roots") recuperating project, a linear progress is not what is meant here. As McKittrick also specifies, Wynter's "anticolonial vision is not [. . .] teleological—moving *from* colonial oppression and *upward toward* emancipation—but rather it consists of knots of ideas and histories and narratives that can only be legible in relation to one another" (McKittrick 2015a, 2, emphasis added). A different texture then—knotted and intra-relational rather than cut apart and gradually ascendant—characterizes Wynter's critical thought-practicing.

What crystallizes from this first inquiry into the modality of Wynter's critical project of *after-toward* is then that in *being after*, in coming after and thereby exposing the coloniality of Being as "our present biocentric descriptive statement [. . .] linked to the law-like normalization of the corporeal features of Western Europeans in their now ethno-class bourgeois, aesthetic configuration" which writes us all because "the West *did* change the world, *totally*" (cited in Wynter and McKittrick 2015, 18, emphasis in original), Wynter literally pushes to *move after*; to finally move past that very configuration of the West. Her work wants to let go of monohumanism; this canon based on violence which aligns also so neatly with the canon of critique itself: modern, white, bourgeois, colonial, with a scientific-evolutionary confidence to claim universal validity. Her multidisciplinary texts are after a cognitive shift; a shift of those critical registers that (so far) prevent "us" from moving past monohumanism. Wynter herself calls this shift the "autopoietic turn/overturn" of the dominant genre of the human as Man (e.g., Wynter 2015), a turn toward another figuration of human—*homo narrans*—no longer as noun or substance but a "being human as praxis" (Wynter and McKittrick 2015).

24 Kathrin Thiele

It might feel adequate to interpret Wynter's rhetorical pushing as nothing but a critical stance *against* the coloniality of Being—politically urgent as that is. Yet, I want to slow down my reasoning and move more carefully here. Rather than interpreting Wynter's critical push as so clearly sided against, I place her autopoietic turn/overturn within the context of her occidentalist approach, and thus read it as a more implicated, a more systemic critical move. Wynter's use of "autopoietic turn/overturn" throughout her texts always comes with a reference to Humberto Maturana's and Francisco Varela's introduction of the concept of autopoiesis in the 1970s (see Maturana and Varela 1980). But her use of it differs from the more mainstream systems theory in which autopoiesis operates descriptively as a given systemic function.[5] In contrast to this, Wynter's proposition of autopoiesis acts more performatively, it is about what it *does*.[6] According to her, a systemic perspective needs to remain charged with such a revolutionary spirit that also Maturana originally gave to autopoiesis when, in the single-authored "Introduction" to *Autopoiesis and Cognition*, he entangled the research on finding an adequate language for systemic processes of the living with the political events taking place in Chile since the late 1960s (Maturana 1980). So, what Wynter's performative activation of autopoiesis seems to speak for is that her anti-colonial criticality does not describe from the outside the violence of the coloniality of Being. Instead, her use of autopoiesis as a systemic and/as performative force *after* Man aims for a more disruptive transformation: autopoiesis here aims to turn/overturn the commonly assumed unique willful critical agent with his (!) rational powers itself: Man.[7] As performatively systemic, autopoietic turn/overturn is a move that both shifts, tips over and stays with. It is moving us "after," yet, only by way of rewriting and shifting, not replacing. In emphasizing autopoiesis in the performative sense, Wynter's vision of change is not reliant on the classical critical Subject (Man) as the singular agent in the (desired) processes of transformation. Rather, the systemic shift that she proposes *affects* the very order of Man (or the coloniality of Being) itself. And it is by way of this systemic push that her critical project and its potential for transformation are no longer (or at least no longer so easily) recuperable into "the World as we know it" (Ferreira da Silva 2014, 81).

After these first two moves of *being after—coming* and *pushing after* the hegemony of Western liberal monohumanism—let me still add a third modality of "after" that in my view also drives Wynter's critical project "towards the human, after Man": to *look after*, to care for, the human as praxis and thus to care for (a different) humanism by cultivating a different imaginary and (at)tending to and caring for that which is continually kept "unthought" (Sithole 2020, 21). If the above presentation has shown how Wynter's work critically exposes and pushes after what is counted as human (as noun) in Western humanism—Man—then I want to add now that she does not do this for the sake of letting go of the dimensions of the human or even of humanism itself.[8] As recurrent critical statements in her texts make abundantly clear, be it from Frantz Fanon's *Black Skin White Masks* (1986)—"How do we extricate ourselves?," "What is to be done to set man free?" (e.g., in Wynter 2015)—or the reiteration of an unwavering belief in the urgent and possible manifestation of Aimé Césaire's project (articulated in *Discourse on Colonialism* [Césaire 2000]) as a "humanism to the measure of the world" (e.g., in Wynter 1984 and 2003), it is the human as *wor(l)ding* dimension that Wynter precisely *looks after*. Fanon and Césaire are central to Wynter's critical project to "rewrite knowledge" (Wynter 1994). These anti-/decolonial critics are her counter-cosmogenic sources to cultivate an alternative horizon for the human. In their company, she looks after the human as praxis; she attends to and cares for a humanism that is no longer focused monotonously on Man but has become "ecumenically human" (Wynter 2015, 193). Yet, also this third modality of "after" is not a U-turn gesture—a simple return to a supposedly less violated or purer "before" the genre of human as Man. Wynter clearly states in the interview from which I already quoted before: "For us it's not a return. IT IS A QUESTION OF GOING AFTER 'MAN,' TOWARDS THE HUMAN" (in Wynter and Thomas 2009, 48, emphasis in original). Thus, her project *is* a move in a direction where "we" have never been. But, at the same time, it is also not leaving what is already there, and thus not a linear surpassing. Thinking with Wynter means I cannot ever fully abandon the horizon within which the critical question of a humanism "to the measure of the world" and the necessity to "extricate ourselves" has emerged: the coloniality of Being. And yet, her work moves me somewhere I have never been. It is from this complex critical move—an *e/affective* superimposing of past and/as future in order to approach the present, troubling "our" habitual mono-linear mind frame—that Wynter's critical, that is, material transformative, question becomes:

> [H]ow can we come to have knowledge of socio-human existence outside the terms of the answer that we at present give to the question of who-we-are as an alleged *purely biological being*, as one in whose *genre*-specific *naturally selected/dysselected* symbolic life/death terms we now performatively enact ourselves as *secular* and, thereby, necessarily Western and westernized bourgeois subjects—including us as academics/intellectuals? (Wynter 2015, 206, emphasis in the original)

While gaining an answer to this critical question would be of great interest, I cannot take this route.[9] My task here does not primarily lie in delineating *what* Wynter concretely proposes as the project of human as praxis and/as a different, ecumenical humanism. Rather, I want to attend still further to the pedagogy of her thinking in order to determine still more clearly *how* her critical thinking actually moves (us) in(to) the world. In view of this more methodological horizon, Wynter's criticality in the quote above lies in my eyes in the force to, on the one hand, allow for (or even request) a push toward an "outside the terms"—that is, moving past the hegemonic narrative of biocentrism that has naturalized itself as thought horizon—and yet, on the other hand, to stay with "the question of who-we-are," especially as "academics/ intellectuals," within the systemic frameworks that continually write "us all." Wynter always keeps more than one force in play; forces which at first might seem to contradict each other in directionality; yet taken together they actually harbor the potential for the systemic move that I claim is transformative. To read Wynter is to always be pulled in more than one direction. And holding on to this more-than-mono-directionality is what methodologically constitutes her critical intervention. This critical vision seems to me also what McKittrick stresses when reflecting more concretely on Wynter's political position:

> The worldview Wynter enables hinges on her ability to turn a hopeful intellectual project invested in emancipation in on itself. To paraphrase Wynter, as she reflects on the promise of civil rights, black is beautiful, feminism, and other "left-leaning" social movements of the 1960s and 1970s: these political projects might be analyzed not through the profits and successes of various "identity" studies [. . .]. Instead, we might see these movements as the *incomplete challenge to* the conception of Man itself and thus unfinished. (McKittrick 2015b, 151, emphasis in original)

"Turning in on itself" implies the awareness that the emancipatory (academic and political) projects that have emerged since the 1960s still fall into the "biocentric model (racial-anatomical difference)" (151). Contrary to what they officially claim, these projects do not yet sufficiently disrupt the linear-bio-evolutionary narrative that keeps the coloniality of Being in place. Their incomplete challenge cannot just be remedied by a move to more inclusivity. What remains insufficient is precisely that the ground(ing) has not yet been shifted enough (biocentrism with its dys/selective consequences in view of the human).[10] No straightforward correction will ever do. Only a more complex un-working and/as rewriting of the colonial scientific order, and thereby working toward a *different imagination*, or an alternative "spacetimemattering" (Barad 2007), will initiate such a shift.[11] Turning in on itself is a version of the autopoietic turn/overturn that I have described before: an autopoietic being after and/as a pushing after, which also implies the continuous looking after. It is to be after Man in order to break (t)his order. But in that move to also remain committed to—as in "staying with"—the (troubling) notions of the human and humanism *as* critical projects.[12] Wynter never turns away from the human. Rather, she works with a turn/overturn that to me resonates with how Karen Barad characterizes "re-turning," as in "*turn it over and over again*, iteratively intra-acting, re-diffracting, diffracting anew, in the making of new temporalities (spacetimemattering), new diffraction patterns" (Barad 2014, 168 emphasis added).[13] If such (over)turning and superimposing moves are moves of criticality, then we here depart from the classical model of critique based on the competition of sides, the opposition of old *versus* new. Instead, facing the systemic conditions of the colonial order of Being, Wynter attends to wherefrom (or whence) to begin to ask critical questions. And it is by way of this cognitive shift that we who listen might come to sense the inherent *systemic liminal spaces* that always/already harbor a potential for disruption and an imagining otherwise—*besides/para*, that is, literally *to the side of*, the colonial-phallogo-capitalist fantasy which relies on the sequentiality to (linearly) move on and abandon.

RE-TURNING

I pursued my investigation into the three modalities of "after" in Wynter, on the one hand, to exemplify how the teleological narratives of linear progress are still dominant in "this World as we know it." And, on the other hand, by looking closely into the critical potential of *being, pushing and looking after* with Wynter, I hope a different critical sense has emerged. This critical move, that not only questions what will replace the linear-teleological order with its ground(ing) violence, but also critically focuses on how to *e/affect* visions of transformation, meaning, and mattering. Introducing in this context quantum registers as systemicity's intra-acting consistency, as my reading above briefly gestured to already, might be a useful tool to further dive into Wynter's criticality as turn/overturn. Not in order to add something that is missing, but rather in order to slow down once more and further explicate how the proposed systemic critical approach initiates nonlinearity, and therefore a non-teleological, nonsequential temporality that at the same time also does not let go of the haunting and haunted-ness of all matters.[14] To critically disrupt the ontological order of biocentrism and to show how biocentrism relies heavily on hu/man exceptionalism, it is not sufficient, as Vicki Kirby also shows, to merely reject the hegemonic modern epistemological order (ranging from the coloniality of Being to Newtonian physics to Cartesian subjectivity). In her recent discussion of "Un/Limited Ecologies," Kirby poignantly argues that "Cartesianism isn't an accusation that can be remedied with a corrective because both its affirmation and its critique install the cogito [Man] as the site of claim and counterclaim" (Kirby 2018, 123). To critically demand the replacement of one order by another one, will always keep us wedded to the very teleo*logy* of the genre of the human as Man which requires the very exclusivity of human agentiality.[15] In order to *e/affectively* move somewhere else, a different shift has to be found:

a com*pli*cated thought-practice of moving after-toward as spacetimemattering praxis. This systemic shift, as Wynter clearly shows in her work, will not make things easier. The complexity of "being human as praxis" as *who-we-are* is impossible to translate without frictions into a world based so heavily on the split between an individualized agent (Man/*S*ubject) surrounded by his (!) social (human and nonhuman) environment. And yet, the act of thoughtfully initiating this shift—practicing it—can spark a different sensibility in view of how change and transformation are said to take place.[16] As Ferreira da Silva says, it is the beginning to "ask [. . .] different questions, methodological rather than ontological ones" (Ferreira da Silva 2015, 104). It is a move away from identity-based claims of "who and what we are" in order to finally "go deeper into the investigations of *how* we come up with answers" (104, emphasis added).

This last point leads me to another question, one that addresses more directly still the matter of why I claim that sounding out resonances in-between critical posthuman(ist) (e.g., Barad, Kirby) and de-/anti-colonial perspectives (Wynter, Ferreira da Silva, McKittrick) helps to further concretize the complex or systemic critical powers I am myself after in this chapter. Earlier, I mentioned in passing that Wynter's work is very much guided by Fanon's existential critical question "How do we extricate ourselves?" (Fanon 1986, 12).[17] Throughout her work, Wynter also consistently follows his answer to this question; that it is *sociogeny* (next to phylogeny and ontogeny) which needs to be closely attended to in order to get to the human *as* praxis.[18] Yet, if sociogeny is approached in a manner in which it is kept categorically separate both from what is called nature and from what is taken as the sovereign sphere of the self (as most social constructivists would argue), then a repetition of hu/man exceptionalism (coloniality of Being), and with it the violent ontological classification of "what is," will be unavoidable.[19] But, what if we read the Wynterian-Fanonian intervention otherwise, inspired again by Kirby's discussion of *un/limited ecologies*? Kirby's arguments for a more expansive eco- rather than socio-logical subjectivity resonates with Wynter's concern for sociogeny. Continuing from the earlier quote that questions mere "corrective" approaches, Kirby rephrases and thereby *rewrites* the very notion of sovereign selfhood and subjectivity itself. She argues that "[i]f the subject is not a pre-existent entity *in* a field of social, political, and historical forces, if the social is not outside the subject, then the interiority of the individual is constitutively alien or, more accurately, uncannily familiar" (Kirby 2018, 123). In Kirby's quantum one-ness (entanglement writ large), agentiality is not severed from the social. Instead, *who-we-are* is indeed a sociogenic matter which no longer comes after phylo- and ontogeny but is with/in them.

In terms of their specific critical legacies, Wynter's and Kirby's thought horizons might not align without friction. But by diffracting their diverging theoretical registers with each other, what is made clear is that "our" critical desire for change and transformation must first of all turn/overturn the very teleological question of *what* comes after the subject/Man so that it can open up *toward* a different subjectivity and/as (more-than-human) agentiality. Reading Wynter with anthropo-critical ecological sources helps to concretize how her move of turn/overturn and/as re-tu(r)ning is able to indeed effectuate a *different critical key*: for a futurity that does not merely play at the horizon (progressive narrative based on the logic of Man); but a horizon of futurity as ethico-onto-epistemological in/determinacy (never just bound to the human and always/already interior) that plays (out) in the here and now (systemic turn/overturn as intra-active re-tu(r)ning).

HOPE AT THE END OF THE WORLD AS "WE" KNOW IT?

Shifting to a different key is also necessary now in order to not end my discussion in a way that would suggest that the proposed quest for criticality as a systemic shift is something which requires high abstract thinking on time and temporality in order to get (to) it. Nothing lies further from what I hope to achieve in this chapter. I quite frankly believe that what I have argued up to here is not at all new, if "we" were only more accustomed to listening less genre-specifically hu/man, and to paying more attention to the majority of this planet's other life-forms. When I look around, simply turning to less hegemonic onto-epistemological critical narrations of *who-we-are*, there is actually no difficulty to see that such praxes exist; they happen in quite a variety. Hence, I want to end my discussion with what might be taken as another beginning: (re-)tu(r)ning my attention to critical projects which I read as sharing in more systemically *turning* the ways or *tuning in* another way to envision change.

A horizon of futurity characterizes critical endeavors. So, José Esteban Muñoz' queer(ing) rewriting in *Cruising Utopia* of Ernst Bloch's utopian horizon of hope as the "no-longer-conscious" and a "not-yet-conscious" (Muñoz 2019, 28) layers of presence is a good place to return to and newly tune in. This central place of hope in Muñoz might at first be felt as slightly *out of time* today. Yet, this affirmative belief in the possibility of change and transformation in the here and now is, as Muñoz shows, a *performative critical* requirement. It cannot be pictured as a straight(forward) future to come. Instead, it is an enacting, a praxis. The critical hermeneutics of hope that Muñoz is after is "more akin to what Derrida described as the trace" (28); it is a critical mode that "call[s] into question what is epistemologically there and signal[s] a highly ephemeral ontological field that can be characterized as a *doing in futurity*" (26). Letting myself now feel-think what this different tonality of "doing in futurity" could mean, I also pay closer attention to the question why Muñoz uses Bloch as the source for queering time. Turning (to) the German idealist, who certainly is not known as a common reference in queer (of color) theorizing, comes as a surprise. But Muñoz makes a methodological, and perhaps even a pedagogical, *critical* point of it. His queering endeavor must not start from a safe outside or beyond the normative. Rather he explicitly "look[s] for queer relational formations *within the social*" (28, emphasis added).[20] Instead of the straight(forward) criticality to overcome and replace the order of Being, the latter is here rather, in Wynterian terms, "turned in on itself." Or, as I want to call it, Muñoz' critical project is to dive into the systemic formation of *who-we-are*, reemerging with a horizon of futurity in the here and now, yet also always to the side of it (no-longer-not-yet-conscious). Queer(ing) is all about attending to and staying with a multilayered, open approach: "Queerness's form is utopian" (30), Muñoz says. Instead of merely fitting it with/in (anti-)normative identitarian terms, queerness is a doing as quotidian praxis that allows to "insist on an ordering of life that is not dictated by the spatial/temporal coordinates of straight time, a time and space matrix in which, unfortunately, far too many gays, lesbians, and other purportedly 'queer' people reside" (31).

The tonality of Muñoz' queering as critical force leads me also to Fred Moten's "blur" (Moten 2017) as yet another praxis of *critical tu(r)ning*. In today's all too hopeless and exhausted times, the Fanonian existential question remains: how to get out? As by now should be clear, the common imaginary of the dividing line that cuts apart, in order to gain clarity and then move on, will fail (us). Tuning into Moten's "in the blur," I hear a different critical suggestion. He characterizes it in *Black and Blur* as "a slide, a *glissando*, in which the ensemble of nonsingle being is differentially revealed" (254).[21] So, instead of the familiar conceptual sequentiality—separating out, proposing as clear-cut idea, so that change and transformation can be initiated step by step (measurable and individualized)—something much less predictable and willful is proposed as disruptive force: a slide, a glide. And, as Moten further specifies, this disruptive potential is to be pursued very differently (if one even can say this) than what the binary order of self/other and Western metaphysics have suggested for so long:

> What's at stake here is neither a bringing forth in itself nor a bringing forth out of an Other, but a bringing forth out of or against self and Other, a bringing forth in defiance of the metaphysical foundations of relation. To bring forth in the blur, out of the blue, in and out of entanglement, through nonlocality's absolutely nothing—that breath, that anima that $\varphi\psi\sigma|\sigma$—is [. . .] essential: a general,

generative, differential repeatability that you could call music, if you decided that you didn't want to call it poetry. (254)

In the registers of classical critique, "to bring forth in the blur" might not be perceived as a very powerful strategy. It probably is also disregarded as ethically insufficient. Nobody tells us here how to act. And could we ever fully grasp what is happening in the blur? And yet, as disruptive critical intervention, this different tonality of transformation unhinges by refusing the *genre-specific* oppositional scenario that so persistently dominates visions of how change occurs, also within critical thinking. Moten's blur cannot be fix(at)ed, but it is not leaving things as they are. He dissolves right in front of our eyes the image of ideational clarity as the prerequisite to meaningful action, but with it also its illusion of change and transformation as overcoming or replacing. In difference to the latter, Moten's perhaps "poet(h)ical" (Ferreira da Silva 2014) criticality teaches us that

> [t]he dissolve resolves nothing; there is no easy solution, no phantasmatic melding; but, at the same time, dissolution is not desolation, either. We feel the blur of a general entanglement and the question is, simply, what are we to make of it? (Moten 2017, 254)

Would this queering force (with Muñoz) of Moten's blur as "a slide, a *glissando*," always *in/determinate* (with Barad) because "the question is, simply, what are we to make of it?," not also be relatable to Édouard Glissant's (non-)concept of *opacity*? That is, Glissant's seminal yet also discomforting political claim, in *The Poetics of Relation*, of "the right to opacity for everyone" (Glissant 2010, 194) as a crucial poet(h)ical dimension to any post-/decolonial project that attends to global differentiality? Before turning to opacity, Glissant explains that no matter how much "thinking" attends to differences and/as the coloniality of Being, "difference itself can still contrive to reduce things to the Transparent" (2010, 189). So, is opacity as the poetics of refusal to (be) fully grasp(ed) essentially required to (be) shift(ed) and to bring forth a slide to the side of the normalized and naturalized approach of "the Transparent" as a totality "threatened with immobility" (2010, 192)?[22] In Kara Keeling's *Queer Temporalities, Black Futures* (2019), Glissant's opacity is indeed called upon as a "reinvigorated concept of knowledge production" (2019, 15). Keeling reads opacity as a "politicized cultural strategy" that "assert[s] the existence in this world of another conception of the world, incomprehensible from within the common senses that secure existing hegemonic relations" (31). While one cannot so easily read Keeling in a universalist manner—her focus on the specificity of Blackness here is as strong as is Moten's—I still want to give words to my own feeling of being interpellated by her as a critical thinker, sharing her assertive belief in another thought-practicing the world. Change and transformation are also here not linked to any safeguarded outside. Keeling neither searches for untouched territories nor for fundamental other times that are supposed to save "us" from the here and now. Rather (with Muñoz and Moten), Keeling once more asserts that her critical project "emerges [. . .] as a way of indicating an investment in the risk that already *inheres in social life*—an antifragile investment in the errant, the irrational, and the unpredictable [. . .] 'Black Futures' are here in every now" (32, emphasis added).

What matters to me in these briefly evoked otherwise critical keys at the end of my discussion of the problem of time and transformation in critical thinking is to concretize what I have pursued as my critical wager in this text: to move after humanism by way of a criticality envisioned as systemic shifting and calling on a different temporality as crucial to such a project. In ways that strongly resonate with Wynter, Muñoz' queer(ing), Moten's "in the blur," Glissant's opacity and Keeling's "Black Futures" critically shift (us) by putting the brakes on the dominant vision of time as sequential teleological progression. Queer(ing) and blur(ring), as much as claiming opacity, are critical strategies that are not about moving on and forward to the next thing. How could they be! Instead, and in resonance with what I explored in this text as the different modalities of *after* in Wynter (diffracted with Barad and Kirby), these moves suggest forms of being critically after, of pushing and looking after without falling prey to linear progressivism. What I hope to have shown, then, is that as (aspiring) critical thinkers "we" can intervene otherwise; in ways that allow for another critical *para*-logic disruptive of the mono-tony of classical critique.

Yet, before ending, there is one more voice that I would like to include in my interference pattern of critical thinking, composed after the end of critique. It is the voice of Lauren Oya Olamina, the main protagonist in the Afrofuturist dystopian novel *Parable of the Sower* by Octavia Butler, written in 1993. Being set in the future of 2024, it feels eerily contemporary to us today when we encounter "our" future in this book. A multiplicity of natural and sociopolitical disasters force Laurel to live the end of "the World as she knows it." Trying to survive and adapt to this critical planetary condition, she starts writing a book, *EARTHSEED: THE BOOK OF THE LIVING*, and she opens it with the following aphorism:

> Prodigy is, at its essence, adaptability and persistent, positive obsession. Without persistence, what remains is an enthusiasm of the moment. Without adaptability, what remains may be channeled into destructive fanaticism. Without positive obsession, there is nothing at all. (Butler 2019, 2)

Wit(h)nessing today's current planetary condition, it seems to me that by holding on to critical thinking I look for such prodigy, consisting of adaptable yet insisting alliances for think-practicing another futurity.[23] *"It is time . . ."* to start investing in frictional relations with/in critical thinking in order to disturb the established comfort zones that keep rather than that they change the order of "today."[24] De-/Anti-colonial critiques and critical posthumanisms as they have figured together in this chapter might be said to differ too significantly. Yet, as contemporary critical praxes, they are *after* the genre of the human as Man in a systemic, multidirectional sense. If one of the tasks of critical thinking today is to unsettle the monotony of the hegemonic ways, to conceptualize, politicize and un-work the logic of Man, then multi-perspectival systemicity as the horizon of theory-practice is key. What my reading of Wynter's "towards the human, after Man" and its reverberations throughout this chapter hope to foreground is that an *e/affective criticality* initiates a different spacetimemattering—plurivocal and happening all at once. It is a deep concern with tempo, rhythm, and tonality with/in critical thought-practices that continually pushes me to look for further interferences between ever more diverging thought-practices instead of searching for the one formula that gets "beyond." Holding on to the possibility of critical thinking as such an open and generous praxis, I cherish frictional polyvocality and a non-harmonious pluriverse of theory and practice with a view to change.

NOTES

1. "The philosophers have only interpreted the world, in various ways; the point is to change it." Thesis XI of *Theses on Feuerbach* (https://www.marxists.org/archive/marx/works/1845/theses/theses.htm).

2. Speaking of "affective" here, I need to stress that while I indeed take recourse to a Spinozian heretical thought tradition (with followers up to today's "affective turn"), I do not use this terminology as if "to affect and be affected" is written within a framework of equality or direct reciprocity. I agree with more hesitant takes on affect as a dimension and not as a solution to relations of power (see also Thiele 2017).

3. This section of the text continues from an earlier presentation of Wynter's critical project in "Critical Matters: Auto-, Sym- and Copoiesis in Ettinger, Haraway and Wynter," in Thiele (2021).

4. See esp. Wynter (2003) for a detailed explication of the hi/story of Man1 and Man2, and the rewriting of the coloniality of Being toward a different humanism.

5. I speak here of the Luhmanian version of systems theory, which was also a central part of my own education in Sociology at the University of Bielefeld. While also Luhmanians rely on Maturana/Varela's concept of autopoiesis, they do so in order to describe how systems function, that is, they use autopoiesis as a definition of

systematicity and not as a *performative* quality in the way I see at work in Wynter. For more political uses of autopoiesis in Luhmanian Systems Theory, see Rasch and Wolfe (2002) and more recently Nassehi (2020).

6. More than once in her work Wynter refers to Judith Butler's performative understanding of gender as an "illuminating redefinition of gender as a praxis rather than a noun" (cited in Wynter and McKittrick 2015, 33). While Wynter's relation to (Western) feminisms is ambivalent (also at this occasion she raises the criticism that Butler delimits the "performative enactment" only to gender and not to "*all our roles*"), the significance of a materializing performativity is unquestioned in Wynter it seems: "All as praxes, therefore, rather than *nouns*. So here you have the idea that with being human *everything is praxis*. For we are not purely biological beings!" (33–34).

7. In her introduction to the volume *Sylvia Wynter: Being Human as Praxis*, McKittrick also writes: "Being human, in this context, signals not a noun but a verb. Being human is a praxis of humanness that does not dwell on the static empiricism of the unfittest and the downtrodden and situate the most marginalized within the incarcerated colonial categorization of oppression; being human as praxis is, to borrow from Maturana and Varela, 'the realization of the living' " (McKittrick 2015a, 3–4).

8. Wynter represents for me here a long tradition of Black Studies, where authors such as Lewis Gordon, Paul Gilroy, Stuart Hall, but also Black feminists such as Ferreira da Silva, Hortense Spillers, Saidiya Hartman, or Katherine McKittrick develop(ed) and stress(ed) the existence of other humanisms, to the side of the dominant liberal versions.

9. McKittrick spells out Wynter's "scientific challenge" as a "threefold" answer: "[T]o explore how the governing code of Man-as-human is implicit to how the human *organism* biologically feels and experiences and creates; to think through how questions of physiology, neurobiology, physics, math, and other areas allocated to the natural sciences can be conceptualized *in relation to* human activities (rather than as naturally pregiven); and to denaturalize biocentricity and its attendant fallen/dysselected castoffs while honoring the science of functioning living systems" (McKittrick 2015b, 146–147).

10. In view of the question of (un-)ground(ing) I can also briefly exemplify where Wynter differs in relation to Michel Foucault's genealogical counter-enlightenment project. Wynter's onto-epistemological work might show similarities to the ways in which Foucault's archaeology of the European epistemic regime has pictured the history of Man (Foucault 1994). But I follow Ferreira da Silva once more when she argues that Wynter "fissures Foucault's account of the modern episteme" (2015, 91), because Wynter's critique "allows us to appreciate the ethico-political significance of Man's being as *an empirical thing* and how it . . . [became] the signifier of European difference" (91–92, emphasis added). So, in a more differentially aware manner— refusing *any* ideational universality of human as Man, because of the always asymmetrically structured *reality* of the question who counts as hu/man—Wynter's critical analysis cuts deeper than Foucault's. Wynter explicates the colonial order and/as anti-Blackness as the very ground(ing) of modern biocentrism and thus also as the very ground(ing) of human as Man; thereby "cutting together-apart" what Foucault

seems to only "cut apart." The terminology of "cutting together-apart" is, according to Karen Barad, a move that undoes the dichotomous setting of difference as "cutting in two" (Barad 2014, 168).

11. In Barad's different "spacetimemattering," or agential realism, "[m]atter, like meaning, is not an individually articulated or static entity. Matter is not little bits of nature, or a blank slate, surface, or site passively awaiting signification; nor is it an uncontested ground for scientific, feminist, or Marxist theories. Matter is not a support, location, referent, or source of sustainability for discourse. Matter is not immutable or passive. It does not require the mark of an external force like culture or history to complete it. Matter is always already an ongoing *historicity*" (Barad 2003, 821, emphasis added). To read Wynter with the help of posthuman(ist) quantum theorizing seems to me helpful to permeate the complexity of Wynter's post-monohumanist project. I also aim to test out possible alliances between decolonial and posthuman(ist) thinking which I find also in other Black feminist scholarship. See, for example, works by Denise Ferreira da Silva, Evelyn Hammonds, Zakiyyah Iman Jackson, Kara Keeling, or Katherine McKittrick.

12. This formulation is inspired by Donna Haraway's *Staying with the Trouble* (Haraway 2016).

13. See also Kaiser and Thiele (2018) for a discussion of "returning (to)" in relation to both Barad's and Wynter's work. And to add one further sound-cloud for the critical move I try to bring across here: re-turning also resonates with re-tuning. Re-tuning is not about merely tuning back in/to what was before. Rather, it is about attending to interferences that need to be accommodated or tuned in anew, over and over again. For such a sound-cloud of retuning, see Griselda Pollock on feminist artist-theorist Bracha L. Ettinger, whose work on matrixial borderspaces Pollock describes as "not the opposite to the phallic order's preferred terms" but as "subject to perpetual *retuning* . . . never stabilized as a cut, split, or division" (Pollock 2006, 19 emphasis added). And Pollock continues: "Retuning opens onto acoustic, sonorous, and tactile potentialities that themselves move beyond the limits of bodies and the boundaries between inside and outside, suggesting wavelengths and frequencies that resonate and come into and move out of connection without ever being completely held or lost" (20).

14. Barad uses Derrida's hauntology as pushing after the metaphysics of presence in Barad (2010) and (2018).

15. Though ideationally committed to nonlinearity, there are quite some posthuman(ist) and new materialist interventions, in which (un)consciously the argument of replacement based on a constructed categorical opposition, a safe outside to which "we" could refer, prevails. But as Kirby in a recent interview on her work explicates: "[T]he denigration of the past as exhausted and even foolish has the effect of leveraging its replacement . . . with almost automatic importance and authority. The trap for the unwary is that replacing what is moribund with what is vital, or what is exclusionary with what is generous and inclusive, relies on the same logics and methodological strategies said to be exhausted" (Kirby and McLoughlin 2019, 264).

16. I explicate this point of how thinking *is* worlding more thoroughly in Thiele (2015). For more on "sensibility" as critical force, see O'Leary in this volume.

17. Since Wynter uses an older translation of Fanon's *Black Skin, White Masks* (by Charles Lam Markman [1967] 1986), I stay here with the phrasing given in her texts. The more recent translation of the work by Richard Philcox gives the original "*Comment s'en sortir?*" as "How can we break the cycle?" (Fanon 2008, xiv). In the following, I work with the more recent translation of *Black Skin, White Masks*.

18. "Alongside phylogeny and ontogeny, there is also sociogeny" (Fanon 2008, xv); for a more detailed discussion of Fanon see also Kaiser in this volume.

19. For an insightful discussion of Wynter's systemic (not social constructivist) use of sociogenesis, also in resonance with feminist posthumanisms, see Hantel (2018). For a more critical reading of Wynter's use of Fanonian sociogeny, see also Marriot (2018, 278–313).

20. For insightful contributions to the question of "antinormativity" in queer theory, see also Robyn Wiegman and Elizabeth Wilson's edited special issue for *Differences* (2015).

21. Moten evokes here of course also Édouard Glissant whose relational ontology (as hauntology) of "consent not to be a single being" binds together Moten's recent Trilogy (*Black and Blur*, *Stolen Life*, and *The Universal Machine*). I will come back to Glissant in what follows.

22. In a short aphorism on the notion of *Poetics*, Birgit M. Kaiser in a different context stresses specifically the very unscalability of "the poetic" as a worlding force "infinitely small and infinitely large at the same time, and always in the plural" (Kaiser 2020, 41). She also links this understanding to Glissant's *Poetics of Relation* in which he demands a poetic thinking that is "a thought that 'beneath the fantasy of domination [. . .] sought the really livable world' " (cited in Kaiser 2020, 41).

23. For the notion of "wit(h)nessing," see Bracha L. Ettinger's *The Matrixial Borderspace* (Ettinger 2006).

24. "It is time . . ." was the title of the last season in Terra Critica's *ReadingRoom* (co-organized with *Casco Art Institute: Working for the Commons* in Utrecht, NL), interrupted half-way by the COVID-19 related shutdowns in 2020. In relation to my claim for coalitions and a frictional coalition politics in theory and practice, I want to recall black feminist Bernie Johnson Reagon who in reflecting on her political activism once stressed that doing coalition politics means that "[m]ost of the time you feel threatened to the core and if you don't, you're not really doing no coalescing" (Reagon 1983, 356).

BIBLIOGRAPHY

Atwood, Margret. 2019. "Greeting, Earthlings! What Are These Human Rights of Which You Speak?" In *The World as It Is in the Eyes of Margret Atwood, Wole Soyinka, Ai Weiwei*, 9–23. Amsterdam: Nexus Institute.

Barad, Karen. 2003. "Posthumanist Performativity: Towards an Understanding of How Matter Comes to Matter." *Signs: Journal of Women in Culture and Society* 28 (3): 801–831.

———. 2007. *Meeting the Universe Halfway: Quantum Physics and the Entanglement of Matter and Meaning*. Durham, NC: Duke University Press.

———. 2010. "Quantum Entanglements and Hauntological Relations of Inheritance: Dis/Continuities, Space Time Enfolding, and Justice-to-Come." *Derrida Today* 3 (2): 240–247.

———. 2014. "Diffracting Diffraction: Cutting Together-Apart." *Parallax* 20 (3): 168–187.

———. 2018. "Troubling Time/s and Ecologies of Nothingness: Re-Turning, Re-Membering, and Facing the Incalculable." *New Formations: A Journal of Culture/Theory/Politics* 92: 56–86.

Butler, Octavia. [1993] 2019. *Parable of the Sower*. London: Headline Publishing Group.

Césaire, Aimé. [1955] 2000. *Discourse on Colonialism*, translated by Joan Pinkham. New York: Monthly Review Press.

Derrida, Jacques. 2019. *Theory & Practice*, translated by David Wills. Chicago: The University of Chicago Press.

Ettinger, Bracha L. 2006. *The Matrixial Borderspace*. Minneapolis: The University of Minnesota Press.

Fanon, Frantz. [1952] 1986. *Black Skin, White Masks*, translated by Charles Lam Markman. London: Pluto Press.

———. [1952] 2008. *Black Skin, White Masks*, translated by Richard Philcox. New York: Grove Press.

Ferreira da Silva, Denise. 2014. "Toward a Black Feminist Poethics: The Quest(ion) of Blackness Toward the End of the World." *The Black Scholar* 44 (2): 81–97.

———. 2015. "Before *Man*: Sylvia Wynter's Rewriting of the Modern Episteme." In *Sylvia Wynter: On Being Human as Praxis*, edited by K. McKittrick, 90–105. Durham, NC: Duke University Press.

Foucault, Michel. [1966] 1994. *The Order of Things: An Archeology of the Human Sciences*, translated by Alan Sheridan. New York: Vintage Books.

Glissant, Édouard. [1990] 2010. *Poetics of Relation*, translated by Betsy Wing. Ann Arbor: The University of Michigan Press.

Hantel, Max. 2018. "What is it Like to Be a Human? Sylvia Wynter on Autopoiesis." *Philosophia* 8 (1): 61–79.

Haraway, Donna. 2016. *Staying with the Trouble: Making Kin in the Chthulucene*. Durham, NC: Duke University Press.

Kaiser, Birgit M. 2020. "Poetics." In *Counterclaims: Poets and Poetries, Talking Back*, edited by H. L. Hix, 41–42. McLean/Dublin: Dalkey Archive Press.

Kaiser, Birgit M., and Kathrin Thiele. 2018. "Returning (to) the Question of the Human: An Introduction." *Philosophia* 8 (1): 1–17.

Keeling, Kara. 2019. *Queer Times, Black Futures*. New York: New York University Press.

Kirby, Vicki. 2018. "Un/Limited Ecologies." In *Eco-Deconstruction: Derrida and Environmental Philosophy*, edited by M. Fritsch, Ph. Lynes, and D. Wood, 121–140. New York: Fordham Press.

Kirby, Vicki, and Daniel McLoughlin. 2019. "Interview with Vicki Kirby." *Theory, Culture & Society* 36 (7–8): 261–271.

Marriott, David. 2018. *Whither Fanon? Studies in the Blackness of Being*. Stanford: Stanford University Press.
Marx, Karl. 1845. "Theses on Feuerbach." Accessed January 30, 2021. https://www.marxists.org/archive/marx/works/1845/theses/theses.htm.
Maturana, Humberto R. 1980. "Introduction." In *Autopoiesis and Cognition: The Realization of the Living*, edited by H. R. Maturana and F. J. Varela, xi–xxx. Dordrecht/Boston: D. Reidel Publishing Company.
Maturana, Humberto R., and Francisco J. Varela. [1972] 1980. "Autopoiesis: The Organization of the Living." In *Autopoiesis and Cognition: The Realization of the Living*, 63–134. Dordrecht/Boston: D. Reidel Publishing Company.
McKittrick, Katherine. 2015a. "Yours in the Intellectual Struggle: Sylvia Wynter and the Realization of the Living." In *Sylvia Wynter: On Being Human as Praxis*, edited by K. McKittrick, 1–8. Durham, NC: Duke University Press.
———. 2015b. "Axis, Bold as Love: On Sylvia Wynter, Jimi Hendrix, and the Promise of Science." In *Sylvia Wynter: On Being Human as Praxis*, edited by K. McKittrick, 142–163. Durham, NC: Duke University Press.
Mignolo, Walter D. 2015. "Sylvia Wynter: What Does It Mean to Be Human?" In *Sylvia Wynter: On Being Human as Praxis*, edited by K. McKittrick, 106–123. Durham, NC: Duke University Press.
Moten, Fred. 2017. "The Blur and Breathe Books." In *Black and Blur*, 245–269. Durham, NC: Duke University Press.
Muñoz, José Esteban. [2009] 2019. *Cruising Utopia: The Then and There of Queer Futurity*. New York: New York University Press.
Nassehi, Armin. 2020. *Das große Nein: Eigendynamik und Tragik des gesellschaftlichen Protests*. Hamburg: Kursbuch Verlag.
Pollock, Griselda. 2006. "Femininity: Aporia or Sexual Difference?" In *The Matrixial Borderspace*, edited by B. L. Ettinger, 1–38. Minneapolis: The University of Minnesota Press.
Rasch, William, and Cary Wolfe. 2002. *Observing Complexity: Systems Theory and Postmodernity*. Minneapolis: The University of Minnesota Press.
Reagon, Bernie Johnson. 1983. "Coalition Politics: Turning the Century." In *Home Girls: A Black Feminist Anthology*, edited by B. Smith, 356–368. New York: Kitchen Table Press.
Sithole, Tendayi. 2020. *The Black Register*. Cambridge: Polity Press.
Thiele, Kathrin. 2015. "Theorizing is *Worlding*—Teaching New Feminist Materialisms in Contemporary Feminist Theory Courses." In *Teaching with Feminist Materialisms*, edited by P. Hinton and P. Treusch, 99–109. Utrecht: ATGENDER.
———. 2017. "Affirmation." In *Symptoms of the Planetary Condition: A Critical Vocabulary*, edited by M. Bunz, B. M. Kaiser, and K. Thiele, 25–29. Lüneburg: Meson Press [Open Access].
———. 2021 (forthcoming). "Critical Matters: Auto-, Sym- and Copoiesis in Ettinger, Haraway and Wynter." In *Human After Man*, edited by S. Witzgall and M. Kesting. Zürich: Diaphanes.

Wiegman, Robyn, and Elizabeth Wilson. 2015. "Queer Theory Without Antinormativity." *Special Issue Differences: A Journal of Feminist Cultural Studies* 26 (1).

Wynter, Sylvia. 1984. "The Ceremony Must Be Found: After Humanism." *Boundary II* 13 (1): 19–70.

———. 1994. "'No Humans Involved': An Open Letter to My Colleagues." *Forum N.H.I.: Knowledge for the 21st Century* 1 (1): 42–73.

———. 2003. "Unsettling the Coloniality of Being/Power/Truth/Freedom: Towards the Human, After Man, Its Overrepresentation—An Argument." *CR: The New Centennial Review* 3 (3): 257–337.

———. 2015. "The Ceremony Found: Towards the Autopoietic Turn/Overturn, Its Autonomy of Human Agency and Extraterritoriality of (Self-)Cognition." In *Black Knowledges/Black Struggles*, edited by J. R. Ambroise and S. Broek, 184–252. Liverpool: Liverpool University Press.

Wynter, Sylvia, and Greg Thomas. 2009. "Yours in the Intellectual Struggle!" In *The Caribbean Woman Writer as Scholar: Creating, Imagining, Theorizing*, edited by Keshia N. Abraham, 31–69. Coconut Creek: Caribbean Studies Press.

Wynter, Sylvia, and Katherine McKittrick. 2015. "Unparalleled Catastrophe for Our Species? Or, to Give Humanness a Different Future: Conversations." In *Sylvia Wynter: On Being Human as Praxis*, edited by K. McKittrick, 9–89. Durham, NC: Duke University Press.

2

The Most Difficult Task

On the Idea of an Impure Pure Nonviolence in Derrida

Leonard Lawlor

While my work on this aspect of Derrida's thought—his late lecture courses on the death penalty in particular—is motivated by general political concerns about prisons and the death penalty, what really motivated me is the idea of forgiveness. It seems to me that, if somehow, we were able to abolish the death penalty all over the earth, this event would imply a worldwide forgiveness of criminals. This connection between the abolition of the death penalty and forgiveness led me back to the problem of the gift. For Derrida, one cannot conceive forgiveness without conceiving the gift. So, the majority of the paper that follows considers the gift, but with an eye toward forgiveness. As is well-known Derrida says that forgiveness (or an act worthy of that name) takes place only in relation to an unforgiveable injury. If the injury can be forgiven, then the injury can be measured, and if it can be measured, then the forgiveness is commensurate with the injury. For Derrida, this is not forgiveness; it is an exchange. Forgiveness must be unconditional just as gift-giving must be unconditional: if I expect reciprocation for a gift I have given you, then we have an exchange. We have a commercial transaction. Derrida argues that the unconditionality of the gift and forgiveness is a conceptual necessity, but I also think he intends this necessity as an ethical necessity. I have found this double necessity of unconditionality (and Derrida will say at times without sovereignty) to be very attractive, just as I have found Kant's moral philosophy attractive: never treat others as a means to an end (i.e., never treat them as a condition for your action), but only ever treat them as an end in themselves (treat them unconditionally). This search for unconditionality—even though it is impossible since there seems always to be conditions—has motivated a lot of my work over the last fifteen years.

***

In his final courses at the Collège de France, *The Beast and the Sovereign*, Derrida says that his deconstruction of sovereignty follows the rhythm of what is happening in the world at the end of the twentieth century (2009, 76). What has been happening in the world are so many events, like terrorism, that disturb the sovereignty of nations. Following that rhythm, Derrida's deconstruction of sovereignty disturbs the concept of sovereignty. Most basically, the sovereign is someone who decides to make an exception. The sovereign is indeed someone who decides to make an exception—but for that decision to function it must be dictated, it must be uttered. For the decision to have its effect, it must be recognizable by the sovereign's subjects, which means the proclamation must repeat recognizable forms. But then, its function is undermined by the very thing that makes it possible: iterability. The recognized form opens the utterance to interpretations other than those intended; its meaning becomes divided from its intended meaning.[1] The sovereign then becomes subjected, as Derrida would say, to the "dissemination." And a sovereign subjected is no longer sovereign (Derrida 2009, 76–77). Thus, like so many of his deconstructions, Derrida's deconstruction of sovereignty shows that the condition for its possibility is at the same time the condition for its impossibility. However, the deconstruction of sovereignty seems to be different from the other deconstructions. Even though Derrida says that sovereignty must be renounced (2005, xiv), he wants to maintain what has constantly been associated with it: unconditionality. He wants to dissociate unconditionality from sovereignty. Unconditionality must be maintained because unconditionality is the condition for the possibility of a genuine or real decision, a decision that is an event and an event which produces effects. In fact, I think the point of this deconstruction is knowledge or know-how. Derrida wants us to know, he wants us to really know how to make a decision without being sovereign (since, no matter what, it is impossible). Similarly, the analysis of what a gift must be according to Derrida—it too must be unconditional in order for it not to be an economic exchange—provides, I hope, the know-how of gift-giving (a know-how which includes knowing how to pardon, the most important act of gift-giving). Therefore, the ends of critique, for me, consist in learning how to make genuine or real decisions, *without* exercising power over others. In short, the purpose of critique lies in taking sides for the least violence, even though violence is irreducible.[2]

At the beginning of his career, in what may be his most important essay, "Violence and Metaphysics," Derrida lays out the idea of transcendental violence. The adjective "transcendental" means pre-ethical violence, a violence prior to anyone's decision or will to harm another creature. Transcendental violence is then a priori. Indeed, as a priori, it possesses a logic, a phenomenology. Here is the logic. The first premise of this logic is the phenomenological insight (shown by Husserl in the Fifth Cartesian Meditation) that I have no direct or immediate access to the interior life of the other; the result of this insight is that every other is a singularity or wholly other (Derrida 2008, 82–87). Yet, I would not even have *indirect* or *mediated* access to the other, unless the other becomes a phenomenon. In fact, if the other never entered into my sphere of experience, I would not be able to speak of or to the other. The necessity of appearing is an openness to the other. This necessity is the only way that I am able to *give* something to the other. In other words, the necessity is the only way for me to be nonviolent to the other. The other must be *understood* under the general meaning of alterity; it must be understood *as* other. However, insofar as I understand (*comprendre*) the other as other, I take (*prendre*) the other into the meaning, into the general meaning, into the concept, or even into the category of alterity. In this way, the singularity of this other is lost. This necessary grasping (*prendre*) of the other is transcendental violence even as it makes possible nonviolence.[3]

Is it possible to have some sort of ethical response to transcendental violence? Given that this violence is transcendental, necessary, a priori, it seems not. In fact, many years after "Violence and Metaphysics," in "Passions," Derrida says that the most urgent questions are those of the ethicality of ethics, the morality of morality, the essence of responsibility (1995, 16–17). These urgent questions are also transcendental questions, questions prior to actual prescriptions. Thus, Derrida's thought seems to remain in the domain of what we usually call meta-ethics. Then, the attempt to find something like a prescriptive in Derrida seems useless, and perhaps impossible. Nevertheless, when faced with this irreducible violence, Derrida seems to "take sides" (*parti pris*); he sides with nonviolence to the other. For instance, in *The Gift of Death*, Derrida states that "deconstructionists" remain "disquieted" by those who display good conscience in the face of the suffering of others (2008, 85). But he continues that, while all societies would condemn the sacrifice of one's son to God (Abraham), these same societies do not condemn the constant sacrifice of others through starvation and diseases so that one does not have to sacrifice oneself; these others are victims of a "letting die," of neglect. As he says, this worldwide sacrifice "will necessarily be recalled to those who just as necessarily forget it" (Derrida 2008, 86). Derrida is suggesting that he is one of the voices "calling" these societies "back" (*rappeler*) from their good conscience. Similarly, in the death penalty lectures (*Death Penalty 1*), Derrida is clearly siding with the abolitionists (even though he is deconstructing abolitionism) (2014, 82n19, 254–259).

Therefore, if Derrida seems to be taking sides with nonviolence and therefore with the abolitionists of the death penalty, and even though Derrida *never* says this anywhere in his writings, then taking the side of nonviolence—or taking the side of others—requires a kind of impure, pure nonviolence. An impure, pure nonviolence would be a nonviolence that aims at complete nonviolence—this is why it is pure—but also a nonviolence that is still violent. It must be violent since violence is irreducible, making the action impure. This chapter attempts to explore this idea (inspired by Derrida) of an impure, pure nonviolence. The idea of an impure, pure nonviolence implies an attempt to determine the golden mean. Indeed, as Derrida says in *Given Time*, finding the "golden mean" (*aurea mediocritas*) between economy and gift-giving is "perhaps the most difficult task" (1992, 64). Throughout most of this chapter, we are going to confine our exploration to Derrida's first published book explicitly on the gift, *Given Time* (*Donner le temps*). You can already see, I hope, why I would privilege this one book; violence for Derrida consists in a taking, and thus nonviolence must be found in the direction of giving. Thus, another way of expressing this idea of an impure, pure nonviolence is through the idea of the gift. A gift is excessive in relation to economic exchange—this is why it is pure—but it is also an exchangeable commodity—since no gift can be completely outside of exchange, making the gift impure. To anticipate a bit, we can say that the model of the impure, pure nonviolence is the giving of *counterfeit money*. But, as we shall see when we turn to Derrida's death penalty lectures, Derrida considers a compromise with the death penalty (suggested by Camus in his "Reflections on the Guillotine" [Camus 1960]). If we understand this compromise correctly, it amounts to something like a counterfeit death penalty.[4] We shall end with a consideration of this impure pure non-cruelty.

THE LOGIC OF THE GIFT IN *GIVEN TIME*

In this first section, we are going to reconstruct Derrida's logic of the gift (just as we reconstructed the logic of transcendental violence above).[5] This logic starts with our pre-understanding of the gift, or even the commonsense view of the gift. First, "our logic and language" (common sense) state the basic structure of the gift: someone wants or desires, someone intends-to-give, to someone. We would say that "some 'one' " (A) intends-to-give B to C, some "one" intends to give or gives "something" to "someone other" (Derrida 1992, 11). For the gift to be possible, this compound structure is indispensable. Second, and more importantly, our pre-understanding of the gift tells us that the gift must not be motivated by any gain; it must not be bound to the economic exchange of commodities; it must not be a purchase (of a gift given back, of love, of honor, or recognition). Thus, our pre-understanding also tells us that the gift must be—this is its most basic or primary condition—*unconditional* (Derrida 1992, 123).

While unconditionality is the primary and first condition of the giving of a gift, the list of conditions for a gift are contradictory.[6] Because of the contradictory nature of the conditions, Derrida calls the giving of a gift an aporia or a paradox. Here is the list of aporias that Derrida indicates in *Given Time*: (1) the conditions of possibility are simultaneously the conditions of impossibility (Derrida 1992, 26). This formula means that a gift must be exchanged or be a phenomenon (condition of the gift's impossibility) and a gift must be excessive and non-phenomenal in relation to exchange (condition of possibility). In other words, if there is no gift (no recognizable gift), there is no gift; if there is a gift (recognized as such), again there is no gift (because it is recognized, it demands a counter-gift, which reduces the gift to a commodity being exchanged) (14–15). (2) There is a double violence to the gift. Here we return to the language of "prendre." There is the violence of the circular exchange (the gift is understood [*compris*] as a gift and thus demands the counter-gift) and the violence of the gift's sur-prise (*surprendre*). (Overall—this claim is true of *The Gift of Death* [*Donner la mort*] too—Derrida is trying to show that giving and taking cannot be isolated from one another. He shows the same in the death penalty lectures where taking life and giving death are inseparable [Derrida 2014, 238].) In any case, when I give a gift as such, recognized as such, the recipient is taken into the trap of being in debt; and when I give a gift as such, I give a surprise. The literal meaning of "surprise" means "to take over." This "taking over" or "grasping" (*la prise*) is why the surprise which interrupts exchange is violence, just as the exchange is the violence of the same. (3) Time—recall that the title of the book is *Donner le temps*—makes the gift (a remainder) be reversible from good to bad or vice versa. Derrida frequently refers to the gift as the *pharmakon*, which can be either a cure or a poison. As we can see from this list, the aporias imply that it is impossible for a gift to be a pure gift. A pure gift would completely exceed economic exchange. But as such, it would not be recognized as a gift. Again, if there is no gift recognized as such, there is no gift. Therefore, the aporias imply that all gifts are impure. But as we said above our question is: is it possible to give an impure *pure* gift? If such a gift-giving is possible, then critique would be defined as taking sides for the least violence, even though violence is irreducible.

In *Given Time*, Derrida also indicates a number of conditions for a *pure gift*. Here is the list of the pure gift's conditions.[7] As we have seen, the primary condition of any gift is that the gift must be unconditional. If it is to be pure, the gift would have to escape completely from any logic of economy. This primary and negative (unconditional) condition of the pure gift implies a series of additional *negative* conditions. These conditions can be systematized into those regarding the giver and those for the recipient. In fact, there is only one condition for the recipient, and we have seen this already: when received, the gift must not be recognized as such. If it were recognized, the recipient would feel obligated to return a gift, to reciprocate and restitute.

Reciprocation would transform the gift into a commodity of exchange. And, if reciprocation implies a kind of equality in the exchange, then, and positively, the gift itself must exceed equality so that it cannot be reciprocated. The requirement that the gift given be excessive takes us to the side of the giver. In fact, the majority of the conditions are for the giver. They tell us what is required in giving in order to have the result of no recognition in the recipient. Here is the list of conditions for the donor, for the giving of the pure gift. (1) The giving of the pure must not be calculable (and conversely and positively, the giving must involve chance or the aleatory); it must obey a principle of indetermination (Derrida 1992, 24, 124). (2) And this follows from the first condition: the giving of the gift must follow no program (162). (3) The pure gift must not be motivated by any moral obligation, including the obligation to be generous; in this sense, the giving of the pure gift is anti-moral (162). (4) The giving of the pure gift must not be caused by anything like a natural inclination like maintaining one's survival; in this sense, the giving of the pure gift is anti-natural (162). (5) The pure gift must not be given as a sacrifice in the sense of an offering offered in exchange for a future reward (137) (although in *The Gift of Death* Derrida attempts to isolate the conditions of a pure sacrifice, that is, a sacrifice that does not resemble a purchase [Derrida 2008, 64–65]). The principle (if we can call it this) of all of the giver's conditions is the following: the giving of the gift must not be subjected to the principle of reason (Derrida 1992, 123). The principle (again if we can call it a principle) for all of the conditions, those for the giver as well as for the recipient, is the following: the pure gift must not be present or be a present; it must be outside of time understood as a circle (of exchange) (8–9). As early as *Voice and Phenomenon*, Derrida had "deconstructed" the conception of time based on the present (or presence) (Derrida 2011, 51–59). Here, in *Given Time*, when Derrida says that the pure gift must tear time apart, he is implying that the pure gift must "interrupt" the temporal synthesis which produces a present (Derrida 1992, 9, 147). The pure gift must be a-synthetic, which means that when it is given it must interrupt the flow of memories which leads to the anticipation of the future. If there is anticipation in the giver, then he will expect that the gift will or should be reciprocated in the future. If there is anticipation in the recipient, then he will expect a certain kind of gift; he will then measure the gift given in terms of the expectation and thereby will assess the right kind of gift with which to reciprocate. Again, reciprocation transforms the pure gift into exchange, making it impure.

Positively, on the side of the recipient, the gift must exceed the horizon of expectation; it must be unforeseeable and excessive. This excess is why Derrida speaks of an "absolute surprise," one not relative to any expectation (Derrida 1992, 122, 156). This absolute surprise explains why Derrida says that the pure gift must be given in an *incalculable* instant and produce an unprogrammed event (146–147).[8] As we shall see, the instant is at the center of Derrida's reflections on the death penalty but here he is concerned with the idea that the instant can be calculated. In any case, by *breaking apart*—here is the surprise's violence—the temporal synthesis of memories and expectations, the pure gift must be one that is forgotten immediately, on the side of the giver and on the side of the recipient. The giver must forget it so that he does not expect reciprocation, and the recipient must forget it so that he does not feel obligated to reciprocate. The surprise of the gift must be so surprising that the gift is forgotten in an instant (147). In fact, Derrida says that—this must be one of the most paradoxical ideas in *Given Time*—this forgetfulness must be absolute (16). By this "absolute," Derrida seems to mean that this forgetfulness must be complete, allowing for no memory of the giving or receiving to return in a memory image. In fact, the memory must be more than repressed. It must be repressed so thoroughly that it cannot come back even in a dream. Clearly, this kind of forgetfulness is impossible. Thankfully, Derrida also speaks of the desire to forget (35). Desiring to forget, at least that is possible. Here, we return to our question. If the pure gift is impossible—it cannot be completely forgotten and thus it can never completely escape from exchange—then what is possible? Is there a way to approximate the pure gift? What must be prescribed for an impure, *pure* gift?

THE IMPURE PURE GIFT: COUNTERFEIT MONEY

In order to develop the idea of an impure pure gift, we must follow Derrida's analysis, in *Given Time*, of Baudelaire's story "Counterfeit Money" ("La fausse monnaie"). Briefly, Baudelaire's story consists in two friends exiting a tobacco store; they encounter a beggar; the friend (not the narrator) gives a silver coin to the beggar; when the narrator asks the friend to justify his excessive generosity, the friend says, "It was a counterfeit coin."

Derrida's analysis of the story amounts to an analysis of counterfeit money itself and thus of money itself. It is clear that money is part of the economy and exchange. Derrida says that there is no money without faith or credit; "Everything is an act of faith" (Derrida 1992, 97). When you give me paper money or metal coins, I have to believe that the money will allow me to purchase something else. This is the convention that supports money. Counterfeit money is clearly still money insofar as "counterfeit money [*fausse monnaie*: false money] must be taken for true money and for that it must give itself for correctly titled money" (84). Therefore, appearing as true money, counterfeit money enters into exchange. But, if it is discovered as counterfeit or false, it can no longer be exchanged. Counterfeit money seems to be at once inside exchange and outside exchange. In other words, the gift of counterfeit money is recognized as true money, but necessarily it cannot be recognized as counterfeit money—since it would no longer function as true money. In giving counterfeit money, one has the intention or desire to give, but not the intention to give true money. This negation of intention at least begins to escape from the principle of reason. It at least cannot be explained by the intention of giving true money. There is nothing honorable in giving counterfeit money to a beggar; the giver cannot congratulate himself for being generous. In fact, the giver has given nothing. The lack of self-congratulation at least opens the possibility of forgetfulness: I gave him nothing; there is nothing to remember. While this is not absolute forgetting, it still amounts to something like desire for forgetfulness. Thus, the gift of counterfeit money satisfies several conditions for a pure gift. Even though the gift of counterfeit money is not pure since it gives itself off as true money, making it exchangeable, the gift of counterfeit money, *as counterfeit*, is outside of exchange and therefore exceeds it. It also allows for forgetting, which stops the anticipation and the obligation of reciprocation. And, there is chance (or no program) since the giver cannot predict what will happen to the beggar in the future. It obeys the principle of indetermination. Most importantly and consequently, the gift of counterfeit money interrupts the cycle of time. As we see in the Baudelaire story, there is chance in this gift since the "friend," the one who gives does not know and cannot know—no program—what will happen to the beggar in the future. The gift of counterfeit money then is not simply present since its effects (gift-effects) are unpredictable. In this way, counterfeit money gives time (*donner le temps*), that is, time within which the beggar is able to do things. Here, with the noncircular movement of time—no foreknowledge—we have the possibility, the "perhaps," of the gift becoming good or bad for the beggar.

This "perhaps" makes possible two polar outcomes for the beggar. Either the counterfeit money is taken as true money and the beggar will increase his fortune; or the counterfeit money is discovered to be false, and the beggar's fortune will be diminished. These possible outcomes mean that, beyond the initial surprise of the silver coin, there is going to be at least one more surprise or event in the beggar's life. The beggar will probably not be able to forget this combination of surprises (actual and possible). But here too, the beggar can desire to forget. If the silver coin is discovered to be false money, then, it seems, the beggar will feel no need for reciprocation. He was given nothing; he owes nothing to the person who gave it to him. If the coin is never discovered to be false, then, it seems, the beggar might again feel no need for reciprocation. The beggar might not feel the need for reciprocation, because the excess of the gift might be beyond his ways of measuring gifts, meaning that the beggar will not know how to reciprocate. I think the logic of this claim is probably flawed, since, if the beggar increases his fortune, it seems more likely he will feel an obligation of reciprocation.

But we should return to the side of the giver. Derrida speculates about the "friend's" statement, "It was a counterfeit coin." One of his speculations is that we can "credit" the "friend" "with feeling innocent of having given a counterfeit coin" (Derrida 1992, 149–150). He might feel innocent since, by giving a counterfeit coin, "he withdrew from the cycle of the gift as violence." This withdrawal from the cycle of the gift as violence refers to the cycle of exchange, of required reciprocation. Here too, we have to keep in mind the fact that the friend gave nothing to the beggar and thus he, the friend, is "*pure* of any mastery" over the beggar (150, emphasis added). Having given him nothing (no true money), the beggar owes the "friend" nothing. And, even if the beggar increases his fortune, the beggar will still owe the friend nothing, since, again, the friend gave nothing in the first place. Therefore, with this withdrawal from the cycle of the gift as violence, with this possible innocence, we perhaps come closest to a pure gift, or, at least to a gift that has reduced (or attempted to reduce) its impurity and violence.

Before we turn to the conclusion, we should note that, for Derrida, the possible innocence of the friend is only one possible interpretation of the friend's statement that "it was a counterfeit coin." Immediately after suggesting the innocence interpretation, Derrida continues by proposing an "inverse hypothesis": "It is the hypothesis of the *worst violence*. At little cost [it was a counterfeit coin], while giving the poor man his chance, he has indebted that man who can do nothing about it, he has surprised his friend not only by the force of his calculations but also by the calm force of his confession" (Derrida 1994, 150, my emphasis). The inverse hypothesis claims that the friend had calculated how to produce the most violence at the smallest cost. In this interpretation, the friend has tried to turn the incalculable into the calculable or the unpredictable into the predictable. With violence, he has behaved as a capitalist: low cost, high profit. The giving of the counterfeit coin is then an act of mastery. As we shall see in a moment, Derrida's real objection to the death penalty is that it attempts to master time and in particular the future.

THE MOST DIFFICULT TASK

In *Given Time* (within a discussion of Mauss's *The Gift*), Derrida quotes Mauss, who in *The Gift* speaks about the golden mean (*aurea mediocritas*), the good rule, the good economy between economy and non-economy, the "not too much," "neither too much this or too much that," "a good but moderate blend of reality and the ideal" (Derrida 1992, 63). Concerning the golden mean, Derrida says that it would be thoughtless to laugh at the mediocrity:

The moderation of this *mediocritas* signals perhaps the most *difficult task*. Better—or worse—it announces perhaps a sort of paradoxical *hubris*, the *hubris* of the right measure (who dares to fix the right measure?), and even announces that vocation of the impossible to which all responsibility and every effective decision has to answer. (64, emphasis added)

Therefore, and again no one should laugh at this, for Derrida, the attempt to determine the golden mean is the impossible itself. This impossibility means that the friend in Baudelaire's story and we who give gifts are never truly innocent. We are always at fault for having always erred by being excessive on the side of exchange or by being excessive in non-exchange. As always for Derrida, there cannot be and there should not be any good conscience. Yet, if we have correctly understood Derrida's analysis of counterfeit money (the story and the thing), then it seems that Derrida is siding with the friend's giving of counterfeit money. We think this because he speculates that the friend might be innocent of mastery and at least of the violence of exchange (Derrida 1992, 150). As in "Violence and Metaphysics," in *Given Time*, Derrida says that violence is irreducible: "The violence appears irreducible, within the circle or outside it, whether it repeats the circle or interrupts it" (147). But again, if we are right about *Given Time*, then the friend has used the violence of the surprise (the sur-prise) against the violence of the cycle: "violence against violence" (Derrida 1978, 117). Or, he produces an impure, pure nonviolence. Even though determining the golden mean is impossible, this kind of impure, pure gift seems to get very close to the *aurea mediocritas*. The gift of counterfeit money is a pure gift because, if it is not discovered as counterfeit, it exceeds exchange insofar as no one can predict its effects. In this way, the giving of counterfeit money is a surprise and therefore violence, but a surprise aiming at nonviolence (the possible innocence of the friend). But of course, it is also impure because it really enters into exchange; the silver coin is equivalent to or the same as so many commodities. It therefore enters into the violence of the same.

Strange consequences result from the mediocre idea of the pure, impure gift. Indeed, if we prescribe this kind of gift-giving, the consequences are perhaps terrible. These consequences reinforce the feeling of no good conscience. Overall, the model of giving an impure, pure gift seems to prescribe to all of us that, if we want to be on the side of the poor, we should give counterfeit money. This would seem to be the surest way to release them from any obligation to reciprocate, from any debt to the giver. However, is giving counterfeit money really a good response to beggars? Is this giving innocence and a reduced violence or is it the height of guilt and the worst violence? Does this mean that we should not give true money, even though true money might keep the poor from starving to death? The impure, pure gift also resembles

Aristotle's purported statement about friendship: "oh my friend, there is no friend" (Derrida 1992, 164). Of course, Derrida analyzes this statement at length in *Politics of Friendship* (Derrida 1997). More generally, the statement implies that it is better not to be the friend insofar as friendship binds and obligates: not being a friend unbinds. Is this "not being friends" really what friendship means? Finally, we can move from friendship to love. The epitaph to chapter 3 of *Given Time* is a quotation from a chapter in Balzac's *Splendor and Miseries of Courtesans*, called "How Prostitutes Love." Of course, prostitutes or courtesans give themselves off as loving, but they do not truly love. Therefore, their love resembles counterfeit money. They love without loving. But, if giving counterfeit money is prescribed, then the love of prostitutes is prescribed. Can we really say this love is what love should be?

ON THE DEATH PENALTY

We are now going to extend the idea of an impure, pure nonviolence to Derrida's lectures on the death penalty. We can make this extension since the death penalty is a gift of death (*donner la mort*). This extension to the death penalty lectures follows directly from the discussion of the gift since what is at stake in the death penalty is "donner la mort," giving or putting to death (Derrida 2014, 237).[9] Here too, with the death penalty, we have a question of economy. At the beginning of the seventh session, Derrida recalls that the word "penalty" (*peine, poena*) had first of all the economic sense of ransom, repurchase, or redemption of the punishment meant to pay for damages: "penalty is a payment" (166). Thus, to give death, to inflict the death penalty is to be economical. This economy has two aspects. On the one hand, it is a question of equivalence, the equivalence between the crime and the punishment. This is the talionic law "an eye for an eye, a tooth for a tooth." Like the *aurea mediocritas*, the talionic law attempts to find a middle or an equivalence between a crime and a punishment. In the case of the death penalty, the talionic law poses an *equivalence* between a murder and the death of the murderer: a death for a death. Here, again, we see the *hubris* of determining this kind of equivalence. We should note, as Derrida does but without commentary, that, in his "Reflections on the Guillotine," Camus suggests that the punishment of death penalty would be equivalent to the crime if the murderer warned his victim in advance of the hour at which he would be murdered and while he waited for his murder he would have to watch the construction of the apparatus that would put him to death (Derrida 2014, 267; Camus 1960, 154). But even though Camus's suggestion seems to come close to the golden mean, such an attempt at equivalence seems absurd. Who would ever believe in this equivalence, who would ever believe that one life is equivalent to another's (Derrida 2014, 152)? On the other hand, the economy of the death penalty concerns interest or surplus value. A common argument made in favor of the death penalty is deterrence of future crimes. This argument then depends on a calculation of cause and effect; it depends on a kind of knowledge of determinations of outcomes; it therefore attempts to make the future determinate; it is an attempt at mastery of time.

Thus, it seems that if one wants to abolish the death penalty universally, one would have to break free of this economy. More precisely, as Derrida expresses quite strongly, one would have to challenge the knowledge of the future. The hinge of this knowledge is the knowledge of the instant of death.[10] Derrida argues that the death penalty presupposes that the objective knowledge of the instant of death coincides with the subjective experience of death (Derrida 2014, 220). Without this coincidence of the objective and the subjective, one cannot calculate the equivalence of the talionic law, and, it seems—I think this is Derrida's argument—one cannot calculate future effects of the death of the condemned. In short, the argument seems to be that if we do not know exactly when the prisoner has died, then we cannot know when this death will produce effects, and we cannot know what kinds of effects will occur. According to Derrida, this knowledge is impossible. We can see why if we recall that the phenomenological insight that we have no direct intuition of another's interior life. Or, one need only think of people who are "brain dead," but still on life-support devices to see that we lack this sort of knowledge (242). Simply, as Derrida says, "never more so than today . . . has this knowledge [of the instant of death] been as problematic, debatable, [and] fragile" (239). Thus, if there is something like an instant of death, this instant remains and must remain indeterminate and unknowable (cf. Derrida 2014, 219, 256, on the principle of indetermination). To think that it can be made determinate and knowledgeable is a "phantasm of omnipotence" (219).

Therefore, to put this knowledge of the instant of death in question, according to Derrida, is to challenge "the principle of the death penalty" (Derrida 2014, 50). He "deconstructs" the current abolitionist discourse because it does not challenge this principle (89n). Most often, the abolitionist discourse provides arguments based on the death penalty being "cruel and unusual punishment." But this sort of argument merely attacks the mode of the death penalty's application; the mode of application is merely modified by the use of anesthesia. Nevertheless, at the end of the first set of lectures, Derrida considers a "compromise with the death penalty," suggested by Camus again in his "Reflections on the Guillotine" (Derrida 2014, 281–282; Camus 1960, 179). Following the model of Socrates drinking the hemlock, Camus says that the prisoner should be provided with an anesthesia, an absolute anesthesia (one from which one would never awake) "for at least a day," and then he would "freely" take the anesthesia at some later moment, slipping from life to death. Because the compromise takes the determination of the instant of the prisoner's death out of the hands of the authorities, making it at least for them indeterminate, this compromise seems to break the economy of the death penalty. We are tempted to call this compromise a "counterfeit death penalty." Nevertheless, what Camus's compromise really resembles is suicide, and, thus again, it is based in a phantasm of omnipotence and a desire for mastery over the instant of one's own death.[11]

Camus suggests this compromise with the death penalty while we are awaiting its universal abolition. As we said at the beginning, there is no question that Derrida sides with the abolitionists and with the universal abolition of the death penalty. Yet, Derrida says that, even if there is a historical tendency toward the universal abolition of the death penalty "the question of what the universal abolition of the death penalty would mean [. . .] will remain intact" (Derrida 2014, 70). Derrida provides something like an answer to this question in the tenth lecture.[12] There, Derrida says, "the death penalty is always, by definition, death that comes from the other, given or decided by the other, be it the other within oneself" (250). The death penalty or "la peine de mort," the pain of death, is therefore always a gift from the other. But this gift of death is not the strangest consequence of Derrida's lectures on the death penalty, and perhaps of all of his reflections on the gift. Here it is. If we were to universally abolish the death penalty, this abolition would mean eliminating or even killing the other, and if the death by the other is death from the other within oneself, the universal abolition would amount to suicide (250). But, one can never really eliminate the other and especially not the other within oneself. This impossibility explains why Derrida concludes the first set of lectures by saying that, even if we could universally abolish the death penalty, something like it would survive. Thus, it is possible that what we commonly call a natural death cannot be rigorously distinguished from a gift of death. Thus, we mortals will never be able to determine precisely whether we are condemned to die or condemned to death (218).

That some form of the death penalty will survive or that death will survive indicates that violence can never be removed completely. But is the death penalty the worst violence? This is an open question since one can easily imagine that prolonged torture or a lifetime of solitary confinement is worse than lethal injection. This open question demonstrates the difficulty involved in trying to achieve the ends of critique: the reduction of violence to its lowest or even best level. How can we determine the lowest level of violence? The indetermination of the lowest level of violence implies that we cannot even form a mental picture of what the lowest level looks like. Nevertheless, this reduction is what critique must work toward. It must also realize that it cannot rest in good conscience. We will never be able to do enough to reduce violence to its lowest level. This bad conscience must even recognize that if we forgave everyone who has ever harmed us, this universal forgiveness would still not be enough. Like the gift, forgiveness is never pure. It is always possible that I have unconsciously placed you in a relationship of exchange. I have locked you into a logic of economy. But this possibility (which makes forgiveness impossible) finally implies that when I forgive, I must also beg for forgiveness for that very forgiveness. My future work will focus on this problem of how to forgive, or, more precisely how not to forgive.

NOTES

1. The utterance is also immediately divisible because the instant of time, even if it is razor thin, is necessarily connected to a memorial aspect which can be repeated since it is recallable. This repeatability (or iterability again) makes the instant projectible into the unforeseeable future.

2. This article continues the work I undertook on Derrida in *This Is Not Sufficient* and in *From Violence to Speaking Out* (Lawlor 2007 and 2016). This article also has two companion articles, "The Gift of Time: The Question of the Death Penalty in Derrida," *Southern Journal of Philosophy*, forthcoming 2020, and " 'Unique as Immediately Iterable': Derrida's Attempted Dissociation of Unconditionality from Sovereignty," for *The Oxford Handbook of Modern French Philosophy*, forthcoming 2021. A portion of this article was previously published in *Studia Phaenomenologica*, 2020.

3. In *Totality and Infinity*, Levinas makes use of the verb "prendre" to express violence: "violence bears only upon a being both graspable [*saisisable*] and escaping every hold [*prise*]" (Levinas 1969, 223).

4. Derrida says that this compromise is "both serious and flimsy [*leger*]" (Derrida 2014, 281; see also, 50: "strong and weak"). The compromise is serious because it seems to reduce the cruelty or violence of the death penalty. It is flimsy or superficial because it allows the death penalty to continue. It only changes the technical modality of the death penalty; it does not strike at the principle of the death penalty. Throughout the first set of lectures, Derrida constantly criticizes the arguments against the death penalty based on its cruelty (see, for example, Derrida 2014, 72). In this chapter, I am taking the compromise seriously as Derrida suggests. I acknowledge that it does not dismantle the death penalty as such.

5. Michael Naas provides a lot of insight into the logic of the gift by analyzing Derrida's essay, "Khora." See Naas (2003, 22–36).

6. Anthony Steinbock lays out some of these conditions in his *It's Not about the Gift* (Steinbock 2018, 103–108).

7. Derrida lays out some of these conditions in *Glas* (Derrida 1986, 243).

8. The question of the instant is very important for understanding all of Derrida's later works. The two most important text for this question are "Demeure" (Derrida 1998) and *Death Penalty I* (Derrida 2014, 218–225, 256). The central feature of the

instant in Derrida is the imminence of death, as in the instant immediately prior to being executed—but beyond which one survives.

9. Here Derrida mentions *The Gift of Death* explicitly. He also mentions *Given Time* (Derrida 2014, 129). These lectures themselves directly extend the analysis of the Abraham and Isaac story in *The Gift of Death* (whose French title is *Donner la mort*), where Derrida analyzes the Abraham and Isaac story, since Isaac (albeit unknown to him) has been sentenced to death (Derrida 2008).

10. The volume *Deconstructing the Death Penalty* contains many interesting articles on Derrida's lectures, although the instant is hardly mentioned in any of the essays (Oliver and Straub 2018).

11. Derrida reminds us that Camus says in *The Myth of Sisyphus* that the only serious philosophical problem is suicide (Derrida 2014, 274).

12. Lisa Guenther provides an interesting analysis of the tenth lecture in her "An Abolitionism Worthy of the Name" (Oliver and Straub 2018, 247–252).

BIBLIOGRAPHY

Camus, Albert. 1960. "Reflections on the Guillotine." In *Resistance, Rebellion, and Death*, translated by Justin O'Brien. New York: The Modern Library, pp. 131–180.

Derrida, Jacques. 1978. *Writing and Difference*, translated by Alan Bass. Chicago: University of Chicago.

———. 1986. *Glas*, translated by John P. Leavey, Jr., and Richard Rand. Lincoln: University of Nebraska Press.

———. 1992. *Given Time: 1. Counterfeit Money*, translated by Peggy Kamuf. Chicago: University of Chicago Press.

———. 1995. *On the Name*, translated by Thomas Dutoit. Stanford: Stanford University Press.

———. 1997. *Politics of Friendship*, translated by George Collins. London: Verso Books.

———. 1998. *Demeure: Fiction and Testimony*, translated by Elizabeth Rottenberg. Stanford: Stanford University Press, pp. 13–103. This volume also contains the English translation of Maurice Blanchot's "The Instant of my Death."

———. 2001. "On Forgiveness: A Roundtable Discussion with Jacques Derrida." In *Questioning God*, edited by John D. Caputo, Mark Dooley, and Michael J. Scanlon. Bloomington: Indiana University Press, pp. 52–72.

———. 2004. "Death Penalties." In *For What Tomorrow*, translated by Jeff Fort. Stanford: Stanford University Press, pp. 139–165.

———. 2008. *The Gift of Death, Second Edition*, translated by David Wills. Chicago: University of Chicago Press.

———2009. *The Beast and the Sovereign, Volume One*, translated by Geoffrey Bennington. Chicago: University of Chicago Press.

———. 2011. *Voice and Phenomenon*, translated by Leonard Lawlor. Evanston: Northwestern University Press.

———. 2014. *The Death Penalty, Volume 1*, translated by Peggy Kamuf. Chicago: University of Chicago Press.
Lawlor, Leonard. 2007. *This Is Not Sufficient*. New York: Columbia University Press.
———. 2016. *From Violence to Speaking Out*. Edinburgh: Edinburgh University Press.
Naas, Michael. 2003. *Taking on the Tradition*. Stanford: Stanford University Press.
Oliver, Kelly, and Stephanie M. Straub. 2018. *Deconstructing the Death Penalty*. Bronx: Fordham University Press.
Steinbock, Anthony. 2018. *It's Not About the Gift*. London: Rowman and Littlefield.

3

The Changeability of the World
Utopia and Critique
Sam McAuliffe

Central to the Brechtian conception of critique and the encounter with reality for which it prepares the ground is a concern with Veränderbarkeit, *changeability. The efficacy of what Brecht calls a "critical stance"* (kritische Haltung) *rests on this capacity to envisage the state of affairs under interrogation as something variable in nature. Indeed, a stance becomes critical insofar as its viewpoint onto reality makes apparent that the latter's current configuration is not definitive. "Criticizing the course of a river means improving it, correcting it" (Brecht 2015, 195). How is this task undertaken? By isolating the conditions that maintain a state of affairs in its given form and taking aim at their purported "naturalness." The course of a river has not been fixed once and for all. To stay with this metaphor, which Brecht often favors when working through this problem: "It is the same as when a river engineer looks at a river together with its original bed and the various hypothetical* [fiktiven] *courses it might have followed had there been a different tilt to the plateau or a different volume of water [. . .] while he in his mind is looking at a new river" (2015, 241). As an exercise in variability, a tabling of differential forms and prospective scenarios, critique therefore makes use of a certain fictive register and the series of simulations it puts to the test do not simply represent reality but exert a pull on it, redirecting its course. "We will now go further," we read in a late fragment, "turning to the light we must cast on the events among people that we wish to portray so that the changeability of the world becomes visible and gives us pleasure" (2015, 284).*

Now, of all the characteristics associated with this form of critical practice, arguably it is this emphasis on pleasure that is most striking, at least when reading Brecht today. On this point he is unwavering: critique should be a source of pleasure. It is not undertaken for pleasure's sake, but pleasure is what it nevertheless gives rise to, supplementing every critical endeavor as something like the latter's signature. "A critical attitude of this type is an operative factor of productivity; it is deeply enjoyable as such" (2015, 195). It should also be noted that this standpoint is taken up by Brecht in full recognition of the fate that has otherwise befallen enjoyment in the age of "late capitalism," that in its "contemporary historical form" pleasure cannot be experienced as anything other than a commodity (2015, 64). In this sense, the Brechtian critical stance is itself an attempt to develop a practice that channels pleasure through a different configuration, assigning it a different set of social functions.

This brings us back to today. Can it be said that pleasure has retained this role for critique? Is pleasure something a critical endeavor still lays claim to? If not, how has their dissociation come about, with what consequences, and how might their association be reimagined?

***

Any utopian projection, over and above the particular vision that it brings into view and regardless of the specific field in which it comes to be articulated, is always engaged in a work of critique. The impulse that animates such projection, the contexts it finds itself drawn towards, the materials it tests itself upon, and the configuration it ultimately culminates in: all this participates in a critical impetus of sorts, in the formation of a critical perspective. This perspective may not be thematically treated by the projection in question, it may not be explicitly foregrounded there, but it cannot be dissociated from the prospect that this projection brings forth. "The essential function of utopia is a critique of what is present," says Bloch in the course of a well-known exchange with Adorno, the title of which already announces the matter at hand: "Something's Missing" (Bloch and Adorno 1988, 12). Inasmuch as it traces the contours of something irreducible to what is in existence here and now, something that extends beyond the present in its given state, utopia announces the possibility that what is could be otherwise. Whatever it brings forth is constituted in and through this difference. In this sense the possibility it harbors is not something that can be drawn from the reserve of what is actual; it is not sustained or supported by anything that already exists. The fact that it cannot be realized in accordance with the actual is what situates it on the other side of the latter's limits, in the form of the unattainable. It is in this sense that the prospect held out by utopia always points to a gap in the existing order of things. It shows that within the latter's present arrangement "something's missing," something that, were it to come about, would leave this arrangement fundamentally reconfigured, having set the present upon an entirely different course. "Whatever utopia is," Adorno says in this discussion, "whatever can be imagined as utopia, concerns the transformation of the [social] totality" (1988, 3). However fantastic a utopian projection ostensibly appears—and utopia is, by definition, a discourse tied to the register of the fantastic, the fictive or the imaginary—it can always be traced back to an unresolved antagonism in reality, which its configuration thereby indicates in inverse form. As such, the wish-images over which an utopia presides are never indiscriminate. And this is why, whether explicitly or not, utopia levels a charge against the existing order of things. It calls this order to account for leaving this possibility unacknowledged and occluded, for failing to give this possibility its due. That the given order of things should persist in its current form is what a utopian prospect suddenly calls into question, demanding a decision from the present one way or another. It is in this sense that utopia could be said to constitute a crisis for the present to which it is tied.

In *The Principle of Hope*, and again in the course of a discussion of utopia's function, Bloch conceives of this tendency in terms of a "counter-move." This movement becomes discernible through a double gesture. On the one hand, it shows utopia acceding to itself through a process of negation, in the form of a *turn against* the present, a "counter-move to the badly existing [*des Gegenzugs gegen das schlecht Vorhandene*], the mobilization of contradictions which occur in the badly existing, for the purpose of undermining it completely, bringing about its collapse" (Bloch 1986, 148). On the other hand, this same movement precipitates an advance, a turn toward that which lies beyond the present's scope. The counter-move, this passage continues, "is not only negative but equally *contains within it the forward surge of an achievement which can be anticipated and represents this forward surge in the utopian function*" (1986, 148; emphasis in original). This, then, is what constitutes the specificity of utopian critique: it is undertaken on the basis of "the being of That-Which-Is-Not-Yet" (1986, 237). Only insofar as it is itself without place within the present, its *topos* irreducible to any determinable locality, only as such is it capable of indicating here and now that "something's missing." Paul Ricoeur, similarly concerned with utopia's "functional structure," draws attention to the same tendency when he states at the outset of his *Lectures on Ideology and Utopia*:

> What must be emphasised is the benefit of this special extraterritoriality. From this "no place" an exterior glance is cast on our reality, which suddenly looks strange, nothing more being taken for granted. The field of the possible is now open beyond that of the actual; it is a field, therefore, for alternative ways of living [. . .] May we not say then that imagination itself—through its utopian function—has a *constitutive* role in helping us *rethink* the nature of our social life? [. . .] Does not the fantasy of an alternative society and its exteriorisation "nowhere" work as one of the most formidable contestations of what is? (Ricoeur 1986, 16)

The critical perspective traced out here is subject to more than one paradox. If this capacity for "exteriorisation" is what lends utopia its critical impetus, at the same time it is also what deprives this impetus of its force. First of all, is it not true that the prospect traced out by utopian projection only ever appears at a remove from us as though blocked off to us? That we do not know how to access the possibility it harbors, how to render this possible something actual, or even how to provisionally situate it as a possibility in relation to where we ourselves are, since it is always elsewhere, or rather, *nowhere*? If it belongs to utopia to appear as a place without determinable locality, then it is always in danger of being nothing more than this: mere appearance, semblance without substance, a shadowland. As Bloch also insists, there is no way of ensuring in advance that the counter-move through which an utopian tendency makes itself known will not ultimately lend itself to the perpetuation of reality in its present state.

> The question is now, whether and to what extent the anticipating counter-move coincides with a merely embellishing one. Especially when the merely embellishing element, although it definitely does highlight things, has for the most part no counter-move in it at all, but merely dubious polishing of what exists. (Bloch 1986, 148–149)

Unable to locate a point of entry for itself onto the real, incapable of propelling itself across the threshold that separates the possible from the actual, utopia always carries the risk of leaving the present order of things unchanged. (Hence Bloch's concession here that as mere appearance it can end up being reduced to an "apology" for what exists. This is what gives utopia a necessary share in ideology [1986, 149]). In Ricoeur's terms, this sees utopia caught within a logic of "all or nothing": "No connecting point exists between the 'here' of social reality and the 'elsewhere' of the utopia. This disjunction allows the utopia to avoid any obligation to come to grips with the real difficulties of a given society" (Ricoeur 1986, 17).

One of the most far-reaching analyses of this prevarication to which utopian critique is subject can be found in Louis Marin's *Utopics: Spatial Play*. "Utopia," he writes there, "is an ideological critique of ideology" (1984, 195). What does this mean? Firstly, that utopia places in circulation a representation that disrupts the discursive operations underwriting a particular reality's supposed legitimacy:

> Utopia is a critique of dominant ideology insofar as it is a reconstruction of contemporary society by means of a displacement and a projection of its structures into a fictional discourse. It is thus different from the philosophical discourse of ideology, which is the totalizing expression of reality as it is given, and of its ideal justification. (Marin 1984, 195)

A utopian projection is thus the point at which this "totalizing expression" falters. Having brought something altogether other into view it prevents reality from achieving its complete self-determination, standing in the way of the latter's full and final coincidence with itself. And yet at the same time a utopian standpoint is itself ideological inasmuch as it cannot secure the ground of its own elucidation, "does not allow for the exposure of the methodology that would legitimate it," Marin writes. It may well be an instrument of critique, but it cannot give an account of its own application: "the discursive position it necessarily implies, the operations it sets in motion in order to exist, and the historical and theoretical presuppositions that govern it are not presented in the criticism" (Marin 1984, 196). Said otherwise, utopia remains opaque to itself as a critical practice, which is why the "figure" around which its representation is organized is always "blinded" (198).

For Marin, this situation has consequences for utopia's discursive form, for the particular way it finds itself situated in discourse.

> Utopia is a fictional construction [. . .] The utopic figure is a discursive object, not without reference, but with an absent referent, as its name will tell us: it is not the "without-place," "the imaginary" or "unreal place"; rather it is the no-place, the in-determined place, the neutral figure. It refers to a reality that is not said *within* the figure, that is not taken up in discourse as its signified. (1984, 196)

That is to say, a utopian projection makes reference to both a prospective presence and a real absence at one and the same time. Whatever it manifests at the level of discourse, as fiction, is the inverse form of what will have thereby been marked as lacking in reality, the "something's missing." On this account the utopian work finds its referential function split in two, and in such a way that the resulting distribution of relations and their respective operations are not in alignment, cannot in fact be situated in relation to one another. The "distance between the indication of the absent term and the signifying figure" is, Marin insists, "unlocatable": "Utopia is the systematic figure within discourse of a strategy for spatial play: it is between the text's signifying and signified spaces" (197; 198). This is the referential arrangement that constitutes the specificity of utopia's discursive operation, and this, as we have seen, is both its strength and its weakness.

"When it is transposed into the future, not only am I not there, but *utopia itself is also not with itself*," says Bloch in "Something's Missing," in a formulation that encapsulates this double bind (Bloch and Adorno 1988, 3; emphasis added). The specific vision it lends expression to seems always to remain in abeyance, as if estrangement from itself or being out of kilter with itself was ultimately utopia's proper form; and yet it is only on account of this situation that it is able to undertake a critique of what is present. Irreality is not an impediment to this undertaking, but its condition. And this is nowhere more evident than when the possibility borne by utopia does achieve a form of realization: "the fulfillment of wishes takes something away from the substance of wishes," Adorno insists here; "Above and beyond this one could perhaps say in general that the fulfillment of utopia consists largely only in a repetition of the continually same 'today' " (1–2). Or, said otherwise, "Not only is utopia not 'realizable,' it cannot be realized without destroying itself" (Marin 1984, 274). It is in view of this state of affairs that Adorno announces an imperative here, which for him the work of utopian critique should at all times adhere to, if it is not to forfeit its own possibility from the outset. Stated in essence: "One may not cast a picture of utopia in a positive manner" (Bloch and Adorno 1988, 10). Whenever the prospect of utopia acquires a definite, readily identifiable form, whenever something that is missing is explicitly named and decided upon, then the difference from what exists, on which utopia hangs, inevitably finds itself reduced and the potency of the possibility it carries diminished. Having conceded to the terms of what is already, the possible is made to speak in the language of the actual, thereby contributing to the latter's continuation.[1] It is precisely this, incidentally, that accounts for Bloch's insistence on the phrase "something's missing" here: "This sentence, which is in *Mahagonny*, is one of the most profound sentences that Brecht ever wrote, and it is in two words" (15). Its importance consists in having indicated that something is missing without saying what this something is, only that it is missing. Which is not to say that the something must remain unknowable or unsayable; as Bloch also insists here, its openness does not preclude its being able to express a definite wish, which is, after all, what will have led to the sentence being uttered in the first place. Paradoxically, then, a utopia's critical force is exerted to the degree that the figure it delineates remains withdrawn from any recognizable form; its capacity to exercise a hold over reality, to intervene in the course along which reality is unfolding, depends upon maintaining itself in this state. "The utopian moment in thinking is stronger the less it [. . .] objectifies itself into a utopia and hence sabotages its realization" (Adorno 1998, 292–293).[2] This is the aporia to which every utopian effort is subject and that demands from its projection not a solution—it is irresolvable—but a response.

*

It is against this background that I want to turn to Brecht once more, and a particular model of critique that takes shape across his wider work, one that is explicitly tied to the question of utopia understood in this sense. This enigmatic model is long in the making and appears in more than one configuration.

It develops out of Brecht's interest in pedagogics, his experiments in instruction and learning, and the new social functions envisaged for a theatre that has been redesigned to provide these processes with a frame. And if it remains tied to the question of utopia, this is first and foremost because it tends to be treated by Brecht in an anticipatory mode. "The way in which superstructure comes about is: anticipation," he writes in a short text on the political function of culture, and this is one reason for "the revolutionary significance of superstructural work" (Brecht 2015, 107–108). A provisional form of this model can be found, for example, in *The Messingkauf Dialogues* (1937–1951), where the idea of a theatre that would be analogous to a "scientific institute" is broached in some detail by "the Philosopher," the character that Brecht has spoken as the proselytizer for this new theatrical operation. As is made plain in his exposition, the context of such a performance would be not so much "art" as a "science of people's social life":

> Science scans every field for openings for experiments or the plastic representation of problems. They make models showing the movements of the planets; they make ingenious apparatuses to demonstrate how gases behave [. . .] So it struck me that your art might serve to imitate people for the purposes of such demonstration. Incidents from people's social life, demanding an explanation, could be imitated in such a way as to confront one with plastic representations whose lessons could be practically applied. (Brecht 1965, 35)

The institution tasked with housing these representations would therefore have instruction as its primary purpose. "I thought we might use your imitations for perfectly practical ends," says the same character, "simply in order to find out the best way to behave. You see, we could make them into something like a physics (which deals with mechanical bodies), and so work out a technology" (1965, 17). Or, as Brecht suggests in a working note that accompanies *The Messingkauf*, at issue here is a

> theatre for purely didactic purposes, which simply models people's movements (including psychological movements) so that they can be studied, showing the workings of social relationships in such a way that society can intervene [. . .] Criticism of the theatre leads to a new theatre. The whole thrown open to learning, with exercises and experiments. (106–107)

And to be clear, the intention informing such demonstrations is not simply to provide a means of making the structure of reality "recognizable," but something that can in turn be "seen through" (17). "One has to be able to see the laws that decide how the processes of life develop" (27). To see through a structure is to see it in light of the conditions that constitute it, but also to see these conditions in their contingency, as something that can therefore be refashioned.

Now the proposal for an institute devoted to the critical study of social life does indeed appear intermittently in Brecht's theoretical writing on the theatre and its contexts, in the form of what he refers to as *the pedagogium*. When, for example, the call is made in *A Short Organon for the Theatre* (1948) for a technical means of representing reality that sees "the theatre edge as close as possible to the apparatus of education and mass communication," the pedagogium could be considered the projection in which this network of relations has been realized (Brecht 2015, 236). It is by assembling this particular combination of functions in a single institution that a new practice of social critique can be anticipated. Here is Ben Brewster on the nature of this critical apparatus and the protocols that would characterize its use:

> The "pedagogium" [. . .] was to be an institution within a society of the future that would hold in some archived form models of every known and classified form of behavior. Members of the society could go into the pedagogium and draw out a particular action which for some reason concerned them, see it demonstrated and try it out for themselves. [. . . .] But Brecht also thought that its stock should by no means be restricted to socially useful actions [. . .] but should also include quite directly anti-social forms of behavior, models of which would be available on exactly the same basis (that is, the pedagogium would make no judgement as to what is or is not a socially useful action). (Brewster 1991, 199)

Envisaged as such, Brecht's pedagogium would do nothing less than reproduce, in all its intricacy, the overarching social totality to which it is tied (a totality of which it is itself, of course, a part). It would form an immense storehouse of the social order's various concretions, the vast array of behaviors and manners of which the latter is comprised. But it would do so in a space *set apart* from this order, under conditions that facilitate a "critical attitude" by offering up this or that incident of social life as an object of interrogation. Within the pedagogium the immediate, self-evident quality of a behavior or action would be stripped away. It would no longer appear as an unchangeable fact of nature—"milieu as fate," Brecht says somewhere else, "immutable and inescapable"—but as the consequence of a specific organization of social relations (Brecht 2015, 53). And on account of the critical distance it opens up onto the social, the pedagogium prepares the way for the latter's alteration.

In this sense, the representations on which the pedagogical transfer depends here would be analogous to that key constituent of epic theatre, *the Gestus* (arguably the institution in question could just as easily be referred to as a "gestarium") (Brecht 2016, 40). This form of demonstration is defined as follows: "By social gestus is meant the mimetic and gestural expression of the social relationships prevailing between people of a given period"; "the social gestus is the gestus relevant to society, the gestus that allows conclusions to be drawn about the social circumstances" (Brecht 2015, 187, 168).[3] This is what each model of action gives to be read, the point of view it has been constructed to be observed in light of, and in such a way that the act of observation elicits a judgment from the one observing. In the pedagogium, an action would be detached from the field of social reality, bracketed off in this space apart, precisely so as to let the socially determinant element within it become discernible, since ordinarily this element remains dissimulated. The critical perspective onto this action rests with this "ability to abstract," a prerequisite "for grasping societal processes" (Brecht 2003, 259).[4]

A key feature of the demonstration undertaken for the purpose of instruction is the technical innovation referred to by Brecht as the *alienation effect* (*Verfremdungseffekte*). "The V-effect consists in turning the object of which we are made to be aware, to which our attention is to be drawn, from something ordinary, familiar, immediately accessible, into something peculiar, striking and unexpected" (Brecht 2015, 192). Alienation, making strange, is thus a technique "designed to free socially-conditioned phenomena from the stamp of familiarity which protects them against our grasp today" (242). Detachment and displacement, the operative principles around which this representational form is structured, are the means by which the social process is made explicit and knowledge concerning this process is produced. "The object of the V-effect is to estrange the social gestus underlying every incident" (187).

It follows that the deployment of this technique is necessarily disruptive, "combative" Brecht says (2015, 261). The idea is central to a short text of Roland Barthes devoted to establishing a typology of the various critical practices found within Brecht's work. For Barthes, this technique makes contact with reality in a highly particular way: by opening up the received discursive order within which the subject's social existence is inscribed. He writes:

All that we read and hear covers us like a layer, surrounds and envelops us like a medium: the logosphere. This logosphere is given to us by our period, our class, our métier: it is a "datum" of our subject. Now, to displace what is given can only be the result of a shock [. . .] Brecht's work seeks to elaborate a shock-practice (not a subversion: the shock is much more "realistic" than a subversion); his critical art is one which opens up a crisis: which lacerates, which crackles the smooth surface, which fissures the crust of languages, loosens and dissolves the stickiness of the logosphere; it is an epic art: one which discontinues the textures of words, distances representation without annulling it. And what is this distancing, this discontinuity which provokes the Brechtian shock? It is merely a reading which detaches the sign from its effect. Have you ever seen a Japanese pin? It is a dressmaker's pin whose head is a tiny bell, so that you cannot forget it once the garment has been finished. Brecht remakes the logosphere by leaving the bell-headed pins in it, the signs furbished with their tiny jingle. (Barthes 1989, 213–214)

This is one way of envisaging how reality might be modelled by the pedagogium. Each discrete action or behavior would appear bearing the critical mark which punctures the "smooth surface" that everyday experience ordinarily lends it. Through this mark, its constructed nature would be made conspicuous. The question then becomes how to find the precise point at which to "pin" an action, such that the social mediations determining its given form are brought to the fore. This "shock-practice" entails a marked change in the way that discourse functions: "Hence, better than a semiology, what Brecht leaves us with is a seismology" (Barthes 1989, 214). Such is the form of knowledge required for the critical study of social life undertaken by the institute in question, and it shows the extent to which Brechtian critique derives an understanding of its object by drawing the latter into this state of "crisis."

There is more to say on the nature of the pedagogic practice envisaged by Brecht here. If the demonstrations in question are composed with a view to instruction, they only function as such through the active engagement of the participating subject.[5] The pedagogium's demonstrations would not simply be contemplated at a remove, but taken in hand, tried out, *practiced*. This recalls the terms of an early fragment, "Theory of Pedagogies" (1930), and its proposal for an educational exercise based around "play-acting" (*Theaterspielen*), in which participants would stage a course of action in such a way that at the same time they themselves could scrutinize it (Brecht 2003, 89). The aim of this practice is not to achieve the greatest possible degree of verisimilitude with the representation in question. The model of instruction is neither treated as a template nor imitated as an ideal. Rather, in the learning situation it takes on the function of a prop, a means for probing the composition of the action under interrogation, the reasons for its given form, what gives this form its apparent consistency, but also the extent to which this form can be reworked, and on what basis. The *Short Organon* gives a further intimation of how this exercise might function in this institutional setting:

> The laws of motion of a society are not to be demonstrated by "perfect examples" [*Idealfällen*], for "imperfection" (inconsistency) is an essential part of motion and of the thing moved. It is only necessary—but absolutely necessary—that there should be something approaching experimental conditions, i.e., that a counter-experiment should now and then be conceivable. Altogether this

is a way of treating society as if all its actions were performed as experiments. (Brecht 2015, 245)

It is in this sense that the model of instruction around which the critical exercise revolves here would not have a fixed form. It is variable in essence. Indeed, it must be capable of tolerating a degree of variation that allows it to be treated as its own counter-case. This is what it means for a representation to be *praktikabel*, to use Brecht's favored term here, "workable." It is structured to facilitate a practice and an understanding as to how this practice can insert itself into reality. And to reiterate, the critical exercises through which this practice is tested and refined are a source of pleasure.[6]

Elsewhere in the *Short Organon*, in the course of discussing the ways in which a dramatic character is handled through the application of the V-effect, Brecht gives a further indication as to how this demonstration would actually manifest itself. The very particular efforts that go into building up the depiction—the character assessed and assembled by the actor through a process of "hypothetical adjustments [*fiktive Montagen*]," its lineaments drawn from the resulting table of variants, each the concretion of a "motive force"—these experiments should not, Brecht argues, simply underwrite the performance. Rather, as the latter's condition they should be integrated into the staging itself, the test material conscientiously left on display:

> The [stage] image that gives historical definition will retain something of the rough sketching which indicates traces of other movements and features all around the fully-worked-out figure. Or imagine a man standing in a valley and making a speech in which he occasionally changes his views or simply utters sentences which contradict one another, so that the accompanying echo forces them into confrontation. (Brecht 2015, 240–241)

Again, the model of action in the pedagogium would have something of this structure: a figure that hangs together but does not necessarily cohere, a figure that constitutively remains *in process*. For Brecht, the formation of a *kritische Haltung*—the "attitude" or "bearing," "stance" or "posture" to which this idea of critique is tied—is drawn out of this differential configuration, and one of the institutional functions required here would be to maintain a record of the "traces of sketching" generated by the pedagogical exercise.

At the same time, it is important to note that this learning situation should not be considered free of the social contradictions it is tasked with analyzing. The span of Brecht's writing concerned with instruction in the theatre draws attention to this circumstance on more than one occasion. On the one hand, the mode of participation required by a theatre designed to instruct implies a "qualitative change" in the nature of spectatorship. In a collection of notes on

"Dialectical Drama," for example, Brecht anticipates a point at which such a performance would no longer be subject to the commodity relation. Its spectators would cease to form "a purchasing collective": "Individuals are not just consumers anymore—they have to produce" (Brecht 2015, 58). Instead, the theatre would become "a public concern," a means by which the collective would be brought before itself with a view to determining what its concerns as a collective are. With this theatre of instruction (*Lehrtheater*), he writes in a striking formulation, "Subject matter is declared common property, it is 'nationalized,' a prerequisite for study, and formal principles—as the means of putting the subject matter to use—are also a crucial aspect of the spectator's work (and study)" (59).[7] This on the one hand. But on the other, and Brecht insists on this with equal force, the collective with which this pedagogical practice is concerned is not reconciled with itself: "Learning has a very different function for different social strata" (113). Thus, in "On Experimental Theatre," a text that looks back over the rapid development of the theatre in this direction, he writes: "Such productions split the audience into at least two mutually hostile social groups, and thus put a stop to any common experience of art. The fact is a political one. The pleasure of learning depends on the class situation" (138). The disharmony to which "bourgeois society" is subject extends to encompass the idea of learning itself. It is a feature of this society, Brecht insists, as well as the process of production governing it, that any connection between learning and enjoyment has been severed. For this society, these are mutually exclusive terms: learning is unenjoyable, enjoyment cannot be learned from (95). The many and varied efforts on his part to develop a pedagogic practice that contests this arrangement—"there is such a thing as pleasurable learning" (113)—is itself a fundamental feature of his own "critical stance."

Returning to the institutional setting envisaged for this study of social life, for the pedagogium to fulfil its critical function, it must reproduce social reality in its totality. It provides a template for all actions, not simply those that are generally presumed to be favorable (to reiterate: the pedagogium's "stock should by no means be restricted to socially useful actions [. . .] but should also include quite directly anti-social forms of behavior, models of which would be available on exactly the same basis" [Brewster 1991, 199]). Here it is worth recalling the inventory of behaviors drawn up by the Philosopher in *The Messingkauf* as possible points of focus for the science in question (not least for the way it passes back and forth between the "good" and the "bad"). It includes but is of course not limited to

> The way [people] get along with each other, the way they develop friendships and enmities, sell onions, plan military campaigns, get married, make tweed suits, circulate forged bank-notes, dig potatoes, observe heavenly bodies; the

way they cheat, favor, teach, exploit, respect, mutilate and support one another; the way they hold meetings, form societies, conduct intrigues. (Brecht 1965, 17)

The pedagogium therefore provides the framework through which the antisocial character of an action could be submitted to interrogation, just as a laboratory provides the setting for a scientist to study a virus within controlled conditions, with a view to developing a vaccine. As with any other action, it too would be actively tried out, but in a forum that cuts it off from its consequences when undertaken in reality. A means of drawing poison from the wound, by allowing the action's motivating force to come into view and a judgment to be formed about it. The "Theory of Pedagogies" fragment also insists on this aspect of the pedagogical practice:

> [I]t is precisely the representation of antisocial behavior by the state's developing citizens that is very beneficial to the state, particularly if that representation is enacted according to exact and magnificent models. The state can best improve upon humanity's antisocial drives—which derive from fear and ignorance—by forcing them out of everybody in the most complete form possible, a form which is almost unattainable by the individual on his own. This is the basis for the idea of using play-acting in pedagogies. (Brecht 2003, 89)[8]

As ever, the "form" that this exercise gives rise to is something to be studied, and the aim of this study is to refashion the subjective arrangement out of which this form was forced. "There is a great deal to human beings, we say, so a great deal can be made out of them. They do not have to stay the way they are; they may be looked at not only as they are now, but also as they *might be*" (Brecht 2015, 243; emphasis added).

This brings us back, finally, to the explicitly utopian aspect of Brecht's proposal. Of course, the pedagogium remains, now as then, a prospect yet to be realized, even if the schema of critique guiding Brecht's vision is discernible in an array of contemporary cultural contexts.[9] To take up Ricoeur's understanding of the critical function of utopia once more:

> Perhaps a fundamental structure of the reflexivity we may apply to our social roles is the ability to conceive of an empty place from which to look at ourselves [. . .] From this "no place" an exterior glance is cast on our reality, which suddenly looks strange, nothing more being taken for granted [. . .] The nowhere puts the cultural system at a distance; we see our cultural system from the outside precisely thanks to this nowhere. (Ricoeur 1986, 15, 17)

With respect to the reality it has been tasked with interrogating, the pedagogium occupies a site analogous to the *nowhere* conceived in these terms. It is utopian as the embodiment of this exterior glance, "an empty place from which to look at ourselves."[10]

But what must also be recognized here is the extent to which the critical practice undertaken in the pedagogium appears to operate in strict adherence with the paradoxical imperative to which utopia is subject, as Adorno understands it in "Something's Missing." "Utopia," he suggests there, "is essentially in the determined negation of that which merely is, and by concretizing itself as something false, it always points at the same time to what should be" (Bloch and Adorno 1988, 12). Carried to this extreme, "utopia" stands for nothing other than the open-ended contestation—the *determinate* negation—of reality's present form, a process by which the latter is taken apart on its own terms, without ever looking beyond it. "Insofar as we are not allowed to cast a picture of utopia, insofar as we do not know what the correct thing would be, we know exactly, to be sure, what the false thing is" (1988, 12). Now this is precisely how society's existing arrangement would be treated by the pedagogium. Its "critique of what is present" sets in place the conditions for another world only insofar as it purposely refrains from indicating what the actual content of this transformed world would consist in. That is to say, if the pedagogium coincides with the empty place of utopia, it does not fill it in. It does not cast a picture. Instead, it simply concerns itself with dismantling the "false" forms of life through which the present social order would otherwise continue to reproduce itself. By placing the utopian function exclusively in the service of critique, the pedagogium would ensure that society henceforth had an apparatus through which to observe itself and a site from which to transform itself. To recall our point of departure: "Criticizing the course of a river means improving it, correcting it. Criticism of society is ultimately revolution: there you have criticism taken to its logical conclusion and achieved" (Brecht 2015, 195).[11]

All this implies a redistribution of the categories that organize the utopian effort. In her critical study of the classical canon of utopian discourse, Grosz writes the following:

> Utopia, like the dialectic itself, is commonly fantasized as the end of time, the end of history, the moment of resolution of past problems [. . .] The ideal society, society in its perfection, is represented as the cessation of becoming, the overcoming of problems, a calm and ongoing resolution. While a picture of the future, the utopic is fundamentally that which *has no future*. (Grosz 2001, 138–139)

Contrary to this understanding of utopia, Brecht's proposal constitutes a singular experiment, inasmuch as its projection of the future does not close off the future's further development in the name of a finally attained ideal.

Rather, the pedagogium's primary purpose is to keep the future open and in process, with critique understood as a means of maintaining the variability of social forms. It is this that makes *Veränderbarkeit*, changeability, the watchword of utopian critique.

*

A final question, by way of conclusion. How would a critical practice devoted to the study of socially inflected action be undertaken today? What would be the historically specific typology of behaviors that constitute the object of such a study? In short, what, today, should the critical attitude be brought to bear on? The work of French artist Julien Prévieux has taken significant steps to develop a response to these questions. Of particular interest here is a series of works brought together under the title *What Shall We Do Next?* (2007–2011).[12] The series is based around a number of applications made to the U.S. patent office by various corporate concerns, registering the set of discrete movements required to engage with the interface of newly invented technical objects. These "patented gestures" are then modelled by Prévieux in a variety of forms, from a 3D animation (*Sequence #1*) to a physical performance where the patents are used as a dance score (*Sequence #2*). As the artist explains in a discussion of the work, in each case these demonstrations concern a prospective behavior, an anticipated use of the body (since the device that supports the gesture is not yet in production): "The assumption was that these gestures patented today are the movements we may have to do in the future: patents as an archive of gestures to come" (Will Brown 2016). What Prévieux brings into view with these demonstrations is therefore the extent to which present-day "techniques of the body" are determined by market forces in increasingly refined ways, administered according to a technical standard that is not in common ownership, and which makes of bodily movement itself a prospective expression of exchange value. Structurally speaking, then, these demonstrations are synonymous with the Brechtian *social gestus* ("the mimetic and gestural expression of the social relationships prevailing between people of a given period" [Brecht 2015, 187]). They display human motion in relation to the technical, economic, legal network that conditions it. At the same time, the meticulous staging of this gestic performance, in its own way a form of "play-acting," is immediately recognizable as a source of enjoyment for performer and spectator alike, and it is this juxtaposition of pleasure and instruction, achieved through collective endeavor that places Prévieux's "archive of gestures to come" in the same critical lineage as Brecht's pedagogium. "Why do we move the way we do?" asks the artist in the same discussion, "Who owns our gestures? How will we move in one, 10 or 100 years?" (Will Brown 2016). The critical attitude discernible in these questions is Brechtian inasmuch as it seeks to open up a future different to the one that is being prepared by today's social order.

NOTES

1. For Elizabeth Grosz, this tendency threatens the tenability of utopia as a mode of critique: "The utopian is not the projection of a future at all, although this is how it is usually understood; rather, it is the projection of a past or present as if it were the future. The utopian is in fact a freezing of the indeterminable movement from the past through the future that the present is unable to directly control" (Grosz 2001, 143).

2. Certainly, this axiom has its detractors. See, by way of example, Siegfried Kracauer's account of an exchange with Adorno on this question: "*Concept of Utopia:* I argued that he [Adorno] uses this concept in a purely formal way, as a borderline concept (*Grenzbegriff*) which at the end invariably emerges like a *Deus ex Machina*. In my opinion, I told him, Utopian thought makes sense only if it assumes the form of a vision or intuition with a definite content of a sort. T. was inclined to admit the justice of my argument [. . .] His intention is then to show that the concept of utopia is a *vanishing* concept when besieged; it vanishes if you want to spell it out" (Kracauer 2012, 127).

3. Here Brecht's method shows several points of convergence with Marcel Mauss's understanding of the *habitus*: for Mauss, even in its most prosaic modes of comportment the human body must be understood as a social artefact. Its habitus is shaped by an open-ended exercise in "collective and individual practical reason." Furthermore, the techniques that govern the body, stipulating how it is used, imply a process of *"education"*: "In every society, everyone knows and has to know and learn what he has to do in all conditions [. . .] The individual borrows the series of movements which constitute it from the action executed in front of him or with him by others" (Mauss 1973, 85, 73).

4. Looking across the body of research materials assembled by Brecht on this theme, it is possible to envisage how this act of observation might actually take place in situ: for example, the proxemics it implies could be said to resemble the structure of engagement associated by Schiller with the epic form, in contrast to the dramatic, as outlined in a letter to Goethe that remained a critical point of reference for Brecht in his work on this theme: "A dramatic plot will move before my eyes; an epic seems to stand still while I move around it. In my view this is a significant distinction. If a circumstance moves before my eyes, then I am bound strictly to what is present to the senses; my imagination loses all freedom; I feel a continual restlessness develop and persist in me; I have to stick to the subject; any reflection or looking back is forbidden me, for I am drawn by an outside force. But if I move round a circumstance which cannot get away from me, then my pace can be irregular; I can linger or hurry according to my own subjective needs, can take a step backwards or leap ahead, and so forth" (Schiller, quoted in Brecht 1992, 210). Observation achieved through the mobility of perspective, the ease of transition from one perspective to another,

allowing the representation to be seen from a variety of angles, at a tempo determined by the observer themselves: the pedagogium's spatial arrangement would have to be structured with a view to facilitating these processes.

5. As Brewster notes in his outline of the proposal (199), the idea can be said to have developed out of that singular mode of theatre to which Brecht gave the name *learning play* (*Lehrstück*), and which forms its own unique canon within his theatrical work as a whole. For an expansive survey of the "structural innovations" associated with this experiment—a theatre without set text or definitive form, undertaken through a set of exercises that abolish the "performance/audience gap," so that the theatrical operation extends well beyond the confines traditionally reserved for it— see Roswitha Mueller's "Learning for a New Society: The *Lehrstück*," not least for her suggestion that in their given context these innovations make the learning play a "genuinely utopian project" (112).

6. See the early article "More Good Sport" (1926) in support of this point: what the theatre has to learn from the sporting event, Brecht argues, is that in the latter's case the performer's demonstration of skill is undertaken primarily for the performer's own enjoyment. For Brecht this is what makes the sporting performance involving to the onlooker. If traditional theatre lacks "sport" in this sense, one sign of a critical theatre's emergence is its attempt to cultivate a participatory practice within which pleasure has a role to play (2015, 25).

7. The sense of "common property" invoked here is further elucidated by a closing statement made by the Philosopher in a variant ending to *The Messingkauf*: "The art of acting needs to be treated simply as an elementary human utterance which contains its own purpose. That's where it differs from the art of war, whose purpose is external to itself. The art of acting is one of society's elementary capacities; it is based on a direct social asset, one of humanity's pleasures in society; it is like language itself; it's really a language of its own" (Brecht 1992, 172).

8. This thesis has its counterpart in Félix Guattari's analysis of social practice in *The Three Ecologies*: "Any persistently intolerant and uninventive society that fails to 'imaginarize' the various manifestations of violence risks seeing this violence crystallized in the Real" (Guattari 2000, 58).

9. To take just one of several possible points of reference here, see Nicholas Bourriaud's study of the *relational turn* in aesthetics and the emergence of a model of art production built around "the realm of human interactions." For Bourriaud, this new aesthetic form has not developed arbitrarily, but as a counter-tendency to the "general reification" imposed by contemporary society: "The social bond has turned into a standardised artefact," he writes, and on this account "artistic praxis appears these days to be a rich loam for social experiments, like a space partly protected from the uniformity of behavioural patterns" (Bourriaud 2002, 9). This could be Brecht speaking. Furthermore, utopia has its role to play in this relational model of art, albeit with a further qualification made by the author: in its "universalist" form utopia must be considered obsolete. It can no longer serve as a grand narrative. Any efficacy it still has rests with its capacity to intervene in reality itself, here and now. A "hands-on utopia" in the parlance of *Relational Aesthetics*. "These days, utopia is being lived on a subjective, everyday basis, in the real time of concrete and intentionally fragmented

experiments. The artwork is presented as a social interstice within which these experiments and these new 'life possibilities' appear to be possible" (45).

10. This association can also be understood through Marin: "Utopia as a figure inscribed within a fable-producing discourse puts ideological discourse and its representations into play in a double sense—implicitly but critically questioning them and setting them apart in order to reflect upon the presuppositions of their internal systems" (Marin 1984, 195). This motion of *setting apart* in order to *see through* is the Brechtian gesture of critique in essence, the V-effect in action.

11. Of course this conception of critique belongs to a Marxist lineage, as is already discernible whenever Brecht invokes "the changeability of the world" in this context, a formulation that conscientiously adopts the terms of the Eleventh Thesis on Feuerbach: "The philosophers have only interpreted the world, in various ways; the point is to change [verändern] it" (Marx 1970, 123).

12. For the schematization underlying the various manifestations of this work, see the artist's *Gestion des stocks* (Prévieux 2009, 48–53).

BIBLIOGRAPHY

Adorno, Theodor W. 1998. "Resignation." In *Critical Models: Interventions and Catchwords*, translated by Henry W. Pickford, 289–293. New York: Columbia University Press.

Barthes, Roland. 1989. "Brecht and Discourse: A Contribution to the Study of Discursivity." In *The Rustle of Language*, translated by Richard Howard, 212–222. Berkeley: University of California Press.

Bloch, Ernst. 1986. *The Principle of Hope*, Vol. 1, translated by Neville Plaice, Stephanie Plaice, and Paul Knight. Cambridge: MIT Press.

Bloch, Ernst, and Theodor W. Adorno. 1988. "Something's Missing: A Discussion Between Ernst Bloch and Theodor W. Adorno on the Contradictions of Utopian Longing." In *The Utopian Function of Art and Literature: Selected Essays*, translated by Jack Zipes and Frank Mecklenburg, 1–17. Cambridge: MIT Press.

Bourriaud, Nicolas. 2002. *Relational Aesthetics*, translated by Simon Pleasance, Fronza Woods, and Mathieu Copeland. Dijon: Les Presses du réel.

Brecht, Bertolt. 1965. *The Messingkauf Dialogues*, translated by John Willett. London: Methuen.

———. 1992. *Brecht on Theatre: The Development of an Aesthetic*, edited and translated by John Willett. New York: Hill and Wang.

———. 2003. *Brecht on Art and Politics*, edited by Tom Kuhn and Steve Giles, translated by Tom Kuhn, Steve Giles, and Laura Bradley. London: Bloomsbury Methuen.

———. 2015. *Brecht on Theatre*, 3rd ed., edited by Marc Silberman, Steve Giles, and Tom Kuhn. London and New York: Bloomsbury Methuen.

———. 2016. *Journals, 1934–55*, edited by John Willett, translated by Hugh Rorrison. London: Methuen.

Brewster, Ben. 1991. "The Fundamental Reproach (Bertolt Brecht and the Cinema)." In *Explorations in Film Theory: Selected Essays from Ciné-Tracts*, edited by Ronald F. Burnett, 191–200. Bloomington and Indianapolis: Indiana University Press.

Grosz, Elizabeth. 2001. "Embodied Utopias: The Time of Architecture." In *Architecture from the Outside: Essays on Virtual and Real Space*, 131–150. Cambridge, MA: MIT Press.

Guattari, Félix. 2000. *The Three Ecologies*, translated by Ian Pindar and Paul Sutton. London and New York: Continuum.

Kracauer, Sigfried. 2012. "Talk with Teddie." In *Siegfried Kracauer's American Writings: Essays on Film and Popular Culture*, edited by Johannes von Moltke and Kristy Rawson, 127–132. Berkeley: University of California Press.

Marin, Louis. 1984. *Utopics: Spatial Play*, translated by Robert A. Vollrath. Amhurst: Humanity Books.

Marx, Karl. 1970. "Theses on Feuerbach." In *Karl Marx and Friedrich Engels, The German Ideology*, Pt. 1, edited by C. J. Arthur, 121–23. New York: International Publishers.

Mauss, Marcel. 1973. "Techniques of the Body." Translated by Ben Brewster. *Economy and Society* 2 (1): 70–88.

Mueller, Roswitha. 2006. "Learning for a New Society: The *Lehrstück*." In *The Cambridge Companion to Brecht*, 2nd ed., edited by Peter Thompson and Glendyr Sacks, 101–117. Cambridge: Cambridge University Press.

Prévieux, Julien. 2009. *Gestion des stocks*. Lyon: ADERA.

Ricoeur, Paul. 1986. *Lectures on Ideology and Utopia*, edited by George H. Taylor. New York: Columbia University Press.

Will Brown, A. 2016. "Julien Prévieux: 'Humour is a Good Fighting Trick.'" *Studio International*, February 22, 2016. https://www.studiointernational.com/index.php/julien-previeux-rachel-cook-interview-what-shall-we-do-next-diverseworks-houston.

4

Seeking Intelligent Life in the Time of COVID-19, or, Thinking "Epicritically"

(For Stan Robinson)

Jennifer A. Wagner-Lawlor

Rethinking critique seems all the more urgent at a moment when COVID-19 seems to be doing our work for us, free of any regard for the structures and limits of intelligibility we might have come up with. The virus' imperative is a simple one: to live. It doesn't care what happens to us, and it's pushing us to our limits in several dimensions at once. Against the background of COVID-19 we see, as if in relief, our selves. Especially, how "stupid" we are: the virus makes us (feel) stupid because we keep coming up against how much we don't know. No wonder it is the morning after this chapter is absolutely, positively due, and it's not done.

But "a friend" visited in the form of an essay published yesterday (May 1, 2020) in The New Yorker *online by well-known science-fiction writer Kim Stanley ("Stan") Robinson. Stan* is *a friend, and I had almost emailed him several weeks ago as I was rereading his "Three Californias" trilogy. In the last volume,* Pacific Edge *(1995), a main character, an aspiring novelist in fact, tests positive, allegedly, for HIV upon reentering the United States from Switzerland. He knows it is probably his membership in the American Socialist Legal Action Group and California Lawyers for the Environment that has flagged his reentry; nonetheless, his papers are stamped "Quarantine possible," and he is sent to a "camp" with an order for a second test. Reflecting on his writer's block he thinks—in a way that strikes home—that*

> the problem of an adequate history bothers me still. I mean not just my personal troubles, but the depression, the wars, the AIDS plague. (Fear.) [. . .] maybe the apocalyptics were just a bit early in their predictions, too tied to numbers. Maybe it takes a while for the world to end. (Robinson 1995, 181)

Today, in his own authorial voice, Stan writes:

> *Science-fiction writers don't know anything more about the future than anyone else. Human history is too unpredictable; from this moment, we could descend into a mass-extinction event or rise into an age of general prosperity. Still, if you read science fiction, you may be a little less surprised by whatever does happen. Often, science fiction traces the ramifications of a single postulated change; readers co-create, judging the writers' plausibility and ingenuity, interrogating their theories of history. Doing this repeatedly is a kind of training. It can help you feel more oriented in the history we're making now. This radical spread of possibilities, good to bad, which creates such a profound disorientation; this tentative awareness of the emerging next stage—these are also new feelings in our time. Science fiction is the new realism.* (Robinson 2020)

Maybe what Stan is talking about here, beyond literature, is a certain kind of aesthetic education ("training") toward a more robust sort of intelligence. Not the discovery of an "intelligent life of aliens," that old sci-fi trope, but the uncovering of the alien-ness, the strangeness of our own, living intelligence—should we be prompted to look at it. The unfamiliarity of our very selves, particularly as we encounter something so alien, and yet so intimate, as the virus. As a vaccine is sought that will resist/vanquish/"beat" the virus, the realists—the indefatigable Dr. Anthony Fauci in the United States, for example—are promoting something else: that we "attune" ourselves to the virus. Attunement does not mean passivity, certainly nothing like harmony, in this context; it is more "critical" than that, if differently so. A "critical attunement" then, suggesting a mode of mediation, rather than simply oppositional criticism (let's just kill the damn thing). Stan's notion of "new feeling" here suggests that this mode is embodied—again, a mediation but as an embodied, critical consciousness sensitive to emergenc(i)es of the Anthropocene.

***

In this chapter, I explore a mode of critique that I call *the epicritical*. The term itself registers the impact of philosopher Catherine Malabou on the contemporary interest, across many disciplines now, in *plasticity* and its biological force in terms of *epigenesis*. In pursuing a "deep structure of transformation" in our neurological lives, Malabou (2008, 64) is seeking a new mode of critique. She actually says this: although in the context of today's debates regarding the end(s) of critique, particularly in my world of literary criticism, Malabou's name rarely appears. She is not drawn into current arguments regarding what Chris Castiglia ironically calls academic "critiquiness" (Castiglia 2013). And yet Malabou's work has *always* been about critique, the narratives we tell about it, and the narratives it tells us: histories, and genealogies. Kim Stanley Robinson muses self-reflexively on the role of the sci-fi writer as a critic (though he does not quite put it this way) and as a storyteller; he also describes the co-constitutive role of the reader-participant in these worldings, such that the worldings become both abstract embodiment and embodied abstraction. Malabou's philosophical moves drill down into the science, biological and philosophical, of subjectivity as *embodied consciousness* (Robinson's "awareness" *and* "feeling") to argue for the essential vitality of the epigenetic development of things *and* of thoughts (if such a distinction even makes sense any more).

Is there a Malabou-ian analogue to Robinson's figure of the science-fiction creator of other worlds? Maybe not precisely, but Malabou does introduce a certain figure that sits "at the threshold" of a "new world of questioning" (2008, 54), which contemporary neurosciences are making accessible. She does not associate this figure with science fiction, but she does talk about a philosophical "fantastic" (in *The Heidegger Change*) and "another possible world" (2008, 80). She does not call this figure a critic, but she does identify this figure in terms of critique: she calls it "*this strange critical entity.*" Malabou does not talk about a new realism for literature, but she does talk about "a new genre—open to everyone" (2008, 2) of consciousness and "its 'reality,'" and about the plasticity of time, space, event, historicity. Both Robinson and Malabou are committed to a certain *training* in and of awareness, in thinking and feeling, that recognizes the strangeness of our perceptions and lived experiences of the world, our very selves. They are both talking about the vital power(s) of speculation, from different angles, both describing a kind of observational science that "[sees] into the life of things"[1] using not only the measurements of mechanical instrumentation but also the mediations of biological investment, including the distributed agencies of an embodied consciousness.

In this short space I begin tracing Malabou's genealogy of this *strange critical entity* from its first appearance in *What Should We Do with Our Brain?* (2008), to her most recent book, *Morphing Intelligence* (2019). This entity seems to be Malabou's familiar, as it were, an uncanny figuration of what she is doing with her brain. This figuration represents an image of "becoming conscious" although the point of *Morphing Intelligence*, of her entire career really, is to reconceptualize models of thinking intelligence "after" plasticity, that is, in terms of epigenesis. I focus here on the relationship between epigenesis and critique as represented in and by this figure, this strange critical entity. The work of this entity occurs, Malabou argues, in the space, narrower than we tend to think, between intelligence and *stupidity*. The latter word does not come up too often in polite academic dialogue. But we need to recognize stupidity, our own most especially, because stupidity goes nowhere. It plasticizes thought into rigid forms. Resisting stupidity, exploding these forms (Malabou's "destructive plasticity") requires the epigenetic vitality of the brain, of the body: we have to be able to see and feel what we *don't* know, and sometimes it takes an encounter with the alien, literal *or* metaphorical, "real" or virtual, to be utterly surprised, shocked by the blinders built into our cognitive "frameworks" and constructions. Into the skirmishes regarding whether or not we are post- or post-post-critique, beyond critique or limited by it, I want to draw Malabou's strange critical figure into the arena.

Extending one possibility of Malabou's thought, I propose that from the epigenetic model of consciousness developed so carefully in her work, we might consider something called *epicritique*, which names the essentially critical nature of thinking. Recent challenges to critique by critics Rita Felski and Gayatri Spivak among others, are really asking for a model of epicritique, and a new genre of *epicritical* analysis. What would that be or look like? It might be an approach to literature from the perspective of "morphing intelligence," or a narrative genealogy of the way a text changes us. It might look like an account(ing) of deliberate self-positioning at a "threshold." It might be a riskier enterprise, putting the critic "on the line" as it were, to recognize that the line bends, or blurs, in an encounter with a text. If the strange critical entity is a figuration of the epigenetic structuralization of *consciousness*, which Malabou lately is calling "intelligence," could we talk about our relationship with other such representations—such as art, literature—as "epicritical"? Could we "train" our critical minds to confront persistently the temptation to rest easy in a comfortable cognitive schema, to take on a certain intellectual "regimen"—and to seek in each critical encounter an evolution in our mental habitus? This is the end, the aim, I propose, of Malabou's articulation of the epigenetic process of becoming conscious. We have the capacity to become epicritical, to think epicritically: we just do not know it yet.

WHOSE LIMITS?

At the 2020 Modern Language Association Annual Conference I attended a panel entitled "Has Postcritique Run Out of Steam?" One clear target of the panel was feminist critic Rita Felski, whose *The Limits of Critique* (2015) declares that we are now in a period of "post-critique," thanks to a model of textual analysis that, she argues, is hardened to such an extent that it is inhospitable toward the possibility of other analytic practices:

> Rather than being a weightless, disembodied, freewheeling dance of the intellect, critique turns out to be a quite stable repertoire of stories, similes, tropes, verbal gambits, and rhetorical ploys [. . .] drawing everything into its field of force, patrolling the boundaries of what counts as serious thought. [. . .] For many scholars in the humanities, [critique] is not one good thing but the only imaginable thing. (Felski, 7–8)

Recalling Fredric Jameson's oft-quoted "someone said that it is easier to imagine the end of the world than to imagine the end of capitalism" (Jameson 2003, 76), Felski implies that contemporary critiquiness (Castiglia 2013) is a failure of imagination. She goes further, to the ongoing irritation of those who take themselves to be her targets: her characterization of the smug, "scholar-turned-sleuth [brooding] over matters of fault and complicity [. . .] piecing together a causal sequence that allows her to identify a crime," shades into near-caricature of a dispassionate "quintessential ironist" (Felski 2015, 76). The object pronoun "her" pointedly emphasizes (through reversal of expectation) a persistent association of critiquiness with a "self-flatter[ing]" masculinist fiction of objectivity, the "old dream [. . .] of the view from nowhere" (81). Felski's blunt assessment: Critique today risks becoming another expression of the Harawayan "god trick" (Haraway 1988), ahistorical and disembodied. Dismissive of nonrationalist approaches to interpretation or critique, contemporary academic criticism, she claims, eschews the affective dimension of responding to art and literature, much less entertaining anything so "soft" and apparently uncritical as "hope." Her proposal to plumb the resources of a "rich language of translation, creolization, syncretization, and global flows" (155) that might challenge "notions of the discrete, self-contained spaces"—whether of nation, ethnicity, or the thinking subject—is to be appreciated. Yet by the end of her own "critique of critique" (which she faults in others, and claims not to be doing herself) Felski herself remains vague regarding next steps. Two years later will appear *Critique and Post-Critique* (2017), a generous array of excellent essays by well-known critics advancing various perspectives and approaches, one of which—Heather Love's promotion of the importance of Donna Haraway to the history of critique—anticipates remarks made at the MLA panel by feminist provocateur Jane Gallop.

If the four male MLA panelists (out of six) neglected to mention Felski's admittedly snarky characterization of "the critic," beyond naming her with a jocular dismissal, Gallop, the fifth panelist, did not hold back a pointed feminist salvo. She called out the panel's implicit "oedipal theory of ideas," which presumes to "dethrone" the "post-critical" by "declaring it 'out of steam' or otherwise lacking in phallic juice" (Gallop 2020, 533).[2] Gallop instead calls for "a different temporality of critique and appreciation than that presupposed by our panel title, a less oedipal temporality, one less based in thesis followed by antithesis," less linear, less rigid (533–534). Less masculinist. The history of feminist criticism, she continued, is "arguably the most widespread and successful of the various strands of critique" (534) in the twentieth to twenty-first centuries, exemplary in its resistance to models of literary canonization that valorize a succession of "strong readings," for example, of literary sons in competition with literary fathers. Gallop rejects the impact of certain presumptions regarding the linearity implied by this genealogy, and rejects a style of criticism that denies *embodied* experience any relevance to the presumed rationality of critical analysis. Feminism's triumph, Gallop declares, is not only the recovery of other texts that do not conform to static critical principles, but also the appreciation of the body as a force of critical intelligence.[3]

The philosophical repression of the body and the hardening of the mind are at the heart of Malabou's long-time investigation of the biological origins of becoming conscious, or more recently, of *intelligence*. This process has been related to a notion of critique and to the "nature" of a critical subject. Introducing *this strange critical entity* in 2004, when the French original of *What Should We Do with Our Brain?* was published (as *Que faire de notre cerveau?*), the figure gradually is fleshed out, as it were. The entity is not a rhetorical figuration, nor even a strictly philosophical one.[4] Its work, however, is characterized as a philosophical task: "to think new modalities of forming the self" (Malabou 2008, 14), also articulated memorably as the "plastic challenge": "[to] construct and entertain a relation with their brain as the image of a world to come" (82). Not the world as it is; that only takes us up to the limit. Foucault urges that we "move beyond the outside-inside alternative; we have to be at the frontiers" (Foucault, qtd. in Malabou 2019, 129). On the matter of limits, Jacques Derrida writes the following: "At the limit, everyone writing is taken by surprise" (1997, 160). Might Malabou want to rephrase this, to replace "writing" with "thinking"? But something about the passive voice in Derrida's formulation does not sound quite right for Malabou: might she write, instead, "At the limit, everyone thinking surprises *themselves*"?

Plasticity is by definition about limits: about when or where exactly one form morphs into another, and where the impulse to reform comes from, inside or outside. Malabou states that plasticity is "situated between two extremes: on the one side the sensible image of taking form (sculpture or plastic objects), and on the other side that of the annihilation of all form (explosion)" (70). In between, plasticity means adaptability: not flexibility, which, following Roland Barthes, Malabou understands to be an agent of passivity, submission to control. Plasticity is something else, "an agency of disobedience to every constituted form, a refusal to submit to a model" (6). In focusing on brain plasticity, Malabou wants to understand the brain's capacity to adapt, to receive shocks, and to repair and reform: "It is precisely because [. . .] the brain is not already made that we must ask what we should do with it, what we should do with this plasticity that makes us, precisely in the sense of a work: sculpture, modeling, architecture" (7). Through this "plastic organic art," which offers "a possible margin of improvisation with regard to genetic necessity," we can entertain, she argues, the possibility of taking control of our own "self-fashioning," "self-sculpting."[5] To do so, however, is to acknowledge the historicity of one's own brain, as it is interdetermined with pregiven structures of knowledge, organization, ideology. To become conscious of the limits set up by these structures is to gain a *useful* sense of self-alienation, an objective sensibility based not in anything conventionally transcendental—no more "god-trick" operations—but in a negotiation of difference and an emergent regenerative force that Malabou calls the process of epigenetic thought.

In terms of the three roles of plasticity within the brain—developmental, modulational, and reparative—the work of this strange critical entity seems most closely associated with the modulational "field of action," at which level "there is a sort of neuronal creativity that depends on nothing but the individual's experience, his life, and his interactions with the surroundings" (21–22). The capacity to modulate synaptic efficacy at this embodied level demonstrates plasticity's capacity, in both giving and receiving form, to "impose itself with the greatest clarity and force in 'opening' its meaning" (21). Metaphors of space emphasize this "opening" as a place, a "locus" of "transdifferentiation"; these transformations over time can be "mapped" (59), not just through image technologies but perhaps in aesthetic representations as well (with Barthes again, Malabou frequently reminds us that plasticity has a deep, even "essential," relation to the aesthetic). Modulational plasticity, "by analogy with process that stem cells undergo" (24), makes (in the active sense of the word) a crucial difference: it "constitutes the differentiating or transdifferentiating force of neuronal plasticity" and is thus "always capable of changing difference, receiving or losing an imprint, or transforming the program" (24). Perhaps the strange entity is best characterized, at this point of Malabou's thinking, as the abstract embodiment of "an ongoing reworking of neuronal morphology" (25) that leads, eventually, in the "plasticity of time" (39), from cognition toward consciousness or "mentality."

As a figuration of ontologic "stem cells" for self-consciousness, the "strange critical entity" works through (across; by means of and in resistance to) limits of cognitive schema. Perhaps the entity is best characterized, at this point in Malabou's thinking, as an abstract embodiment of the "ongoing reworking of neuronal morphology" (25). This is the *epigenetic* process of transmission and transdifferentiation, according to her: and to "read" that process, as we now can, reveals the historicity of our own brain, of consciousness itself. Spatial references in *What Should We Do with Our Brain?* are most common, especially in terms of determining the "locus" of transdifferentation, and the brain's "mapping" of its activity as mentality, or even as self-representation (59). But it is the "plasticity of time" (39) that comes into play in the reengagement of "remembered" stimuli as synaptic traces that can be displaced, modified, or transformed in response to later stimuli. Malabou is interested in the relationship of this process, this neuronal life-long learning, on "survival" or "resilience" (3).

Following Damasio closely here, Malabou traces an account of the progress from proto-self, to conscious or autobiographical self, to "conscience"

(60)—a knowing-with oneself. As a self-representation, the autobiographical self constitutes a "second-order" awareness of "object-organism interaction. [. . .] the account of the *causal relationship* between object and organism can only be captured in second-order neural maps" (Damasio, quoted in Malabou 61). Damasio concludes that this "accounting" constitutes a kind of narrative: "*that of the organism caught in the act of representing its own changing state as it goes about representing something else*" (Damasio, quoted in Malabou 2008, 61). Malabou redescribes this recognition as "grasping the nature of this becoming, which permits the transformation of the proto-self into a conscious element" (63); but at the same time warns against leaving unthought the *interpretive* aspect of such an account. What are the conditions that would orient the development of a pattern toward an image, or a "disposition" toward a schema, without which conditions that image or schema would *not* form? By neglecting to locate a "deep structure of transformation" we are not "thinking it through," not really understanding the connections or the motives orienting transition. We might end up, Malabou says, explaining ourselves as a product of "the wisdom of nature" (2016, 64), relying on some preformed explanation or, in Roland Barthes's terms, on a myth (Wagner-Lawlor forthcoming 2021). But, as it is for Roland Barthes, for Malabou that reliance on myth is a mistake:

> Not to interpret is still to interpret. By wishing not to construct a hermeneutic schema capable of explaining, at least provisionally, the relations between the neuronal and the mental, by wishing not to recognize the necessarily meta-neurobiological dimension of that schema, one exposes oneself, whether one recognizes it or not, to ideological drift—for example, and above all, to that of mental Darwinism or psychological Darwinism. (2008, 64–65)

This is a fundamental point for Malabou, this "transition" from earlier to later, into "maturity," supporting her distinction between a "weak" plasticity in flexibility, and a "strong" plasticity of transdifferentiation. And it returns her to the interface or "space between" the promises envisioned in "this continent known as cerebral plasticity" (67), and the external conditions of the broader field on and within which we as individual subjects *and* as part of much broader political and cultural networks are able to operate: "What remains mysterious [. . .] is therefore the deep structure of transformation, the transition from a universal self, not yet particularized, to the singular self, to that which I am, that which we are" (64).

Malabou declares her dissatisfaction with the "story" told by neuroscientists thus far, who are reluctant to consider how the historicity of their "interpretations," how their own "reading" of what they observe, or how the instruments of observation themselves might not only impact the shape of that narrative but might itself replicate or "legitimate a certain social and political functioning" (68). Attuned to Donna Haraway's proposition on the mediate positioning of a "more objective" observer, Malabou reiterates the imperative that we reposition ourselves, over time, that we may bring ourselves to account.

THIS STRANGE CRITICAL ENTITY

Before Tomorrow (2016, published originally as *Avant Demain* in 2014) elaborates Malabou's argument that the biological paradigm of epigenesis functions as a mental paradigm as well: that is, "the origin of thinking flows from this relation [between] genetic determinism and the 'environmental selective imprint' on the individual" (2016, 11). Kantian "innatism" is "relinquished" once this is understood, the circularity of his notion of the transcendental broken. Malabou wants to locate the generative point in between, *entre-deux*, at the point of resistance, wherein "every form carries within itself its own contradiction" (2008, 71) of form and deformation; and where a past trace can change meaning, or "change difference" (also the title of her 2009 monograph, *Changing Difference*). This narrative of thinking-through-plasticity constitutes a "theory of the transition" from proto- to experiential plasticity that, she asserts throughout *What Should We Do with Our Brain?*, is the "theoretical bedrock" (69) to an understanding of consciousness. This theory of transition marks out the condition for the possibility of "saying no," of resisting conformity, of exerting agency.

But what of *this strange critical entity*, to go back to my original question? Does that mean that it, too, is dialectical? Yes and no. Identity, as a stable form (if only temporarily), is a kind of settlement of "the dialectical play of the emergence and annihilation of form" (72): "all current identity maintains itself only at the cost of a struggle against its autodestruction," and adds that "identity is [in this sense] dialectical in nature" (71). But the "strange critical entity" is itself not an "identity." If anything, it is a form of time, a "momentum" (later, the term "motor of thought" will appear). The strange critical entity is never named in *What Should We Do with Our Brain?*—though its "plastic" quality is established. But interestingly, a second, contemporaneous book appears in France during the same year (2004) as *Le Change Heidegger* (as *The Heidegger Change* in 2011). While her resources in the first book (*Que faire de notre cerveau?*) are primarily neuroscientific, in the second (*Le Change Heidegger*) they are not only philosophical but also "fantastical," with references to myth (Ovid's *Metamorphoses*), to literature (Kafka's *The Metamorphosis*), to art (painting and sculpture). Reading the books with and/or against one another, we can compare their respective emphases on the biological and the philosophical, as she works to make these domains commensurate.

While the word *plasticity* does not appear, interestingly, in *The Heidegger Change* this book is entirely about metamorphosis and change, without the overlay (or interweaving) of neuroscience. But we can recognize in this work Malabou's intuition regarding the importance that *epigenesis* will ultimately have to her work, as we recall that the strange critical entity is constituted by its *becoming conscious* in and through changing difference:

> My proposal is that *Ereignis*,[6] when cast in and clarified by the light of the late Heidegger's interpretation of himself, must be envisaged as an *interchange* in which the elements that circulate or "play" stop seeking to exercise mastery *on* each other and being of value *for* each other. At bottom, *Ereignis* is only the name given the possibility of an exchange *without violence* between the elements that it appropriates: *Dasein*, God, world, earth. The possibility of such an exchange constitutes for me the *ethical* dimension of Heidegger's thought. This "exchange" leaves no room for *identification*: the instances present in it are neither identical nor identifiable with each other. What is at stake is an exchange, in the triple sense of a *contemporaneousness*, a *mutability*, and a *passage* into the other. At once "neither this nor that" and "everything at once." [. . .] At stake in *Ereignis* is a structure of address and reception, the instances at work in it remaining unique and mysteriously incomparable. (Malabou 2011, 127–128, emphasis in original)

This provocative passage replaces terms of opposition with words such as *interchange, circulation, play, exchange, invitation*, all of them, she notes, "*without violence between the elements that it appropriates*" (127, emphasis added). Earlier in the book, these figures of exchange are said to belong to "the *ontological metabolism* that renders possible all its changes, mutations, and transformations. I call such a point of access *fantastic*" (2011, 11; emphasis in original). What she means by "the fantastic" has to do with an "opening up" toward the "not-yet," as German philosopher Ernst Bloch has it throughout his work on the principle of Hope (Bloch 1986). In this particular context, Malabou claims that the fantastic

> *designates at once a kind of approach to change and the very strangeness of what changes and is going to change. It also manifests, by consequence, the uncanniness of the fantastic to itself: its irreducibility to a genre or category of discourse, its resistance to every relegation of itself to a conventional domain... The philosophical fantastic is contemporary with the bringing to light . . . of the ontological difference and, by way of consequence, the possibility of thinking being without beings. It never designates* "*an element exterior to the human*

world" ... *but describes the foreigner on the inside, the whole of the metabolic force that sleeps without sleeping in what is, the very face of being that concepts cannot say without losing face.* (2011, 12–13, emphasis in original)

"The strangeness"; "the foreigner inside"; irreducible to genre: these are terms we have seen, in the other 2004 book, *Que faire de notre cerveau?* And then, here, she qualifies it again: "*unlocatable, undatable, and unthinkable, it [the philosophical fantastic] is nonetheless the motor of thought.* I would like us now, you and me, to engage together its unforeseeable, constantly changing motility" (2011, 13). "The motor of thought" is a "surprising image" of the "dividing line of change" (14) she notes; and almost immediately, the word "change" is revised to "exchange" (15). In the preference for "exchange," Malabou registers the interaction between differing and changing. The "meeting point" between the "epigenesis of cognition, the autonomy of the practical subject, and the creativity of life" (Malabou 2016, 95) is the site of a critique that cannot be objective in any *fixed* sense. To claim that it is—that we can read absolutely objectively—is to become unconscious of a past "that has become rigid," and in effect to turn one's back against the vitality of subjectivity. The fantastic does not refer to the fanciful or utopian; nor is the "metabolic force" simply metaphorical. The metabolic economy of the body, Malabou shows us, is more than a conversion of one form of energy to another, but also involves the traceable changes in the structures of thought, as "the other thinking" (2011, 21).

As Malabou has consistently argued, a different temporality (anticipating Jane Gallop) is being articulated. The critical entity is a *temporal* engagement, before it is an ontological matter(-ing), based not in the a priori but in an a posteriori: "Structure, or the structural nucleus, thus arrives in some sense after that which it structures" (2012, 21–22). The critical event constitutes itself, with each repetition, as a strangeness of the "structural kernel," "already in itself a *deconstructive affirmation*" (29, emphasis added). Why an affirmation? Because "by thus opening structure onto its future" (21), thought resists the rigid plan of the preformed: meaning and interpretation find form in a consciousness of difference that is anticipated by Bloch's notion of the *novum* as a figuration of radical futurity. The paradigm of epigenetic regeneration "mobilizes" (her word) a regenerative force not only at the cellular/biological level, but at the level of mentality and consciousness. The temporalities of epigenesis are the theoretical bedrock of what I take to be her "new genre" of critique as regenerative, not defensive or violent, but mobile, plastic—epicritical. Epicritique recognizes and appropriates both epistemological and ontological pluralities: the surprising "motor of thought."

Malabou understands this in her earliest book *The Future of Hegel* (1996), which concludes by theorizing the essential subjectivity of objectivity:

"Clearly [plastic reading] is a conception of reading that will invalidate any idea of readerly 'objectivity' if by 'objectivity' we mean the attempt to bring to light, once and for all, what the text 'means' "—an act Malabou calls an "interpretative *violence*" (2005, 181; emphasis added). The intervention of the "knowing I" in reading does not mean "mastery" of a text: in such a case a reader would end up "writ[ing] what he or she reads." Instead, we should think of the intervention as a kind of accident, this "knowing I" is brought into tension with a text as "by accident": "Progressively, in the course of reading, the reader's subjectivity is formed into a substantial accident, a style, a plasticity" (183). Fifteen years later, Malabou will describe this entity yet again—but give it another name: *intelligence*. "Intelligence is not," Malabou claims, "logic that turns its back on life; rather it is what comes to occupy the space between logic and life" (2019, 11).

So here again, we arrive at this site, placed within

> both a biological and a social arrangement that seals the union of brain and body as the original site of intelligence. The process of practical and plastic formation [. . .] requires the connection of heterogeneous instances—nature/culture and biology/history—and this connecting offers one possible definition of intelligence. (65–66)

This idea too has been with Malabou from early on:

> Plasticity is a name for the originary unity of acting and being acted upon, of spontaneity and receptivity. A medium for the differentiation of opposites, plasticity holds the extremes together in their reciprocal action, enabling the function of a structure of anticipation where the three terms of the temporal process are articulated. [. . .] The meaning of the notion of plasticity is the same as its way of being. [. . .] Indeed, the originary operation of receiving and giving form is not a rigid and fixed structure but an instance which can evolve, which means that it can give itself new forms. (2005, 186)

Plasticity is thus simultaneously spatial and temporal—a "structure" and an "instance": a structuralization of thought. An "epigenetic development of intelligence," according to Malabou, understands the brain to be a "cultural organ, the space of interaction of the biological and symbolic along with the original possibility of 'acquired dispositions' [or *conditionality*]" (2019, 58). Consciousness forms as a dynamic engagement "between the biological and the social [. . .] and this connecting offers one possible definition of intelligence" (65), not to be simply measured, but "still observable" (66).

NEW LOGI(ISTI)CS OF CRITIQUE

As far back as *The Future of Hegel* (2004), Malabou asserts that it is "freedom that is in question here" (2011, 3)—a freedom, she is suggesting, without violence: this applies to the practice of critique, avoiding the metaphors of attack and defense. The opportunities of a "liberating transformation" depend on our seeing that "new logics of resistance" are necessary, "to structure each moment in terms of specific agonistic modes: confrontation, self-criticism, interruption" (2019, 16). What is different in Malabou's notion of critique is that it avoids previous metaphors of attack and defense (to which Felski and Spivak object), by proposing a figuration that generates a field of negotiation, synthesis, and revision, rather than mastery. Malabou's "strange critical entity" is constituted by its *becoming conscious* in and through "the thought (or thoughts) of difference" (2005, 21), marking the historicity of consciousness insofar as "it differentiates itself and thus temporalizes itself" (14). The strange critical entity is what allows us to say not only "I am not that person any more," but also, "I think differently now."

Ultimately, the "regenerative force of reading that I call plasticity" (2012, 22) might be the best definition of critique, at the same as it is also its best "methodology." Plastic reading, as Malabou develops the concept from Hegel, would meet Foucault's challenge for a

> criticism [that is] no longer going to be practiced in the search for formal structures with universal value, but rather as a historical investigation into the events that led us to constitute ourselves and to recognize ourselves as subjects of what we are doing, thinking, saying. (Foucault, quoted in Malabou 2016, 106)

This strikes me as an accurate description of the procedure that Malabou herself carefully has developed, as she considers, from the very first book, the nature of thinking as a "speculative oscillation" (2005, 178) between subject and predicate. Malabou continues to investigate, revisit, revise her own philosophical genealogy, each monograph extending the narrative of her own becoming-self, describing her own intellectual evolution by becoming conscious, from another horizon of thought, of the historicity of that progress. Following Bergson's proposal that we look to life "itself"—particularly the capacities of adaptation—to find "a real genesis of intelligence" (2019, 4), Malabou's most consistent object of study is her own becoming-intelligent.

The autobiographical idiom of her work is perceptible early on: Derrida notes this even in the introduction to *The Heidegger Change*, this tendency of hers to adapt her own work to the very grounding of philosophy itself. Having developed over thirty years a notion of life and/as plasticity, "mobilized" by a biological imperative for epigenetic change, Malabou arrives at "a description of intelligence on its own terms" (2019, 10). This very process becomes the narrative of her own epigenetic development as a thinker. Tracking the history of her responses to Hegel, Heidegger, and Kant from the site of her own "epigenetic turn," her books in particular *perform* the critical process that constitutes "epigenetic becoming." The recent books in particular, *Before Tomorrow* and *Morphing Intelligence*, appear as adaptations of earlier positions regarding plasticity, becoming-consciousness, and critique. In *Morphing Intelligence*, this includes the recognition that she has *gotten something wrong*, realizing to her own surprise, that a long-standing resistance to regarding "artificial intelligence" *as* a form of intelligence was a blindness. Stubbornly unreflective and thus maintaining the "vulgarity" (2005, 191), she refused to "put [AI] in play" with her increasingly sophisticated notions of embodied consciousness. Until she saw it otherwise, and changed her mind:

> I was indeed mistaken in *What Should We Do with Our Brain?*: plasticity is not, as I then argued, the opposite of the machine, the determining element that stops us from equating the brain with a computer. As I have said, that opposition can only derive from the old critical conflict it claims to challenge. As such, it still belongs to the *testudo* [defense] strategy. (2019, 113)

From the perspective of a "critical intelligence," there will be no comfortable place: observing "from the edge," Malabou favors the Bergsonian notion of *intuition* as "instinct that has become disinterested, self-conscious, capable of reflection upon its object and of enlarging it indefinitely" (Bergson 1998, 176). Insofar as we are able to do that, we remain critical, discerning sameness and difference while refusing any reduction to a singular or "transcendent" meaning. To use a word Malabou previously deployed, we must "mobilize" our own intelligence, drop the habitual defenses, and "believe in an emancipation of intelligence by intelligence" (2019, 13). This emancipation, again, is *epicritique*.

It seems appropriate as I finish this during (*still*) the days of COVID-19, that we entertain Malabou's challenge that we pay attention to stupidity, particularly "our own"—personally and collectively. It is interesting to watch Dr. Anthony Fauci, world-renowned expert on infectious disease, model a practical intelligence by telling both what we do know, and also what we don't know. His appearances on television, before the U.S. Senate, anywhere he is given a platform, stress again and again not to be stupid, though he is smart enough not to put it that way. "Emancipation of intelligence by intelligence"? Is it possible that the virus itself might be "read critically" as the "strange entity" that is defamiliarizing the world? We are, as Stan Robinson said, living in a science-fiction *reality*—which urges us to reflect on the fictions we live by. ("We'll be back to normal.") However disorienting it may be to "live" it and "think" it, I embrace Stan Robinson's faith (his word) in *"this tentative awareness of the emerging next stage—these are also new feelings in our time"* (2020). Stan Robinson is at heart an optimist, inviting these "new feelings" and emergences; Catherine Malabou's investigation of plasticity, temporality, consciousness, and intelligence strikes me as similarly optimistic. These positions, I suggest, represent the purpose of a new kind of critique. In the "radical spread of possibility" (Robinson), or the regenerative possibilities of epigenetic thought (Malabou), we have the best possible end of critique: to *think epicritically*.

NOTES

1. William Wordsworth, from "Lines Composed a Few Miles above Tintern Abbey, On Revisiting the Banks of the Wye during a Tour. July 13, 1798."
2. I am grateful to Jane Gallop for sending these remarks to me in advance of their publication.
3. Similarly, in her 2012 *An Aesthetic Education in the Age of Globalization*, Gayatri Spivak also resists a mode of critique (including Marxian) that affirms the "[dialectical] circle of self-foundation and self-responsibility" as a "test of the self-reflexive circle that consists in taking itself for its object" (Spivak 2012, 51). Simply replicating a philosophical repression of "the body as the seat of the mind" (57) is inadequate.
4. "The figure of epigenesis—irreducible to a simple theoretical device—in fact determines the fate of the transcendental" (Malabou 2016, 34).
5. See Hugh Silverman's excellent article, "Malabou, Plasticity, and the Sculpturing of the Self" (2010).
6. In Heidegger, this technical term is "translated variously as 'event' (most closely reflecting its ordinary German usage), 'appropriation', 'appropriating event', 'event of appropriation' or 'enowning'. [. . .] The history of Being is now conceived as a series of appropriating events in which the different dimensions of human sense-making—the religious, political, philosophical (and so on) dimensions that define the culturally conditioned epochs of human history—are transformed. Each such transformation is a revolution in human patterns of intelligibility, so what is appropriated in the event is Dasein and thus the human capacity for taking-as" (Wheeler 2018).

BIBLIOGRAPHY

Barthes, Roland. 2011. *Mythologies*. New York: Hill and Wang.
Bergson, Henri. 1998. *Creative Evolution*. New York: Dover.
Bloch, Ernst. 1986. *The Principle of Hope*, translated by Neville Plaice, Stephen Plaice, and Paul Knight. Cambridge, MA: MIT Press.

Castiglia, Christopher D. 2013. "Critiquiness." *English Language Notes* 51 (2): 79–85.
Derrida, Jacques. 1997. *Of Grammatology*, edited by Gayatri Spivak. Baltimore: The Johns Hopkins University Press.
Felski, Rita. 2015. *The Limits of Critique*. Chicago: University of Chicago Press.
Gallop, Jane. 2020. "Has Postcritique Run Out of Steam?" *Symploke* 28: 533–535.
Haraway, Donna. 1988. "Situated Knowledges: The Science Question in Feminism and the Privilege of Partial Perspective." *Feminist Studies* 14 (3): 575–599.
Jameson, Frederic. 2003. "Future City." *New Left Review* 21: 65–79.
Malabou, Catherine. 2005. *The Future of Hegel: Plasticity, Temporality and Dialectic*, translated by Lisabeth During. New York, NY: Routledge.
———. 2008. *What Should We Do With Our Brain?* Fordham University Press. (Originally published as *Que faire de notre cerveau?* Paris: Bayard, 2004).
———. 2011a. *Changing Difference*. Translated by Carolyn Shread. London: Polity.
———. 2011b. *The Heidegger Change: On the Fantastic in Philosophy*, edited by Peter Skafish (translator). Albany, NY: SUNY Press. (Originally published as *Le Change Heidegger, du fantastique en philosophie*. Paris: Éditions Léo Scheer, 2004).
———. 2012. "Following Generation." Translated by Simon Porzak. *Qui Parle* 20 (2): 19–33.
———. 2016. *Before Tomorrow: Epigenesis and Rationality*, translated by Carolyn Shread. London: Polity.
———. 2019. *Morphing Intelligence: From IQ Measurement to Artificial Brains*, translated by Carolyn Shread. New York: Columbia University Press.
Online Etymology Dictionary. Accessed March 12, 2020. https://www.etymonline.com/search?q=appreciate.
Proctor, Hannah, and Laura Salisbury. 2016. "The History of a Brain Wound: Alexander Luria and the Dialectics of Soviet Plasticity." In *Plasticity and Pathology: On the Formation of the Neural Subject*, edited by Nima Bassiri and David Bates, 159–193. New York: Fordham University Press.
Robinson, Kim Stanley. 1995. *Pacific Edge*. New York: Orb Books.
———. 2020. "The Cornona Virus Is Rewriting Our Imaginations." *The New Yorker*, May 1. https://www.newyorker.com/culture/annals-of-inquiry/the-coronavirus-and-our-future.
Silverman, Hugh. 2010. "Malabou, Plasticity, and the Sculpturing of the Self." *Concentric: Literary and Cultural Studies* 36: 89–102.
Sontag, Susan. 1966. "Against Interpretation." In *Against Interpretation and Other Essays*, edited by Susan Sontag, 3–14. New York: Picador.
———. 2007. *At the Same Time: Essays & Speeches*, edited by Paulo Dilonardo and Anne Jump. New York : Farrar, Straus, Giroux.
———. 2012. *As Consciousness is Harnessed to Flesh: Journals and Notebooks 1964–1980*, edited by David Rieff. New York: Farrar Strous Giroux.
Spivak, Gayatri Chakrovorty. 2012. *An Aesthetic Education in the Era of Globalization*. Cambridge: Harvard University Press.

Wagner-Lawlor, Jennifer. 2017. "The Persistence of Utopia: Plasticity and Difference from Roland Barthes to Catherine Malabou." *The Journal of French and Francophone Philosophy* 25: 67–86.

———. Forthcoming 2021. "Plastic's 'Untiring Solicitation': Geographies of Myth, Corporate Alibis, and the Plaesthetics of the Matacão." In *Life in Plastic*, edited by Caren Irr. Minneapolis, MN: University of Minnesota Press.

Wheeler, Michael. (2018). "Martin Heidegger." In *The Stanford Encyclopedia of Philosophy*, edited by Edward N. Zalta. https://plato.stanford.edu/archives/win2018/entries/heidegger.

Williams, Raymond. 1977. *Marxism and Literature*. Oxford: Oxford University Press, 1978.

Winterson, Jeanette. 1995. *Art Objects*. New York: Vintage.

———. 2009. *The Stone Gods*. New York: Mariner Books.

Wordsworth, William. "Lines Composed a Few Miles Above Tintern Abbey, On Revisiting the Banks of the Wye During a Tour. July 13, 1798." https://www.poetryfoundation.org/poems/45527/lines-composed-a-few-miles-above-tintern-abbey-on-revisiting-the-banks-of-the-wye-during-a-tour-july-13-1798.

Part II

CRITICAL READING

5

Suspicious Minds

Critique as Symptomatic Reading

Esther Peeren

In 2019, the World Health Organization listed "vaccine hesitancy" as one of the top ten threats to global health (WHO 2019). That same year, there were several measles outbreaks the likes of which had not been seen for decades in, among others, the United States (1,282 confirmed cases in the calendar year, 128 of which required hospitalization) and Samoa (5,697 confirmed cases between September 1, 2019, and January 6, 2020, of which eighty-three were fatal). In 2021, with no end to the global COVID-19 pandemic in sight but various vaccines approved, whether enough people will want to be vaccinated is a matter of great concern (COCONEL Group 2020; Pylas 2021). A BBC article by Michelle Roberts (2019) entitled "Vaccines: Low Trust in Vaccination 'a Global Crisis' " refers to people's lack of "trust" and "confidence" in vaccination programs, especially in higher-income regions, despite "overwhelming evidence" of their effectiveness. The article cites a WHO immunization expert as saying that the best way to tackle vaccine hesitancy is "to have health workers really well trained and able and ready to recommend vaccinations based on scientific truth."

The WHO's use of the euphemistic term "hesitancy" obfuscates that part of what is at stake is an outright refusal to vaccinate on the part of an increasing number of people—a refusal that many actively seek to propagate by spreading misinformation on social media.[1] *"Hesitancy" downplays the entrenchment of the problem both at the individual and the social level. This makes the solution proposed by the expert in Roberts's article seem feasible even though it disregards the fact that the problem is driven precisely by a lack of trust in institutions, health workers, and "scientific fact" as trumping fraudulent science, anecdotes, feelings, and intuitions. Another term often used, including in scientific articles, is "vaccination controversy" which, like "climate change debate," suggests parity between two sides in a rational disagreement, rather than acknowledging the fact that only fringe scientists contest the overall benefits of vaccination programs or deny that climate change is not only real but man-made; or, in Sylvia Wynter's term (to be discussed below), Man(2)-made.*

***

Far from seeing in the current "post-truth" era, in which anti-vaxxers and climate change deniers thrive, a reason to proclaim the end of critique, as Bruno Latour did in his 2004 article "Why Has Critique Run Out of Steam?," I believe that what is called for is a re-intensification of critique through a return to symptomatic reading. Rather than foregoing suspicion and a political stance in favor of a "new modesty" that recoils from casting critics as "warriors" and refrains from looking for hidden or multiple meanings in texts (Williams 2015), the above vignette makes clear that we need to ask what euphemisms like "vaccine hesitancy," "vaccine controversy," and "climate change debate" imply and are symptoms of, and how they stand in the way of preventing and addressing disease outbreaks (including COVID-19) and environmental collapse. It is necessary to insist on the difference between, on the one hand, popular and scholarly caricatures of critique either as absolute relativism, doing away with truths and facts, or as violently imposing a particular politics on a defenseless, nonpolitical text; and, on the other, critique as a situated engagement with a text or world that is always already political and that accommodates various readings, but not just any one. With regard to our world in crisis, the end (as in aim) of critique in the latter mode is to provide a diagnosis of what is going on and to envision potential cures (or at least modes of care) from a position of implicatedness. Critique, we might say, should act like a vaccine in making the critical condition of the world a part of us in order not to let it destroy us, in order to ensure a living-on that is a "living-with" (Haraway 2) rather than a living-*off* others—vaccine refusal, after all, is predicated on taking advantage of herd immunity.

In 2004, Latour, in the above-mentioned article, famously wrote:

> Wars. So many wars. Wars outside and wars inside. Cultural wars, science wars, and wars against terrorism. Wars against poverty and wars against the poor. Wars against ignorance and wars out of ignorance. My question is simple: *Should we be at war, too, we, the scholars, the intellectuals? Is it really our duty to add fresh ruins to fields of ruins? Is it really the task of the humanities to add deconstruction to destruction?* More iconoclasm to iconoclasm? What has become of the critical spirit? Has it run out of steam? (Latour 2004, 225, emphasis added)

Citing a Republican strategist who advised those in his party to keep pointing to the "lack of scientific certainty" (226) about the man-made causes of global warming, Latour worried that his own emphasis on the "social construction of scientific fact" and his desire to "*emancipate* the public from prematurely naturalized objectified facts" (227, emphasis in text) had backfired. He speculated that there may not be any difference between the fanciful explanations offered by 9/11 conspiracy theorists and the way critique—of which the rather incongruous threesome of Jean Baudrillard, Thierry Meyssan, and Pierre Bourdieu are presented as the "French field commanders"—mobilizes a "deep dark below" to put into question what people take to be natural or self-evident (229). In the face of this apparent indistinguishability[2] and of the way critique supposedly humiliates both those who believe in the agency of objects and those who believe in their own agency, Latour's answer to the question of whether scholars and intellectuals should wage war appeared to be a firm "no." This does not mean, as some have argued, that he advocated getting rid of critique altogether. In fact, his proposal was to make critique *more critical* by eschewing debunking and deconstructive modes (associated with the "fact" and "fairy" positions) in favor of assembling, protecting, and caring ones (associated with a "fair," realist, constructivist position) that would, crucially, not evoke associations with waging war and avoid creating "new ruins."[3]

Yet, in a 2018 interview with Ava Kofman of the *New York Times*, headlined "Bruno Latour, the Post-Truth Philosopher, Mounts a Defense of Science," the idea of critique-as-warfare returns with a vengeance as Latour insists that climatologists "must recognize that, as nature's designated representatives, they have always been political actors, and that they are now *combatants in a war* whose outcome will have planetary ramifications" (Kofman 2018, emphasis added). It is not just climatologists who are called upon to take up arms; Latour also posits, in relation to the rise of alternative facts, that it is "a greater understanding of the circumstances out of which misinformation arises and the communities in which it takes root [that] will better equip us to *combat* it" (Kofman 2018, emphasis added). This idea of combating misinformation would no longer seem to preclude, and might even require, the type of debunking critiques dismissed in 2004 together with the idea of the scholar as having to be at war.

In *Down to Earth: Politics in the New Climatic Regime*, to which the *New York Times* interview refers, Latour specifies the war in question as declared by former U.S. president Donald Trump when he withdrew from the Paris Accord, and as being waged "over what constitutes the theater of operations" (2018, 3). Significantly, this identifies the war as one declared by retreat, by refusing to take action even as the ruins of climate change were piling up. The epigraph to *Down to Earth* puts the focus on reading by quoting Jared Kushner, Trump's son-in-law, as saying: "We've read enough books." This could be taken and was probably meant by Kushner to suggest that the time had come to stop studying the situation and to take action (albeit not, of course, on climate change). However, given Trump's infamous admission that he does not read much of anything, and Kushner's statement being taken from a *New York Times* opinion piece by Sarah Vowell (2017) that ends with the affirmation "as with literally every other kind of book, I will never, ever read enough of those," it seems fair to take Latour's epigraph, contrary to what it proclaims on the surface, as an exhortation to keep reading. Because, when it comes to climate change, not doing anything is itself an act of war that needs to be exposed as such and to be countered by critique.

Scholars across the humanities, social sciences, and natural sciences are—increasingly in conversation with each other—presenting incisive readings of this war's "theater of operations" and of how to fight it. A particularly strong salvo is fired by a 2017 volume edited by Anna Tsing and others entitled *Arts of Living on a Damaged Planet: Ghosts/Monsters*, which is also cited by Latour (2018, 116n36). The volume seeks to imagine radical, creative, non-anthropocentric "arts of living" that will enable survival in what are designated as "troubled, illegible times" (Tsing et al. 2017, G10). A partial legibility is restored to these times by presenting, as noted on the cover, "entangled histories, situated narratives, and thick descriptions" of ghosts and monsters—the titles of the two parts into which the volume is split and that work toward each other from the cover, which does not have a defined back or front, to meet in the middle.[4]

Ghosts and monsters, as "figures hiding in plain sight" (M176), resist immediate and full apprehension, necessitating an active attentiveness to their possible presence and a close, careful engagement with the "forms of noticing that crosscut forms of knowledge, official and vernacular, science and storytelling" (M176) that they point to—for ghosts and monsters *always* point beyond themselves and are never (just) what they seem. The editors of *Arts of Living on a Damaged Planet* consider ghosts as the haunting (disruptive and elusive) "traces of more-than-human histories through which ecologies are made and unmade" (G1), and say of monsters that "on one hand, they help us pay attention to ancient chimeric entanglements; on the other, they point us toward the monstrosities of modern Man" (M2). Ghosts and monsters, then, are at once symbols and symptoms of the current planetary crisis that so many people are determined to deny. Ghosts and monsters indicate the need, in the war identified by Latour, to assess and assert the realities on the ground, as well as the status of this ground, by "redescribing the dwelling places that have become invisible" (Latour 2018, 94), an act that manifestly (or, rather, *manifestingly*) goes beyond mere description and involves looking—closely, intently, symptomatically—for what escapes notice at first sight or is deliberately obfuscated.

In what follows, I will read Latour's turn to redescription as an indication that critique-as-deconstruction has not run out of steam and is, in fact, more needed than ever, particularly in challenging, as the contributors to *Living on a Damaged Planet* do, the idea of "modern Man" as abdicating responsibility for the climate crisis while nonetheless considering humankind's survival its main stake; elevating itself over all other species and materialities; and purportedly but never actually including all *homo sapiens*. Without this combative debunking of "modern Man" that is not afraid of generating debris, the current war of the worlds—"there are now several worlds, several territories, and they are mutually incompatible" (Latour 2018, 26)—is unwinnable.

A deconstructive critique of "modern Man" is, of course, nothing new. In the spirit of redescription—which, as Latour's own redescription of Europe at the end of *Down to Earth* shows, inevitably involves going back over the past—I will return to two important milestones in the history of this critique: Jacques Derrida's 1968 "The Ends of Man" and Sylvia Wynter's 1984 "The Ceremony Must Be Found: After Humanism." Both these texts symptomatically read "Man" as a historically and culturally specific construction that has taken different, but always exclusionary forms. Wynter's 2015 follow-up "The Ceremony Found: Towards the Autopoetic Turn/Overturn, Its Autonomy of Human Agency and Extraterritoriality of (Self)Cognition," which revisits the territory of her earlier text and recalls Derrida's in taking his question "But who, we?" as its starting point, is specifically concerned with the intersection between climate change/global warming and the reign of a particular genre of Man: Man(2) or *homo oeconomicus*. This reign is exposed and subverted by Wynter's explicitly demystifying critique, which sets out to reveal— slowly, carefully, insistently, repetitively—what is *"normally unseeable,"* namely the fact that the climate crisis is not due to *"generic* 'human' activities" (2015, 137, 140, emphases in text) but to the "continued enactment and replication of this now neo-Liberal monohumanist conception" (2015, 238) that is the current version of Man(2). Against the background of the recent backlash against close and especially symptomatic reading in literary studies, in which Latour has been mobilized as an ally, I take Derrida and Wynter—together with the Latour of *Down to Earth*—as affirming the need to remain suspicious of what seems self-evident (who "we" are, who "man" is, what form "the world" has, what a war is and how it is to be declared and waged), as well as to remain alert to ghosts and monsters—to what may not be apparent at first glance and what, symptomatically, points beyond itself.

FROM READING SYMPTOMS TO UNCRITICAL DESCRIPTION

When it was first espoused by the New Critics in the mid-twentieth century, close reading was positioned against what Cleanth Brooks calls the "heresy of paraphrase," or the idea that it is possible to "formulate a proposition that will say what the poem 'says' " (1975, 198). According to Brooks, "as his [*sic*] proposition approaches adequacy," any reader would find,

> not only that it has increased greatly in length, but that it has begun to fill itself up with reservations and qualifications—and most significant of all—[. . .] that he has himself begun to fall back upon metaphors of his own in his attempt to indicate what the poem "says." In sum, his proposition, as it approaches adequacy, ceases to be a proposition. (198)

Close reading thus entailed a rejection of modes of criticism that assumed that a text's singular meaning could be straightforwardly read off the page and summarily relayed. As involving, instead, a "respect for the stubbornness of texts," taken to demand a detailed examination of the multiple, complex meanings and effects yielded by the intertwinement of their form and content (and, later on, also their context and that of their readers), close reading was long considered the "sine qua non of literary study" (Culler 2010). In the 2000s, the emergence of distant reading, most notably in the work of Franco Moretti (2013), provided a machine-assisted supplement to close reading but did not fundamentally challenge its position as the preeminent form of critique. More recently, however, close reading as symptomatic reading has been attacked as sidelining aesthetic experience and ordinary readers; harboring unrealistic or hubristic expectations about literary studies as a form of political activism; and disrespecting the text.

Stephen Best and Sharon Marcus present the most pugnacious and influential argument against symptomatic reading in their programmatic introduction to a 2009 special issue of *Representations*, titled "The Way We Read Now." There, they define symptomatic reading as

> a mode of interpretation that assumes that a text's truest meaning lies in what it does not say, describes textual surfaces as superfluous, and seeks to unmask hidden meanings. For symptomatic readers, texts possess meanings that are veiled, latent, all but absent if it were not for their irrepressible and recurring symptoms. (Best and Marcus 2009, 1)

It is difficult to think of any actual literary scholar who would consider textual surfaces as "superfluous" or who would seek, as is implied here, *only* to unmask hidden meanings—and that includes those identified by Best and Marcus as symptomatic readers, like Fredric Jameson, Jacques Derrida, and Louis Althusser. In addition, it is hard to see how pursuing meanings that, while being "veiled, latent, all but absent," nevertheless yield "irrepressible and recurring symptoms" that presumably present themselves to the reader can be considered critical overreach. Similar overstatements and incongruities pervade Best and Marcus's account of symptomatic reading as a masterful, even violent practice in which the critic reads meanings into the text in order to make a political point, while disregarding what the text manifestly says.

In place of the straw man of symptomatic reading that Best and Marcus contest, they propose surface reading, also called descriptive or just reading (in the sense of simply/only reading). Focusing on "what is evident, perceptible, apprehensible in texts" on their surface (Best and Marcus 2009, 9), this mode of reading, per Ellen Rooney's brilliant takedown, "celebrates obviousness" and "disavows reading's own formal activities" (2010, 116), in what might be considered a return to the "paraphrastic heresy" (Brooks 1975, 200). Surface reading not only ignores the difficulty of determining and putting into a proposition what is "evident, perceptible, apprehensible"—as Rooney points out, this may be "a matter of what one looks for, where one stands, and what one expects to see or desires" (2010, 123)—but also the impossibility of establishing where the surface of a text begins and ends, not least because the linguistic sign itself, as Saussure showed, is layered.[5] When do we leave the surface of a text? When we read (some of) the text as metaphorical or allusive, when we take into account the multiple or changing meanings of certain words, when we pursue the "irrepressible and recurring symptoms" breaking through to the surface of the text, or when we consider something that is not in the text as nevertheless relevant to its interpretation?

Just how restricted Best and Marcus's notion of the surface of a text is becomes clear when they propose to let "ghosts be ghosts, instead of saying what they are ghosts *of*" (2009, 13, emphasis in text). Since, as I have already noted, a ghost is, quite literally, the remainder of something else—this is its very definition!—it demands, on the surface if you will, a suspicious reading that asks what this something else is. Best and Marcus's description of a surface as "what insists on being looked *at* rather than what we must train ourselves to see *through*" (2009, 9, emphasis in text) does not hold when a ghost, a symptom, or a habitual liar and master of distraction like Trump enters the stage. At that point, surface reading's claim to modesty is revealed as originating in a dangerous naïveté—about how language, reading and especially description work[6]—and as resulting in political apathy.[7] The call for surface reading absolves readers from having to take responsibility for their reading—for bringing something to the text (including a certain suspicion) and doing something with it and with the ghosts and monsters that may lurk in it, something that exceeds not only objective description but also aesthetic enjoyment or enchantment.

A strident call for the revaluation of enchantment—as what supposedly draws ordinary readers to literature—over "an attitude of vigilance, detachment, and wariness (*suspicion*)" animates Rita Felski's (2015) book *The Limits of Critique* (3, emphasis in text). While she is also critical of surface reading, most of Felski's arrows are aimed at symptomatic reading as the privileged method of what she mockingly calls, in the title of her fourth chapter, "Crrritique." Describing crrritique as "fl[ying] off the tongue like a weapon, emitting a rapid guttural burst of machine-gun-fire" and as "a negative act" of "againstness," Felski presents it as unduly combative, much like the mode of critique challenged by Latour in his 2004 article, which she alludes to (2015, 120–129). Those who practice crrritique are considered party poopers in that, even when things appear to be going well, they refuse to stop being suspicious: "[crrritique] demonstrates, again and again, that what might look like hopeful signs of social progress harbor more disturbing implications" (Felski 2015, 129). In its political optimism and trenchant resistance to what Haraway (2016) might call "staying with the trouble," *The Limits of Critique* marks itself as a distinctly Obama-era text: pre-Trump, pre-Brexit, pre-Bolsanaro and pre-peak-Modi. In light of the current championing of nationalist populism by many world leaders and the resurgence and global spread of the Black Lives Matter movement after the brutal police killing of George Floyd in Minnesota in 2020, the above quote and Felski's dismissal of crrritique's "conviction that [incremental] change is actually harmful in blinding us to what remains undone" makes crrritique sound visionary and Felski positively Pollyannaish (2015, 129). Similarly, read from the present, Felski's stated aim of "bringing critique down to earth and exploring new modes of interpretation" that are "postcritical" (2015, back cover), which entails the espousal of an "affective hermeneutics" that embraces "the language of enchantment, incandescence, and rapture without embarrassment," comes across as an uncannily accurate description of the hermeneutical stance taken by hardcore Trump supporters, especially in its evocation of rapture's evangelical homonym (2015, 178, 175).

For my purposes, it is important to note that Felski calls upon Latour and, more broadly, on actor-network-theory (ANT), to support her argument against "militant reading" (2015, 1). Best and Marcus, too, claim Latour as an ally in their quest against "the excessive emphasis on ideological demystification" (2009, 18). In view of Latour's opposition to critique's "explanations" of "the things really close to our hearts" in the 2004 article (243), this is hardly surprising, and the apparent affinity between his work and that of advocates of surface and postcritical reading is further strengthened by the way the title of his 2018 book echoes Felski's notion of "bringing critique down to earth." However, as I already indicated at the beginning of this chapter, Latour's turn to redescription as part of his combative engagement in the current war of the worlds, which is also a war of words, suggests that his work can no longer be seen as diametrically opposed to symptomatic reading. In fact, given its implicit declaration by Trump's withdrawal from the Paris Accord, the very diagnosis of this war *as* a war depends on symptomatic reading.

Looking closely at "Why Has Critique Run Out of Steam?" shows that already in that text Latour employs a language of depth and seeing-through that is at odds with Best and Marcus's commitment to staying on the surface. Thus, in the discussion of Alfred North Whitehead as the embodiment of the "*fair* position" that Latour is advocating, Whitehead is described as trying "to get *closer* to [facts] or, more exactly, to see through them the reality that requested a new respectful realist attitude" and as proposing "to dig much further into the realist attitude and to realize that matters of fact are totally implausible, unrealistic, unjustified definitions of what it is to deal with things" (Latour 2004, 234–244, emphases in text). Here, matters of fact are what, on the surface (or perhaps hovering above the surface), impede the perception of matters of concern; what is on or hanging over the surface needs to be seen through, dug into—in other words, penetrated—in order to expose matters of fact as deceitful (as clouds to be dispersed) and to make it possible to gather together matters of concern.

Against Latour's assertion that "the critic is not the one who debunks [. . .] but the one who assembles," then, there seems to be a necessary stage of suspicion and destruction: the "powerful descriptive tool" that will deal with matters of concern and that will "protect," and "care" is predicated on an operation that may well be called deconstructive (2004, 246). Upping the suspicion quotient of my reading of the 2004 text, I might also highlight the contradiction between Latour's statement that the "direction of critique" is "not *away* [from] but *toward* the gathering, the Thing" (246, emphasis in text) and the fact that the two examples given of the thing to be taken as a matter of concern are the "shower of debris" signaling the Space Shuttle Colombia disaster (234) and the 2003 military strike against Iraq, both violent, shocking events of ungathering, dispersal and, quite literally, ruin.

In *Down to Earth*, Latour initially describes the "narrative" that "obscurantist elites" have kept "the scientific knowledge" about climate change secret in order to maintain their dominance as one that "appears implausible" and resembles "a conspiracy theory" (2018, 21). However, unlike in 2004, when conspiracy theories and deconstructive critique were both dismissed as sharing an excess of suspicion, now, in a footnote, Latour cites Luc Boltanski's idea that conspiracy theories "sometimes correspond all too well to reality," while referring to Nancy MacLean's book *Democracy in Chains* as making it "tempting to believe this" (2018, 113n21). In the main text, moreover, Latour acknowledges that the narrative about obscurantist elites "is not impossible to document" and that "in the absence of flagrant evidence, the effects themselves are quite visible" (2018, 21, 22). These effects, including "the epistemological delirium that has taken hold of the public stage" since Trump's election and the pervasive chaos of the Trump administration, are seen to demand a reading capable of undoing the denial or denegation of "the proverbial 'elephant in the room' " that is "the enormity of the [climate change] threat," while at the same time not dismissing the understandably suspicious attitude of those deceived by Trump and the rest of the obscurantist elites (Latour 2018, 23).

Latour insists that the present situation of human-induced climate change is, to "a stunning extent [. . .] unprecedented" and therefore requires new stories (2018, 44). However, his formulation already indicates that there are indeed precedents: something that is to a stunning extent unprecedented is not wholly so. In addition, the story he turns to next is in fact an old one, namely Edgar Allan Poe's "A Descent into the Maelstrom" from 1841. For Latour, this story about a sailor observing the aftermath of a shipwreck of which he is the only survivor stresses the necessity, if survival is to be an option for us now, of

> paying close attention to all the wreckage as it drifts; such attention may make it possible to understand suddenly why some of the debris is sucked toward the bottom while other objects, because of their form, can serve as life preservers. (44–45)

It is difficult not to read this as an endorsement of close reading in the symptomatic mode, since it advocates a tracing of the debris beyond the surface of the water. Instead of being admonished to turn away from warfare, it seems, the critic is now urged to fight in a no longer avoidable war that has put the earth's very survival at stake, and to do so using a form of critique that combines construction and deconstruction, care and distrust. What is undone in the process is the spurious opposition of construction—aligned with care and fairness—and deconstruction—aligned with distrust, destruction, and a lack of realism (through the figure of the fairy)—that governed "Why Has Critique Run Out of Steam?"

In *Down to Earth*, the aim is not just to describe what is happening but to uncover the reasons why and to redirect the situation. What complicates this effort is that two descriptions of the world are, according to Latour, in competition: a planetary or Galilean vision that proposes a view from nowhere—"*to know is to know from the outside*" (2018, 68, emphasis in text), from far above the surface—versus a Lovelockian view (named for James Lovelock, who formulated the Gaia hypothesis) from the inside or from below. The latter view's proponents "consent to *face up to* an enigma *concerning the number and nature of the agents at work*" (77, emphasis in text), which include "metamorphoses, processes, entanglements, and overlaps" (76). What the world *is* and how it is properly apprehended, then, is not something that simply appears on its surface to a disinterested or enchanted reader, but an effect of the different modes of reading applied to it. The Lovelockian view that Latour privileges is not descriptive but explicitly interpretative; it confronts the reader of the world with an enigma—something inscrutable—that has to be faced up to, however unsettling. The innumerable agents at work in the enigmatic system of engendering engaged by the Lovelockian view point beyond themselves, in a symptomatic, ghostly manner, to "questions about descendants and forebears" (87). In this system of engendering, the world is never just there, in the present, on the surface, but is becoming, throwing up ghosts of which it needs to be asked what they are ghosts *of*, what pasts (precedents) and futures (afterlives) their hauntings indicate.

Latour's key message about critique in *Down to Earth*, consequently, concerns the need to "*generate alternative descriptions*" of "what makes up the Earth for us" (2018, 94, emphasis in text). The notion of alternative descriptions already separates description from any notion of objectivity, as does the addition of "for us." Alternative descriptions are not paraphrases, but redescriptions aimed at revealing what has "become invisible" (94). They are acts of "unpacking [. . .] before recomposing" and thus deconstructions/reconstructions of territory that proceed "from the bottom up" with "the configurations [. . .] travers[ing] all scales of space and time" (95). Only through alternative descriptions, Latour contends, can an understanding be gained of the "causes and effects of our subjections," of which the capitalist system of production and its seductive narrative of modernization have made us "lose sight, in the literal sense" (96). The emphasis that *Down to Earth* places on returning obscured elements to visibility through redescription belies the alleged closeness between Latour's project and those of Best and Marcus, and Felski.

Latourian redescription must be recognized as, in all but name, a form of symptomatic reading that is not just about going deep, but also about going wide (following horizontally *and* vertically oriented traces), and that involves a deconstruction that is always also a reconstruction. The same is true of the mode of reading advocated by Donna Haraway in *Staying with the Trouble* (2016) under the name of string figures (SF). SFs involve "promiscuously plucking out fibers in clotted and dense events and practices"; following these fibers to "find their tangles and patterns," tangles and patterns that are seen to demand a response, a going-with; and "passing on and receiving, making and unmaking, picking up threads and dropping them" in "surprising relays" that are never done (3). SFs manifest as a suspenseful, symptomatic reading/writing "without guarantees" (Spivak 2004, 532) that, like Latour's redescription and the explicit deconstructions of Derrida and Wynter to which I turn now, hopes to shape a new shared world no longer dominated by man.

DERRIDA AND WYNTER: FROM REREADING TO REWRITING

Derrida's "The Ends of Man" and Wynter's "The Ceremony Must Be Found" and "The Ceremony Found," in having much to say about reading, are important precedents of Latour's redescription and Haraway's SF. Most importantly, these three texts all underline the importance of looking beyond the obvious, which is so often the normative, comfortable, and conservative. Derrida's "The Ends of Man," the most substantial section of which is titled "Reading Us," focuses on what it means to read others, ourselves and the notion of man attentively, accountably, comprehensively, fairly, ethically, but also critically. Early in the text, Derrida describes Sartre's translation of Heidegger's *Dasein* as "human-reality" as a "monstrous translation in many respects, but so much the more significant" because it takes away the "metaphysical presuppositions" of *Dasein* (1982, 115). Sartre's misreading, then, was also a productive rereading that did away with a certain humanism without rejecting humanism altogether. As Derrida notes, in Sartre, "the unity of man is never examined in and of itself" (115). For Derrida, it is only in *Nausea* that Sartre "takes apart" the humanism he elsewhere espouses, through his critical portrayal of the character of the Autodidact who sets out to read the "world library (which is really the Western library [. . .]) in alphabetical order by author's name, and in areas where he is able to love Man [. . .] in the representation of men, preferably young men" (115n4). The Autodidact can be considered a predecessor of the surface, descriptive or postcritical reader who looks no further than what is presented to and enchants him. Derrida's discussion of "the reading or the nonreading of Heidegger" in postwar France by Sartre and others makes clear that what is reproachable is not so much reading-as-nonreading, which may take the reader in the right direction (away from humanism), but rather the seemingly comprehensive, systematic, respectful reading of the established world library on which *Nausea*'s Autodidact embarks, in its refusal to read beyond the *anthropos*, the West and the patriarchal.

This does not mean that nonreading—which refers both to not reading at all and to reading "poorly" (Derrida 1982, 119)—is excused completely: Sartre's productive mistranslation remains "monstrous" and the " 'first reading' of Hegel, Husserl, and Heidegger" in France is seen to have had harmful consequences in overlooking the critique of anthropologism present in these philosophers' work (119). Yet, at the same time, nonreading is understandable, at least when it can be attributed to certain works not having been accessible to a particular audience. Thus, Derrida acknowledges that *Sein und Zeit* was "the only partially known work of Heidegger's at the time" (115) and that Hegel's *The Phenomenology of Spirit* "had only been read for a short time in France" (117).

The corrective rereadings that Derrida pursues in "The Ends of Man" are designed to highlight both the inadvertent "confusion" (120) and deliberate "falsification" (124) that made "the Hegelian, Husserlian, and Heideggerian critiques or *de-limitations* of metaphysical humanism appear to belong to the very sphere of that which they criticize or delimit" (119, emphasis in text). These are symptomatic readings that clearly convey a sense of superiority and mastery, of Derrida being a better reader than those he critiques. However, by emphasizing the way in which texts tend to be read in service of the problems posed by the context of reading, Derrida leaves open the possibility that his readings, too, could be exposed as mistaken or misleading in another time and place.

Significantly, for Derrida, reading Hegel, Husserl, and Heidegger properly entails "taking into account" (a phrase that returns three times) how reading appears in their texts—or, in Heidegger's case, how the meaning of Being is read off (*abgelesen*) certain entities that "interrogate themselves about the meaning of being" (125–126). Derrida calls Heidegger's description of this process in *Being and Time* a "protocol of reading" that reveals itself as symptomatic:

> The process of disengaging or of elaborating the question of Being, as a question of the *meaning* of Being, is defined [by Heidegger] as a *making explicit* or as an interpretation that makes explicit. The reading of the text of Dasein is a hermeneutics of unveiling or of development. If one looks closely, it is the phenomenological opposition "implicit/explicit" that permits Heidegger to reject the objection of the vicious circle, the circle that consists of first determining a being in its Being, and then of posing the question of Being on the basis of this ontological pre-determination. This style of a reading which makes explicit, practices a continuing bringing to light, something which resembles, at least, a coming into consciousness, without break, displacement, or change of terrain. (126, emphases in text)

Taking *Dasein* as a question to be read (or reread) and realizing that this reading (or rereading) is not descriptive, not a taking in of what is simply there (before the asking of the question), but rather an act of "unveiling or development," a "continuing bringing into light," is what reveals "that Dasein, though *not* man, is nevertheless *nothing other* than man" (127, emphasis in text) and what ultimately makes clear how Heidegger's text participates in the "destruction of metaphysical humanism" (134). This, in turn, can only be remarked "if one looks closely" at Heidegger's text, if it is read in a way that recognizes the "subtlety and equivocality" of Heidegger's argument, the overlooking of which—by not reading closely enough—is what "authorized all the anthropologistic defamations in the reading of *Sein und Zeit*, notably in France" (127).

Derrida's endorsement of a close reading that looks beyond the obvious or literal also manifests in his emphasis on "the dominance," in *Being and Time*, "of an entire metaphorics of proximity" that would be misread if seen as "an insignificant rhetoric" (130), as well as in his insistence that Heidegger is not truly read (fully, fairly, responsibly) unless "the prevalence given to the *phenomenological* metaphor," which makes its appearance in "all the varieties of *phainesthai*, of shining, lighting, clearing, *Lichtung*, etc." (132, emphases in text) is noted. The reason why it is necessary to go beyond the obvious and literal is because that level—of what Best and Marcus would call the surface of the text—is precisely where human and man, in "the language of the West," can continue to appear as essentially the same (133).

Toward the end of his text, Derrida does warn that adopting the strategy of "using against the edifice the instruments or stones available in the house, that is, equally, in language" means that "one risks ceaselessly confirming, consolidating, *relifting* (*relever*), at an always more certain depth, that which one allegedly deconstructs" (135, emphasis in text). Here, he acknowledges that deconstruction, which requires an attentive, symptomatic reading beyond the literal may also more deeply embed that which it seeks to dislodge or make tremble. This, however, is no reason not to deconstruct in this manner or in the alternative manner of placing oneself outside, which carries its own risks; what is needed, according to Derrida, is "a new way of writing" that combines these two deconstructive modes (135). At this point, rereading makes way for rewriting, but it is clear that this rewriting is predicated on ethics of reading that posits it as attentive, accountable, and inevitably political, and on a practice of reading closely that moves beyond the literal and obvious.

Wynter's "The Ceremony Must Be Found" and "The Ceremony Found" echo Derrida's endorsement of close, symptomatic reading, despite barely mentioning reading. In the first text, Wynter argues for the need to establish a new *Studia Humanitatis*, something that she argues, following Kolakowski, can only happen through an act of heresy, since "everything that is new grows out of the permanent need to question all existing absolutes" (1984, 21). This constitutes a plea for continuous suspicion, as every "rewriting of knowledge" subsequently establishes "new orthodoxies," which should become subject to critique in their turn (22). What results is not destruction, a trail of ruins, but an infinite process of "destructuring/restructuring" (23).

Reading—or, rather, rereading—comes into play in Wynter's discussion of the Renaissance heresy that brought the original *Studia Humanitatis* into being. She notes that, for Erasmus, the sacrilege consisted in a desire "to get back to a reading of the original text, uncontaminated by some of the later interpretations, back to the simple piety of the early father and to the original Greek texts believed to be able to elucidate pristine meanings" (28). Erasmus, then, is painted as somewhat of a surface reader, a believer in pure meanings that become accessible when looking at the words on the page only, rather than at marginalia and commentaries. While this may appear to have been about assuming a position of modesty in relation to the text, Wynter is quick to note that what it heralded, in effect, was a power grab in which the formerly taken-for-granted authority of theology was replaced by "the authority of the lay activity of textual and philological scrutiny" (28) and the "new template of identity" of "Natural Man" (29). This new template would soon come to seem equally self-evident and unassailable, or, in Wynter's neologism, "lawlikely" (38).

The ceremony that Wynter's title insists must be found would destructure-restructure the valuated binary oppositions (man-woman, culture-nature, white-black, order-chaos) cemented by the new form of Man, no longer subordinated to the divine. The emergence of the so-called New Studies in the humanities in the 1960s did not amount to such a destructuring-restructuring because, as a result of "our non-consciousness of the real dimensions of what we were about," they remained focused on demanding inclusion in the existing *Studia Humanitatis* (38). In order for the real problem—the irrevocable, foundational exclusion of women and black people from Natural Man (later termed Man(2))—to be "brought into unconcealedness" (39), a "suspicion of something automatic functioning beyond the conscious control of the human" was needed (43). Where literary critics had played the role of "theologians" in keeping the "imaginative schemas" of Man(2) "free from aesthetic pollution," Wynter calls for them to begin acting instead as "*rhetoricians*" and "*diagnosticians*" (51, emphasis in text), or, in other words, as symptomatic readers. Literary criticism is assigned the task of operationalizing suspicion through a practice of rereading: "re-reading the texts from the perspective of their configuring function in the rhetoric-symbolic processes of human auto-speciation constitutes for literary criticism its Copernican epistemological break" (52). Only through such re-reading can a new *Studia* be built, one that would not pretend to be *the* truth, but that would present itself as a symptomatic reading from an " 'outer view' which takes the human rather than any of its variations as Subject" (56). This "outer view," for Wynter, is not the Galilean view from nowhere but a Bakhtinian exotopic position that is "at once inside/outside the figural domain of our order" (56) and thus one of immanence, reconcilable with the Lovelockian perspective advocated by Latour.

In the second part of Wynter's manifesto "The Ceremony Found," her account of the "fictively constructed and performatively enacted different *kinds of being human*" (2015, 196n20, emphasis in text) is all about trying to make these genres readable (and, consequently, rewritable or redescribable) for those who enact them, to whom they normally remain opaque because acknowledging their fictiveness would cause "*entropic disintegration*" (227, emphasis in text). The problem Wynter identifies is one of nonreading as not "correctly identifying" narration as narration (216): instead of factual, the world as we see it, is narrative and fictive, yet it does not appear to us as something that requires interpretation. In fact, we ourselves deliberately construct it as something that is self-evident and, as a result, incontestable:

> Each respective fictive *We* can normally never know its no less, always-already cosmogonically chartered order of social reality and/or autopoetic living system *outside* the *genre*-specific perceptual categorization system or mode of knowledge production that each societal order needs for its own enactment and stable replication as such a reality. (238, emphases in text)

That we cannot "normally" know our reality outside of the specific way in which we narratively constitute it, or even see that it is narratively constituted, does not mean that we can never do so, for "*that which we have made we can unmake and consciously now remake*" (242, emphasis in text). Such unmaking-remaking, however, requires an effort of suspicion. It requires that we read opacity—a reading that can only be a penetrating, piercing, and painful symptomatic one, for rendering opacity legible as obfuscation requires repudiating the imperviousness of the "nothing to see here" that it shows us.

At the level of the literal or descriptive, the way in which mankind—within the "neo-Liberal-monohumanist *genre* of being hybridly human *Man*(2)"—is "*rhetorically overrepresented as if it were that of humankind*" remains inaccessible (222, 216, emphases in text). For Wynter, as for Derrida, working with(in) language, exploiting its depth and width (its capacity for metaphor and metonymy), is key to rendering this overrepresentation accessible as an overrepresentation that produces seemingly "*naturally dysselected Others*" (216, emphasis in text) and to make it possible for those Others to challenge it. Thus, one of the tools of Wynter's proposed "*Autopoetic Turn/Overturn*" is semantic inversion practiced from a " 'gaze from below' perspective" as in Bob Marley's song lyrics, which have to be read beyond the literal to reveal the Rastafarian "*counter-cosmogony*" (207, emphases in text). Aimé Césaire's "new science" likewise proceeds through "an original handling of the word" that is not immediately obvious but requires study (209) and is therefore a "science of the *Word*-as-the-*code*" (244, emphasis in text), where the word is never simply what it seems, and where the flesh, in turn, becomes legible as "*code-made-flesh*" (245, emphasis in text).

Both Derrida and Wynter would reject "just reading" in Best and Marcus's sense because they are interested in reading justly, righteously, *for* something (ultimately, a better, more just world) that will not come about if texts are simply accepted and deferred to at face value—especially when, as Frantz Fanon (1968) so powerfully shows, for those dysselected from the category of the human, their own face, in appearing masked, already casts doubt on what such face value would be. Symptomatic reading is required if we are to stop taking the construed opacities that keep humanism in its current non-ecumenical form globally dominant—and that allow this humanism to "guard against the very recognition of its direct threat to the continued livability of our planetary habitat" (Wynter 2015, 234)—for the simple surfaces they present themselves as.

***

As Latour (2018) makes clear, the threat to our planet is now so great that a refusal to take action by a world leader like Trump has to be read, suspiciously, as a declaration of war. Of course, if we are to take symptomatic reading seriously, the figure of war itself should also not be taken for granted. That Latour's use of this term is strategic becomes clear from a short piece he wrote for *Critical Inquiry* on the COVID-19 pandemic entitled "Is This a Dress Rehearsal?" in which he tests the hypothesis that "the health crisis prepares, induces, incites us to prepare for climate change" (2020). After arguing that it does not in fact do so, given that state responses to the pandemic have relied on an outdated form of biopower and unfolded along national lines (neither of which would be effective against climate change), Latour declares the "figure of the 'war against the virus' " so often invoked during the pandemic, including by Trump, "unjustified" (2020). Instead of signaling a return to the stance that critics should not involve themselves in warfare, this "unjustified" war is set off against a war that Latour believes is both justified and necessary—the one against "those who make war on us without declaring war on us" in which "the battle fronts are multiple and cross each of us" (2020). Thus, in another instance of symptomatic reading on Latour's part, the war that is called a war is exposed as not a war or not the main war to be fought, while the war that has not been declared is revealed to be the one that matters. What this suggests is that the figure of war is not, for Latour, a descriptive label, but a way to redescribe both the COVID-19 pandemic and climate change; the figure of war functions, in other words, as a symptom marking not the end of reading, but its beginning.

Similarly, in relation to the issue of "vaccine hesitancy" with which I started this chapter, a symptomatic reading would not stop at pointing out the euphemistic nature of this term. It would also focus on the reluctance to aggressively counter a movement increasingly driven by privileged white subjects prepared to spread misinformation and to weaponize concern about vaccinations in black and Global South communities prompted by long histories of "medical racism" (Morgan 2021). Such reluctance is particularly concerning in the context of a global pandemic that is disproportionately taking and affecting non-white lives. At a time when more and more people are seduced by the hermetic, self-satisfied readings of the world proffered by conspiracy theories, it is vital to counter proclamations of the end of critique with mobilizations of critique in the form of symptomatic readings that maintain a suspicion even of themselves and, consequently, an openness to the possible validity of other and future (re)readings. The ends of this form of critique would be to challenge the self-evidence of the genres of being human-constructed and lived in the past and present, which have so thoroughly devalued certain human and all nonhuman lives, and to propose new genres of being posthuman/decolonial that would make for a more equal, more inclusive, and more sustainable future.

NOTES

1. The WHO's definition of "vaccine hesitancy" as "the reluctance or refusal to vaccinate despite the availability of vaccines" exposes the term as a euphemism (WHO 2019). On the anti-vaccination movement's use of social media, see Wilson and Keelan (2013); Smith and Graham (2019).

2. I write "apparent" because this indistinguishability seems overstated, especially in the supposedly shared "punctilious demands for proof" (Latour 2004, 230).

3. While Latour's explanation of why the fact and fairy positions have failed to convince is apt, the critical gestures he associates with these positions are not representative of any serious forms of deconstruction, which, rather than being only about "*subtraction*" (Latour 2004, 248, emphasis in text), are also about addition, in moving, for example, from either/or to both/and.

4. The page numbers in the Ghosts part are prefaced by G; the page numbers in the Monsters part by M.

5. See Baskin for a trenchant Marxist critique of surface reading that insists on the "constitutive interrelation between surface and depth" (10).

6. See Rooney's painstaking account of how description "partially creates the reality it 'describes' because description depends on the immersion of both subject and object in a whole social process" (2010, 11); and Brinkema, who, in a dazzling

reading of Audio Porn (porn videos narrated for the blind and visually impaired), makes clear that "description is not passive but predictive, [. . .] its energetic line is apt to fill out formulas, always running ahead in an attempt to imagine and produce its object—which of course means it can—in minor, irrelevant, but profound ways—be totally at odds with that which it describes" (2019, 5).

7. In a footnote, Best and Marcus do acknowledge that "there remain things that government powers go to extraordinary lengths to keep hidden, to keep as state secrets, 'extraordinary rendition' being one of them. A hermeneutics of suspicion in which understanding requires a subtle reading of the situation thus remains readily pertinent to the work of critique" (2009, 19n2). Yet, even here they cannot bring themselves to explicitly—on the surface—endorse close or symptomatic reading, using "subtle" instead.

BIBLIOGRAPHY

Baskin, Jason M. 2015. "Soft Eyes: Marxism, Surface, and Depth." *Mediations: Journal of the Marxist Reading Group* 28 (2): n. pag.

Best, Stephen, and Sharon Marcus. 2009. "Surface Reading: An Introduction." *Representations* 108 (1): 1–21.

Brinkema, Eugenie. 2019. "Form for the Blind (Porn and Description Without Guarantee)." *Porn Studies* 6 (1): 10–22.

Brooks, Cleanth. 1975. *The Well Wrought Urn: Studies in the Structure of Poetry*. San Diego: Harcourt Brace Jovanovich.

COCONEL Group. 2020. "A Future Vaccination Campaign against COVID-19 at Risk of Vaccine Hesitancy and Politicisation." *The Lancet*, July 1. https://www.the lancet.com/journals/laninf/article/PIIS1473-3099(20)30426-6/fulltext.

Culler, Jonathan. 2010. "The Closeness of Close Reading." *ADE Bulletin* 149: 20–25.

Derrida, Jacques. 1982. "The Ends of Man." In *Margins of Philosophy*, 111–136. Chicago: University of Chicago Press.

Fanon, Frantz. 1968. *Black Skin, White Masks*. London: Grove Books.

Felski, Rita. 2015. *The Limits of Critique*. Chicago: University of Chicago Press.

Haraway, Donna J. 2016. *Staying with the Trouble: Making Kin in the Chthulucene*. Durham: Duke University Press.

Kofman, Ava. 2018. "Bruno Latour, the Post-Truth Philosopher, Mounts a Defense of Science." *New York Times Magazine*, October 25. https://www.nytimes.com/2018 /10/25/magazine/bruno-latour-post-truth-philosopher-science.html.

Latour, Bruno. 2004. "Why Has Critique Run out of Steam? From Matters of Fact to Matters of Concern." *Critical Inquiry* 30: 225–248.

———. 2018. *Down to Earth: Politics in the New Climatic Regime*. Cambridge: Polity Press.

———. 2020. "Is This a Dress Rehearsal?" *Critical Inquiry*, March 26. https://critinq .wordpress.com/2020/03/26/is-this-a-dress-rehearsal/.

Moretti, Franco. 2013. *Distant Reading*. London: Verso Books.

Morgan, Winston. 2021. "Anti-vaxxers Are Weaponizing the Vaccine Hesitancy of Black Communities." *The Conversation*, January 26. https://theconversation.com/anti-vaxxers-are-weaponising-the-vaccine-hesitancy-of-black-communities-153836.

Pylas, Pan. 2021. "Survey Finds Global Mistrust Could Weigh on Vaccine Rollout." *AP*, January 13. https://apnews.com/article/coronavirus-pandemic-coronavirus-vaccine-united-states-3a6fbf0e8ff3e63917f707aa935b492c.

Roberts, Michelle. 2019. "Vaccines: Low Trust in Vaccination 'a Global Crisis.'" *BBC*, June 19. https://www.bbc.com/news/health-48512923.

Rooney, Ellen. 2010. "Live Free or Describe: The Reading Effect and the Persistence of Form." *Differences* 21 (3): 112–139.

Smith, Naomi, and Tim Graham. 2019. "Mapping the Anti-Vaccination Movement on Facebook." *Information, Communication & Society* 22 (9): 1310–1327.

Spivak, Gayatri Chakravorty. 2004. "Righting Wrongs." *South Atlantic Quarterly* 103 (2–3): 523–581.

Tsing, Anna Lowenhaupt, Heather Swanson, Elaine Gan, and Nils Bubandt. 2017. *Arts of Living on a Damaged Planet: Ghosts and Monsters of the Anthropocene*. Minneapolis: University of Minnesota Press.

Vowell, Sarah. 2017. "The Danger of an Incurious President." *New York Times*, August 9. https://www.nytimes.com/2017/08/09/opinion/trump-fire-fury-north-korea.html.

WHO. 2019. "Ten Threats to Global Health in 2019." *WHO*. https://www.who.int/news-room/spotlight/ten-threats-to-global-health-in-2019.

Williams, Jeffrey J. 2015. "The New Modesty in Literary Criticism." *Chronicle of Higher Education*, January 5. http://chronicle.com/article/The-New-Modesty-in-Literary/150993/.

Wilson, Kumanan, and Jennifer Keelan. 2013. "Social Media and the Empowering of Opponents of Medical Technologies: The Case of Anti-Vaccinationism." *Journal of Medical Internet Research* 15 (5): e103.

Wynter, Sylvia. 1984. "The Ceremony Must Be Found: After Humanism." *Boundary 2* 12/13: 19–70.

———. 2015. "The Ceremony Found: Towards the Autopoetic Turn/Overturn, Its Autonomy of Human Agency and Extraterritoriality of (Self-)Cognition." In *Black Knowledges/Black Struggles: Essays in Critical Epistemology*, edited by Jason R. Ambroise and Sabine Broeck, 184–252. Oxford: Oxford University Press.

6

The Ends of Critical Intimacy
Spivak, Fanon, and Appropriative Reading
Birgit M. Kaiser

In spring 2020, I wrote a first draft of this chapter in "self-isolation" during the start of the COVID-19 pandemic. As I am editing its final version in January 2021, we are still in the middle of the pandemic, again in "lockdown" in the Netherlands and still unsure where all of this takes us. What is quite evident though is that so far the predominant method to "grasp" what is going on has been the count of infected bodies. What is less attended to, at least in media discourse, is how the policy responses to COVID-19 across the globe (will) affect sociality; how they already afflict different social groups very unevenly; in what particular ways the underlying biocentrism (Wynter) of allegedly "protecting all lives" (Hartman) is complemented by the necropolitics that makes "all" not pertain to everyone.[1] It seems to me that beyond statistics and numbers, we also need to ask critically, how pandemic policies tap into the necro/biopolitical, neocolonial, hypertechnologized, security-prone, finance-capitalistic grounds of the early twenty-first century. How is "social" reconfigured in "social distancing" (and is it?) when what we are doing is, as many noted, physical *distancing? What are the "governing fictions" (Fanon) at work in this superposition of "bodily" and "social"?*

The COVID-19 pandemic comes after decades in which neoconservative and neoliberal governance has tried to reconfigure the social as a collection of individual bodies—think of Thatcher's dictum that society does not exist, that there are only "individual men and women and there are families" (1987). Decades which correspondingly have seen drastic defunding of public services such as health care (now exacerbating the pressure on IC-units and the menace of triage) and higher education. In the latter, especially the humanities were hit disproportionally hard and fields associated with critique such as "literature" and "theory" have come under increasing suspicion by university administrations of being useless (i.e., of not generating sufficient external funding from "societal partners"). These intersecting governing fictions of the past decades will have to be read: How do they continue to inform COVID-19 policies? How are they altered by the pandemic? Counting death by disease does not replace understanding the ((un)changing) operations of sociopolitical life in 2021 and beyond. "We" (a grouping that needs to be continuously and critically examined) will have to get a read on the deep grammars of this situation; a reading that does not emerge from statistics. Even a nonhuman agent such as SARS-CoV-2 requires that one reads it: not just its DNA, but also its effects, the conflictual agendas, the conceptions of the social that operate in relation to it. In that light, what follows is a plea for reading as a critical method—always in view of the social.

***

But first, a word on critique. As someone inspired by twentieth-century cultural critique, I cannot but start from the assumption that an end of critique, if not *the* end, is not only to diagnose social ills but also to produce transformative effects "for the better." Especially the critical impetus of feminist and postcolonial analyses of the power/knowledge nexus constituting capitalist-patriarchal-colonial culture (henceforth CPC)[2] have been influential for me in this regard. From that angle, an end of critique is pushing us/the world to move from oppression toward greater social justice. Or, as Sylvia Wynter (2015) argues, especially with Frantz Fanon, the end of critique (which is also its conundrum) is to extricate ourselves from the current colonial-patriarchal-bourgeois-biocentric regime of being/knowledge that constitutes us all, albeit unequally. "*Comment s'en sortir?*" (1952, 9), as Fanon asks in *Peau noire, masques blancs*.

Indeed, how to get out? Merely counting on intellectual insight to be implemented, in the tradition of the Enlightenment hope that understanding will lead to (good) action, has historically proven not very effective; insight into persistent structural racism or sexism does not cause them to disappear, even if discrimination is legally, constitutionally banned. For transformation to actually take hold, more than rational critique and legal certification is needed. With the backing of legal declarations of equality (because without them, not even a first step is taken), also affective-cognitive habits need retraining. "We" need to learn different dispositions.[3] Keeping in mind as an *end* of critique Fanon's interest in "break[ing] the cycle" (Fanon 2008, xiv), which is Philcox's translation of the question cited above, what are the *critical practices* needed to work toward that end? How to affectively and cognitively forge the tools to "extricate ourselves" (Fanon 1986, 12; Markmann's translation of Fanon's question), if critique in its traditional modality has fallen short here? What modes of critique might target the hegemonic corporeal-intellectual dispositions, which have so persistently been molded according to the CPC regime of power/being/knowledge, with recent neoliberal twists, so that we can begin to learn new habits and to revision the formations of the social?

With these questions in mind, this chapter engages, perhaps counterintuitively, with the practice of reading. For Gayatri Spivak, reading itself can become a critical practice that does not primarily increase insight, but that can work toward "the rearrangement of desires, your own, and theirs"—if it trains us "in reading the other(s) carefully enough" (2014b, 164–165). Through reading, Spivak suggests, we can train ourselves away from self-interest and toward a concern for greater social justice. Of course, one might wonder how reading—by definition an act that is tied to textual material usually enjoyed by oneself in silence—can become a site of relearning and especially a site where the social or even social justice come into play. What kind of act or movement is reading, if we conceive of it as invested in retraining affective-cognitive habits? With the help of Spivak—her reflections on aesthetic education, as well as her engagement with Fanon—I will explore these questions, taking reading as a critical practice that invites us to engage intimately with (textual) otherness and that can affectively educate us toward considering others first; that is, train desire toward the social. When engaged in reading (especially in reading *literature*, as the chapter's first part discusses) we can begin to practice breaking the cycles of appropriation and narcissism operative in CPC. Learning to move in critical intimacy is key here, as we shall see. However, critical intimacy is not only at play when reading literature, it also (albeit in slightly different ways) pertains to reading theoretical texts. Taking Spivak's reading of "Fanon Reading Hegel" as an example, the chapter's second part argues that critical intimacy permits an engagement with the thoughts of others that bypasses the established protocols of critical distance and rational critique. Spivak reading Fanon offers a different style of critique and considering Fanon's moves with-and-beyond Hegel, we will see operations of critique that work differently from the traditional notions of critique as opposition, or as the detection and correction of shortcomings in the texts of others. As we shall see, Fanon neither accuses nor attempts to correct Hegel, but instead appropriates Hegel—and thereby paradoxically undercuts a racialized, colonial-capitalist order that thrives on the very appropriation of otherness. The chapter makes, therefore, a plea for reading in the service of transformation.

REFRAIN FROM APPROPRIATION.
READING AS AESTHETIC EDUCATION

When thinking about reading as a practice or an act, the debates around the ethics of reading literature come to mind. Inspired by Jacques Derrida's work on *différance* and the literary, Derek Attridge's engagement with J. M. Coetzee and Spivak's work on Mahasweta Devi, for example, have considered the ethical implications of reading literature. For both, reading is a practice that hinges on a reader's exposure to the singularity or incalculable otherness of a literary text, where one encounters realities that are experienced as different from oneself and which challenge us to make the effort of understanding this alterity, an effort that is difficult and never complete due to the text's composition. In *Coetzee and the Ethics of Reading*, Attridge argues that reading a literary text requires a specific type of responsiveness to what one encounters. For Attridge, reading designates something more specific than what we conventionally understand by it: the act of "scan[ning] or study[ing] writing silently [. . .] by oneself or for one's own benefit" (OED) in order to discern a message. Instead, reading here means engaging with a complex linguistic, narrative texture—riddled with ambiguity and polyvalence so that one clear message is persistently complicated—and designates the very practice or event of acknowledging and responding to these complexities. Therein lies the ethical injunction: "Reading a work of literature entails opening oneself to the unpredictable, the future, the other, and thereby accepting the responsibility laid upon one by the work's singularity and difference" (Attridge 2004a, 9). Each time anew, literary texts activate readers to wrestle with this otherness and if that engagement does not occur, the time spent with a text would not be reading in this strong sense. The ethics of reading consists in this challenge to enter "a process of constant reappraisal and self-redefinition" (Attridge 2004b, 111). Literature invites readers to struggle with their assumptions and challenges them to "understand how little you understand me, translate my untranslatability" (131). Reading is this specific epistemological and affective exercise and Attridge highlights its ethical dimensions.[4] Akin to Attridge, Spivak makes a similar proposition for the ethical element in literary education and reading as a practice. She holds that reading literature demands (but also *in the act* trains) a particular "epistemological performance" (Spivak 2014b, 4), a specific "micrology of practice" (5). Putting before us idioms and fictive realities not easily commensurable with our own, the literary invites us to "suspend our own interest into the language that is happening in the text" (4). As for Attridge, reading consists for Spivak in an exposure to otherness (the text, its language and protocols) that, given the pleasure it evokes, invites us to get close to what is other, to pay attention to "otherwise ignored detail" (7) and to refrain, for a moment, from judgment. Reading literature appropriately consists in such a suspension, it requires us to refrain from appropriating the otherness before us and to become attuned to the complexities invoked.[5]

Hence, the *ethical* consists in the summons to suspend immediate self-interest and the desire to impose our (pre)conceptions onto the text/other, to refrain from the appropriative drive that arrests a world of differences into "the Selfsame."[6] On these ethical grounds of suspended appropriation, Spivak's investment in reading as *aesthetic* education—prominent throughout *An Aesthetic Education in the Era of Globalization* (2012) and *Readings* (2014)—stems from the additional conviction that literary reading also makes possible "a painstaking *learning* of the language of the other" (Spivak 2014b, 6; emphasis added). Literature here becomes one key site to train the imagination and evokes more than an experience of otherness as incommensurable or an experience of the limits of self. Beyond the ethical suspension of self that is central to Attridge's ethics of reading, the turn toward the aesthetic explicates a layer that the ethical implies but does not exhaust. The experience of otherness inherent in the literary is turned here toward the senses or *aisthesis*; toward the possibility of a training that works through affect, an *aesthetic* education that cultivates us to bear (with) otherness and complexity. The collected essays in Spivak's *Readings* express the hope that literary reading can be part of such a deeper training of the imagination (i.e., a tuning or turning that outstrips the experience of limitation) whereby we might "be given habits that deeply relate to others first, the very principle of social justice" (25). Thus, from the perspective of an aesthetic education, reading is not only a site where we (negatively) experience the self's limits of understanding otherness, but a critically affirmative site, where—infinitely slowly and incalculably—desire might be rearranged by *unlearning* appropriation and *learning* to approach the languages of others, by *redirecting* affects toward a desire for responsibility, by *moving* our epistemological disposition toward social justice. Even though Spivak acknowledges that this is "undoubtedly a utopian vision" (22), it is where transformation (can) occur(s): in the moves of un/learning and redirecting which entail a however minute recomposition of the one who undergoes them, of one no longer at the safe distance of judgment or (mere) empathy with others, but one moving and learning with and from others/otherness. This is a vision Spivak affirms not only as an educator and teacher of literature, but also as an organic intellectual thinking with Gramsci and Marx.

As a teacher of literature myself, I affirm this role for literature in an age of globalization, when learning to appropriately (i.e., not in an appropriative manner) encounter and read otherness is a pressing concern, on the affective-cognitive, not merely the conceptual, level. Literature and other (visual, filmic) textualities can help us common readers, in our encounters with (literary) works of art, to practice intimate exposure to what is experienced as foreign and to relearn what sociality—being with and among others *as other(s)*—might mean. Literature (in and outside the classroom) can foster learning *to read* in this sense. Slowly but surely, it might assist us in veering away from narcissistic self-involvement toward thinking with and in view of others first. That at least is the wager for literature and the arts here; and in this veering, this setting in motion, lies its critical, transformative potential. Reading then becomes a little bit like acrobatics or dancing, engaged in teaching us to make different cognitive-affective moves than the knee-jerk concern for self. By attending to literary texts carefully, we can become more adept in negotiating the difficult intimacies that difference and otherness demand.

***

I suggested just now that Spivak is thinking through this with Gramsci and Marx. I want to briefly turn to her "What's Left of Theory?" (2012 [2000]) to illustrate why. Thereby, this chapter will also move from considering reading as a critical micro-practice that is hypothetically enacted in reading *literature* as unlearning appropriation, to the appropriations effected by more specialized readers when reading what is commonly called *theory*. One of these specialized readers is Spivak herself, to whose reading of Fanon, another specialized reader, I will turn momentarily. But for the moment, in conclusion of my first part and with the help of "What's Left of Theory?," I want to highlight again how Spivak's engagement with the micro-practices of reading *literature* as unlearning appropriation is invested in an affective training for social justice. In "What's Left of Theory?," Spivak engages with two key elements of Marx's thinking: his stress on labor-power as abstraction (which Spivak affirms and works with); and his ultimately humanist, Enlightenment trust in reason. It is the latter that is relevant here, because it made Marx assume, Spivak suggests, that once the workers understand themselves as agents of production, their public (social) use of reason must lead to revolution (and the left, in its Engelsian empiricism, followed him in this). In that regard, Marx was a thinker of his time and its unchecked Enlightenment belief in the force of reason. However, writing at the beginning of the twenty-first century and after Gramsci, Spivak can see that what this "left uncalculated was the epistemological burden of training the socialist subject" (2012a, 185). Marx did not pose the question why—once the *Mehrwert* produced through labor-power was understood—"an epistemically unprepared population" (185) should opt for socialism, rather than for improving their capitalist skills or even fascism. Even if we cognitively (or rationally) realized the freedom that inheres in labor-power, namely that its surplus can also be put to use for social(ist) justice and not only for capitalist accumulation, it is unclear why the desire for social justice should follow. Or, if it followed, how it could be sustained and become habit. The enlightened belief in rational insight alone will not do, because we can just as well opt for getting "better and better at making money" (2012b, 198). Therefore, what is needed in order to make change sustainable, if not possible in the first place, is not just (class-)consciousness, but—with-and-beyond Marx—"cognitive tuning" (201) toward a responsibility for the social. "What's Left of Theory?" calls this tuning an "aesthetic education as training the imagination for epistemological performance" (197). Reading literature, which, as we saw, provides a generous exposure to otherness, can be one important element in such an epistemologico-affective training.

With this, we can return to the questions raised earlier: How can reading as an intimate act, tied to a textual material commonly enjoyed by oneself in silence, be a site where social justice comes into play? I hope one can now better see the intimate link between a will for social justice and the type of training that literary reading can foster. The movements one undergoes when reading—wrestling with the incalculable, bearing the incommensurability of a text's idiom with "my" language, paying attention to detail—are crucial not only as a constant reevaluation of the self or a change in individual disposition, but they also tie the intimate activity of reading to the social. When engaging in the micro-practice of reading in the sense outlined, it moves us toward thinking of others first and thus places us within a horizon of the social. "Literary reading has to be learned" (Spivak 2019, 18), but it is *in the learning of reading* that learning to refrain from appropriation is made tangible. Such training of the imagination toward the social is needed to make "revolutions last" (Spivak 2014b, 5). In nano-moves, the practice of reading literature can epistemically prepare readers to bear the complexities of sociality: suspend judgment of characters whose reasons I do not (yet) understand or agree with; endure the indeterminacy or polyvalence of language and yet continue to find my bearing; realize the world's heteroglossia and resist the urge of reducing what are complex idioms to only one story or voice. What such aesthetic, affective-cognitive moves can generate is an orientation toward a desire for social justice—so that, for example, an insight like Marx's into the operations of labor-power might fall onto *those* grounds, rather than onto the will to accumulate or to merely turn the tables. Surely, to say it again: aesthetic education in view of the social is a utopian project because it would be dangerously naïve to think that reading literature will make the revolution. But the thwarting of appropriation that reading demands *as one learns to read* literature can make it more likely that one might keep narcissism in check, tuning readers toward the social and getting us ready for wanting and anticipating a different future. In the meantime, I learn how to learn reading from and with others.

The second half of this chapter now turns to the related, yet distinct practice that was already hinted at above as the (perhaps counterintuitively) *appropriative* mode of reading theory—a mode that Spivak's own reading of Marx (too briefly touched on above) enacts. As we will see, just like *reading literature* in the outlined sense, *reading theory* designates a particular type of operation that is different from interpretation or commentary. But as we will see, the operations of reading theory by what Spivak and Gramsci call "organic intellectuals" also differ from the ethico-aesthetic training highlighted so far. Whereas intimacy with otherness in reading literature is directed at *refraining from appropriation*, the "critical intimacy" (Spivak 2014b, 12) at work when reading theory is instead rather *appropriative*. Reading here means becoming critically intimate with other thinkers so that one can, as Spivak suggests, work with-and-beyond them, generously use their texts in order to turn them around and appropriate them for one's own purposes.[7] So, intimacy here is not the same as intimacy in literary reading. Whereas a literary-aesthetic education trains me to abstain from imposing myself on the text, guiding me to become intimate with an otherness that nevertheless remains different and inappropriable and thus (re)training affects that are critical of CPC's appropriative drive, the critical intimacy when reading theory works quite differently. It thrives on the desire to get into the thoughts of others and, where necessary and appropriate, use them for one's own project. In such an appropriative move lies *its* critical transformative potential. In that vein, Spivak does not discard Marx as a thinker indebted to an Enlightenment trust in reason or the teleology of History, but rather becomes critically intimate with his thought, works with-and-beyond him—as we will see Fanon work with-and-beyond Hegel. As I hope will become clear in what follows, appropriation here is also quite different from the very powerful and voracious appropriation of everything into the sameness of CPC. What I call the appropriative reading of theory instead implies a positionality within and contestation of power relations (of who appropriates what?), while at the same time it refuses to discard certain thinkers or texts even if they clearly have limitations and problems (such as Hegel's racism or Marx's eschatology). I will take Fanon as a case in point here, pursuing Spivak's reading of Fanon in "Fanon Reading Hegel" (2014), interlaced with attention to Fanon's *Black Skin, White Masks* itself, where Fanon takes what he needs from (Freud, Adler and) Hegel. "Reading Hegel" comes down to refusing to refuse Hegel as much as refusing to adhere to Hegel; a readiness to get intimate with another thought that the chapter's second half calls appropriative reading.

Appropriative Reading: Spivak Reading Fanon Reading Hegel

A disclaimer at the start here to avoid opening an unfortunate and entirely misleading opposition between literature and theory. Ultimately, reading is reading: careful attention to the protocols of a text. So, just as with reading literature, when reading theory "[w]e do not bulldoze over the linguistic practice of the theorist's work, making argumentative gist [. . .] we read it as a primary text, not as something that we are going to apply, not instrumentalizing it, but for its own sake" (Spivak 2014b, 77). In distinguishing between the two directions of reading, as I am doing here, my intention is not to classify practices, disciplines, or genres; rather, it is to tease out the different yet related styles of critique inherent in both. If the end of critique is transformation in view of social justice, if we can no longer put our trust (only) in reason and if critique from a distance as correction or fault-finding is neither sufficient nor effective, then we need to ask as precisely as possible: What modes of intimacy are at play in different modalities of critique? And how is reading one such mode of critical intimacy? As this second part argues, much like reading literature, reading theory is also an act of intimacy. It is not an application as if from the outside, or a utilitarian extraction of points or concepts from a theoretical text. Rather, it means to work intimately with a theorist's thought and text, and from that position of critical intimacy to start moving (with) it. However, these two maneuvers of intimacy are slightly different from each other. While I call the intimacy when reading theory appropriative, critical intimacy with literature trains us for the reverse. That said, let us turn to the example of Spivak reading Fanon reading Hegel.[8]

All the chapters in Spivak's *Readings* are based on lectures given at a four-day seminar at the University of Pune in May 2012. In "Fanon Reading Hegel," Spivak closely pursues the relatively short seventh chapter of Fanon's *Black Skin, White Masks* (hereafter *BSWM*), entitled "The Black Man and Recognition," which is divided into subchapters on "The Black Man and Adler" and "The Black Man and Hegel" (2008, 185–197). Spivak tells her audience that although the fifth chapter of *BSWM* ("The Lived Experience of the Black Man") is usually selected as core reading from Fanon's canonical text, chapter seven, where he "reads Hegel," is where Fanon makes a move from negritude (of which chapter five is critical) "into something else" (Spivak 2014a, 30). Hence her focus on this chapter, which she uses to expound what reading means in Fanon's case. How, then, does Fanon read Hegel, according to Spivak? And considering critique no longer as exercising rational judgment within the horizon of universality, the question is also: Where from and what for does Fanon read Hegel? *Cui bono*?

Spivak opens "Fanon Reading Hegel" by noting precisely this positionality, stating that "[t]he Antilles are still not postcolonial" (28). Indeed, the West Indies, or more precisely Martinique and Guadeloupe, are still to this day administrative regions of France. As Spivak's opening suggests, Fanon starts from a concern for the colonial condition; a condition tied to relating to alterity through appropriation, the very mode of relating that literary reading sets out to re(s)train. Spivak makes sure to explicitly tell us where *BSWM* was written from:

Frantz Fanon writes from Algeria, not his place of origin—Martinique—when he is talking to us about Africa. A gentleman, traumatized by not being recognized as a French gentleman in France, wanting to go to a French-speaking country—first choice: Senegal. But Léopold Sédar Senghor does not respond to him. Therefore, Fanon goes to his second choice: Algeria. (28)[9]

Thus, Fanon writes *BSWM* and reads Hegel in chapter seven from that situation—from within French education, not recognized as French, as a gentleman of a certain class from Martinique and later Algeria, in a (blocked) conversation with one of the founders of *négritude*. His engagement with Hegel comes at the end of the book's analysis of the Antillean "identification process" (Fanon 2008, 126) and immediately after chapter six on "The Black Man and Psychopathology" as well as Fanon's engagement with Adler at the start of chapter seven. Thus, on the one hand, Fanon comes to Hegel as an educated man from Martinique who was forced to undergo the lived experience of racism, its "suffocating reification" (89), upon arriving in France (discussed in chapter 5), and, on the other hand, he comes to Hegel as the psychiatrist who speaks back to the discipline of his clinical training. Hegel interests him in light of these perspectives and Spivak rightly notes that Fanon was therefore not trying to "produce a correct description of Hegel" (2014a, 55)—offer commentary or interpretation. Rather, he *reads* Hegel in a strong sense: starting from within a certain concern, Fanon gets—and this is Spivak's argument on reading theory *in nuce*—into the movement of Hegel's text, appropriates his *philosopheme* of the master/slave-relation for the question of Antillean subjectivity and blackness for which psychoanalysis and psychiatry have proven insufficient. He uses Hegel partly against himself, especially Hegel's *Philosophy of History*, and does so from the vantage point of his own interest in sociogeny, over and against Freud and Adler's focus on bourgeois individuality.

Reading Hegel here means, Spivak proposes, that Fanon inserts himself "inside the text of the other, not as her/himself. It is not 'Please, Hegel, be like me!' It is rather 'Hegel, here I come, to ventriloquize you'." (31) At the end of his analysis of Blackness, colonialism and the inability of psychoanalysis to account for the emergence of Antillean self-consciousness, Fanon "*appropriates* and claims the Hegelian text" (31; emphasis added) and thereby performs the only *appropriate* move with which to respond to colonial-patriarchal-bourgeois conceptions of the Subject. In order to "combat [. . . those] governing fictions" (45), Fanon's appropriat(iv)e reading opens conceptualizations of alterity and Man that "turn the [Hegelian] text around" (31). But let us unravel this slowly and keep in sight the question of critical intimacy.

"The analysis we are undertaking" in *BSWM*, Fanon writes, "is psychoanalytical. It remains, nevertheless, evident that for us the true disalienation of the black man implies a brutal awareness of the social and economic realities" (xiv).[10] What Fanon at the opening of *BSWM* calls the disalienation of the Black man informs the entire span of the argument and it is also from this angle that he comes to Hegel in chapter seven. The emergence of self-consciousness of "the black man"—given his [sic] psychological-cum-socio-economic alienation—poses itself as a problem to Fanon, from the vantage point of the Antilles; a problem for which the psychoanalytic tools at hand are inadequate. They are inadequate, because the psychic complexes they describe and are meant to treat have been developed (Fanon explains this in depth in the sixty pages leading up to his engagement with Hegel) with the White, bourgeois European institutions of individual and family in mind. However, as the "Introduction" to *BSWM* already postulates and as the entire text expounds until coming to Hegel, "the alienation of the black man is not an individual question" (xv). Fanon's famous addition of sociogeny to Freud's phylogeny and ontogeny is a response to that insufficiency.[11] We can see that Fanon here thinks *with-and-beyond* Freud, as he will think, for different reasons, with-and-beyond Hegel: while acknowledging Freud's claim of the individual factor for psychiatry as innovative, namely a reaction against what Fanon calls the "constitutionalizing trend" (xv) of the nineteenth century, he also points out its inadequacy to Antillean and Black realities in the twentieth century. Although Freud's claim may have given important impulses for the analysis of psychic ailments of late nineteenth-century bourgeois European society, the isomorphism of individual, family, and nation does not work in the same way for the Antillean, Black child: "Whether you like it or not the Oedipus complex is far from being a black complex" (130). Whereas bourgeois, European society projects the "characteristics of the family environment [. . .] onto the social environment" (121), so that social structures are replicated and can be practiced within the bourgeois-patriarchal family, the Black child, according to Fanon, is made to experience a profound rupture between the two.

> As long as the black child remains on his home ground his life follows more of less the same course as that of the white child. But if he goes to Europe he will have to rethink his life, for in France, his country, he will feel different from the rest [. . .] he is made to feel inferior. (127)

Evidently, Fanon has especially the colonial relation of the Antilles and France in mind here. It is going to the metropole—an experience famously described in "The Lived Experience of the Black Man"—that causes a psychic break, realizing one is and is not part of one's country. Exposure to a predominantly white social environment and its myths around Blackness/whiteness needs to be taken into account, in order to understand what Fanon calls the dependency and inferiority complexes of the Black man; and hence, as we heard above, Fanon claims that "[a]longside phylogeny and ontogeny, there is also sociogeny" (xv).

One could think that herewith Fanon's analysis of psychic life of the colonized Antilles—always in full view of the social and economic realities saturating it—has achieved its goal. Since the analysis is stated as psychoanalytical, once readers have followed *BSWM* through its exposure of the links between Black existence, language, and myths of racialization (in chapters one to three), its unraveling of the "massive psycho-existential complex" (xvi) that the apposition of white and black have caused (chapters two to five), and its demonstration that the underlying fictions governing phenomenology, existentialism, and psychoanalysis are inadequate not only to Black lived experience, but also complicit with the maintenance of racism (chapters 5 and 6), that *analysis* is indeed complete. And with it, the fact of supplementing psychoanalysis with sociogeny is established. One might, therefore, take the brief, twelve-page chapter on "The Black Man and Recognition," and especially its six pages on Hegel, at first sight as a mere addendum. But, of course, those pages are more than that. It is, in fact, in this brief final chapter where Fanon *does* what he proclaims in the Introduction, namely that "[b]y *analyzing* it [the massive psycho-existential complex of black and white] we aim to *destroy* it" (xvi; emphases added). Appropriating Hegel for his own project, in this final chapter Fanon moves from analysis "into something else" (Spivak 2014a, 30). It is here that we can watch him turn things around. For sure, the six pages on Hegel only take effect in light of the 190 pages preceding and preparing them, so just a cautionary note to be clear: these pages are not the linear culmination of Fanon's argument. The destruction of the bourgeois-colonial frame of the individual already happens in the claim to sociogeny at the very start and *BSWM* has a similar proleptic temporality as Hegel's *Phenomenology* itself, where the introduction states the project *in nuce* and the text "merely" but indispensably unravels it.[12] *BSWM*'s opening line itself notes that such explosions always occur "too early ... or too late" (xi). So, the point is not to say that chapter six is the core of *BSWM*'s argument, but that we here get to see very closely *how* Fanon moves in critical intimacy with Hegel and appropriates a philosophical tool that may not have been intended for him, but that Fanon puts to use for his own purposes. It is here that we can watch him not only analyze, but also begin to transform (destroy) what Wynter calls the regime of Man2.

Therefore, let me return once more to the questions of reading raised earlier. We already saw *where* Fanon *reads from*: how the fact of Blackness is a matter of concern to him and that to tackle this concern he reclaims psychoanalysis and philosophy from a situatedness "in Postcoloniality" (to invoke one of the subtitles of Spivak's chapter; 2014a, 39). We also saw that the ends of his critical analysis of the "complex of inferiority" (Césaire qtd as epigraph, Fanon 2008, xi) instilled in the colonized is to destroy the entire psycho-existential complex of colonial, racialized modernity. So, exactly how then does Fanon read Hegel with-and-beyond Hegel? How does he put Hegel to use in ways that neither dismiss or find fault, nor merely offer commentary or a right or wrong interpretation, but that rather appropriate Hegel for his own critical ends? Having considered closely *what* Fanon reads for, we can now focus on *how* he does what he does, thus investigating more directly the procedures of appropriative reading.

In a way, Fanon both does and does not take Hegel at his word. The subchapter "The Black Man and Hegel" starts by quoting the opening to Hegel's famous subsection in *The Phenomenology of Mind* on "Independence and Dependence of Self-Consciousness. Lordship and Bondage": "Self-consciousness exists in itself and for itself, in that and by the fact that it exists for another self-consciousness; that is to say, it *is* only by being acknowledged or recognized" (Hegel 229; qtd in Fanon 2008, 191). It is the *mutual* recognition of two men (*sic*; see note 12) that Fanon affirms with Hegel; he highlights as crucial to Hegel's phenomenology of self-consciousness that a recognition has to occur in "absolute reciprocity" (2008, 191). Recognition is therefore something else than being acknowledged within structures where the terms and values are already set and remain unchanged. Recognition is something else, Fanon holds, than being granted freedom in the abolition of slavery, one day in history when the "white masters grudgingly decided to raise the animal-machine man to the supreme rank of *man*" (194); such granting of freedom is not recognition, as it fails to be mutual and thus to destroy the racialized, colonizing regime of power/knowledge that is built on the very exclusion of reciprocity. "The individual, who has not staked his life, may, no doubt, be recognized as a *person*," that is a legal position, "but he has not attained the truth of this recognition as an independent self-consciousness" (194). Although Fanon is clearly conscious of the Haitian revolution (he refers to it in the conclusion) and its revolutionary seizure of freedom from the French, that did not yet destroy racialized, colonial modernity—a fact that is evident not least when thinking from the Antilles, which are to this day administratively French. And it is precisely as a man from the Antilles that Fanon takes Hegel at his word in order to claim the philosophical tool over the historical fact *and* that he turns that *philosopheme* around.

In the pages leading up to his engagement with Hegel, Fanon speaks about that Antillean position at length. He contests Jung's notion of the collective unconscious as something ahistorically archetypical and rooted in "inherited cerebral matter" (165) and shows, taking the Antilles as his case, that quite to the contrary the collective unconscious is a "cultural imposition" (167). It is sociogenic, in that—as we saw above—the family structure is insufficient as analytic frame and the governing fictions that rein the social must be taken into account. Crucially, the Antilles are in that regard in what Wynter calls a liminal position, submitted to French imperial narratives of universal "Frenchness" *and* the lived experience of Blackness. It is from this position of liminality that Fanon can be heretic, Wynter holds (cf. 2015, 58ff). And also for Spivak that position is crucial to Fanon's reading of Hegel: helped by this contradictory situatedness of Frenchness *and* Blackness, Fanon assumes the right to reciprocity in Hegel's dialectic and he reads Hegel's model of self-consciousness and the emergence of the Subject as *for him*. "Helped by this conviction" (and enabled by his problematic patriarchal notions displayed in chapters two and three of *BSWM*), Spivak writes, "Fanon puts himself in the place of the Hegelian Subject, clear away from the well-placed diasporic" (31). By taking Hegel at his word, Fanon is reading him against himself in a double fashion. Hegel's account of history as world spirit in his *Philosophy of History* (1822–1831, published 1837) infamously relegated African civilization to the early stages ("childhood") or outside of human history. Its apologetic argument for the institution of slavery gave "expression and legitimacy to every conceivable European racist myth about Africa" (Ngũgĩ 1986, 30 note 15).[13] Yet, although Hegel did not have Fanon in mind as one of his potential addressees, *BSWM* does not discard Hegel for his delusions about History and Western civilization. Instead, Fanon simply refuses that (non)address and uses what he needs from Hegel's *philosopheme*, neither buying into his racist presuppositions, nor in any way neglecting the history of their onto-epistemological and material violence. However, not stopping at *analyzing* that violence and taking Hegel as one case in point, Fanon "is doing something more: he is combating governing fictions" (Spivak 2014a, 45), with Hegel (because insightful) and beyond Hegel (because necessary). Contesting the teleology and white supremacy of the Hegelian idea of History, from his double-edged male position Fanon puts himself in the place of the self-consciousness that Hegel's *Phenomenology* unravels. He asserts the position of man that Hegel's *Philosophy of History* would deny him. So, although *BSWM* analyses at length the excruciating onto-epistemological and corporeal violence of the "zone of non-being" (xii) reserved for Blackness in Hegel's universe (and CPC), Fanon refuses its ascription and affirms himself as (new) man: as a being who "is not only the potential for self-consciousness or negation [but also] a 'yes' resonating from cosmic harmonies" (xii). A "[y]es and no" (197) that Fanon returns to on the last page of chapter six: "We said in our introduction that man was an *affirmation*. We shall never stop repeating it. Yes to life. Yes to love. Yes to generosity" (197). Thus, even if he was not the *Phenomenology*'s implied reader and the *Philosophy of History* tried to consolidate his place as non-addressee (to say the least), Fanon, a gentleman from Martinique, refuses to be "a prisoner of History"

(204) and claims reciprocity as a philosophical tool from Hegel in order to put it to use for decoloniality and disalienation. Rather than finding fault with Hegel from a critical distance, Fanon enters the protocols of Hegel's text to such an extent that he comes to be "in a position neither to excuse [. . .] nor to accuse [. . .], but to locate a place where you think the text will allow you to turn it round and use it—to use its best energies for the project at hand" (Spivak 2014b, 161–162). In *BSWM*, and in demonstrable fashion in chapter six, Fanon is a most engaged reader, "claiming the text as the other's text *for me*" (Spivak 2014a, 35; emphasis added). What he does is "affirmative sabotage" (49).

THWARTING GOVERNING FICTIONS

"Fanon is able to see, on both sides—the European mistake and the Antillean suggestion of invincible uniqueness. There *are* competing and governing fictions. This is what gives him his power" (Spivak 2014a, 45; emphasis added). The reciprocity on which Fanon insists, *using* Hegel, permits him to claim his right to be a man, *simpliciter*, not a black man. It is a reciprocity that must ultimately eliminate the dualities of black/white. "Superiority? Inferiority? Why not simply try to touch the other, feel the other, discover each other?" (Fanon 2008, 206). Fanon does not merely apply, reverse, or imitate Hegel here, rather he morphs what Hegel thinks he says into what Fanon can use to speak for decolonization, using Hegel's best energies (the insistence on reciprocity) and putting them to work for his own project. That is, he reads appropriatively.

By refusing to work only with negation, as we saw, Fanon "deliberately makes a mistake" (Spivak 2014a, 44), but it is a "mistake" that helps him refuse to accept the *Phenomenology*'s master-slave dialectic as a "description of what happens" (44). In his insistence on reciprocity as philosophical booty, Fanon contests the historically implicit epidermalization of the master/slave dialectic, with-and-beyond Hegel himself.[14] Spivak warns that "[t]he specialists will stop you. Someone who really knows Hegel will say, 'Ah!' But in fact these mistakes tell us something about what to *do* with philosophy" (35; emphasis added). If appropriative reading is making mistakes, it makes them in critical intimacy: that is, as a result of a generous-critical engagement that becomes so intimate with the thinking of others that the latter becomes one's own "mental furniture" (Spivak 2014b, 77). It makes errors perhaps in view of a thinker's established reception. However, whether one gives a right or wrong interpretation might not be the appropriate measure or the most important point. Rather, appropriative reading intends to claim that "mental furniture"—affirmatively—for one's own project at hand. Thus, "mistakes" are not a shortcoming, but the effect of training oneself carefully enough in the idiom of the other; they stem from having "learnt to make the reading movements dictated by the text," however, crucially, "without the guarantee that we are correct" (Spivak 2014a, 57). Certainly, there is a very fine line between misunderstandings or misreadings and "mistakes" in an appropriative reading.

> The mistake that was made with Marx's philosophy was—thanks to Engels who did not understand Marx's counter-intuitive genius—to use it as if it were a blueprint for unmediated imitation in statecraft. That is the exact opposite of "claiming the text" by entering its protocols. (35–36)

In line with Marx and Feuerbach, the point of appropriating appropriately might not be to interpret the work of others. Instead, it might be to use it well, that is to make of reading a practice which aims to transform one's present, not an application of ready-made concepts from thinkers of the past.

Thus, when reading theory in critical intimacy, the move is to make the thought-figures of another part of our own intellectual habitat, helping us to negotiate their potentials and limits and to forge from them our own (theoretical) weapons. We might not have to discard texts *tout court* because they are limited or problematic in certain respects. It might rather be a question of first getting as close as possible to them, "reading as carefully as possible, without the desire to reclaim" (39, emphasis added). A desire to reclaim (or to dismiss) would only get in the way of reading as carefully and intimately as possible and of then using (or eventually discarding) them well. Inspired by Fanon and Spivak, one might then say that the point of reading as critical intimacy is not to judge theoretical texts as correct or false, but to work with them, even if they may not be intending to speak to *me*; even if they have problematic presuppositions that make it necessary to deconstruct them and turn a text around. If those moves can help detect and thwart some of our own governing fictions, including the categories of individuality, identity (politics) and sociality that dominate the early twenty-first century, then it seems worth "entering their protocols."

When reading literature in critical intimacy, as I have suggested, a slightly different task is put to us, namely to refrain from appropriating the text's idiom and thus move affective-cognitive habits away from the quick discarding or appropriating of otherness that CPC thrives on. By sitting with a literary text—its idiom, strange fictive universe, or challenging opacity—without making the move to appropriate one begins thwarting a governing fiction of CPC: appropriate what is other. If reading literature moves us to instead bear with otherness, it seems worth the effort of reading. In both cases—reading literary texts or reading theoretical texts—critique turns, as I have been suggesting, into an affective-corporeal practice that is somewhat akin to dancing, sometimes dancing in view of a project at hand, sometimes dancing in view of letting the text be and bearing otherness. Both require us to practice new steps for the future, a new style of critique that works with critical intimacy, moving us/the world rather than aiming to describe, analyze, judge, or dismiss.

In my opening vignette I suggested that the intersecting governing fictions of the past decades will have to be read. Surely, a critical reading of COVID-19—the policies and changes the virus has effected—is not the same as reading texts. But a constellation such as the "corona-era" also operates on (shifting) grids of signification and presupposition. Detecting these grids requires careful attention and degrees of intimacy; thwarting the governing fictions that uphold them will be impossible to do as if from the outside, by judging and dismissing, not least because the complicities here are too messy. The virus, this nonhuman agent at the limit of life, does not permit easy side-taking. It simply makes no sense to be for or against SARS-CoV-2. So can we, I wonder, become intimate enough with the situation inflicted by COVID-19 so as to critique it from the inside? Read it, enter its protocols and turn it, with-and-beyond itself? Can we critically affirm it and learn to move it in other directions than the state-corporate surveillance, intensified immunization of renationalized collectives and prohibition of social intimacies? Can we make use of this blaze that threatens to sweep away the few democratic, civil rights achievements of the twentieth century and turn it around for social and planetary justice in the twenty-first? That surely would seem to be one of the ends of critique.

NOTES

1. For the disproportionate exposure of people of color, poor people or people living in the Global South to COVID-19, but also disease in general, see Andrews (2020); Hartman (2020); Preciado (2020).

2. In its series 2018/2019, the collective ReadingRoom (http://terracritica.net/readingroom/) dubbed the interlocking system of **c**apitalism ~ **p**atriarchy ~ **c**olonialism CPC. I will use the acronym hereafter.

3. The use of "we" here is inspired by Derrida's "we" as a perpetual question (Derrida 1972, 136), that is, a category in need of continuous reexamination, and by Wynter's use of "we" to delineate the *systemic* quality of a hegemonic regime of being/knowledge: its epistemic fault lines affecting everyone though privileging only certain groups (who are especially called upon to unlearn privilege and learn different dispositions); for more on Wynter, see Thiele in this volume.

4. Clearly, such an approach to reading differs drastically from the type of activity to which, for example, proponents of "surface" or "distant" reading refer, where

reading is associated with discerning patterns from larger clusters of data or descriptive neutrality. I discuss the pitfalls of these latter in Kaiser 2021; see also Peeren in this volume.

5. To do justice to the argument, I would need to consider in detail how the literary operates in that regard. As that would leave no space for the modi of reading as critique that I am after here, I refer readers for now to Spivak 2019 (on Coetzee's *Disgrace* and how it summons readers to counterfocalize, that is, actively nudges readers to contest the narrative perspective); and Spivak (1995; 2012a, 60–72; 2012b, 209–214; 2014a, 67–76) (all examining how Devi spurs responses to otherness, especially the tribals of India, and moves readers toward suspending self-interest and attending to the idioms of others).

6. Cixous (1986, 79). Cixous offers a feminist reading of Hegel's dialectic. Where Fanon reclaims narcissism, feminist responses to Hegel's death-freedom opposition have turned to Echo as Narcissus's gendered other in order to critique narcissism's patriarchal patterns and think toward self-consciousness for a feminist postcoloniality. For Echo in that regard, see Cixous (2009); Kaiser (2019); Spivak (2012a, 218–240).

7. "With-and-beyond" is used to designate the intimate moves of reading as critique that work with a text or thinker, neither excusing nor accusing, and yet allowing one to move beyond their shortcomings.

8. Fanon is not used by Spivak (nor by me) as a model whose argument we must embrace entirely, but as an example teaching us something about what it means *to read*. In chapters two and three of *BSWM*, for example, Fanon struggles with patriarchal and homophobic presuppositions (I am grateful to Shannon Winnubst for this reminder). That he can affirm "reciprocity" as key tool from Hegel, as we shall see, is conditioned also upon this masculine position. Thus, "[w]hen we read the text of Fanon we have to say to ourselves: That story is not yet at an end." (63) "We cannot imitate him [Fanon] absolutely" (48); we must also *read* him (see note 10 on Spivak's intervention with-and-beyond Fanon on gender).

9. *BSWM* was intended as Fanon's dissertation but rejected by the Faculty of Medicine at Lyon University. It was published in the spring of 1952, after he had defended an alternative dissertation in 1951. Thus, Fanon was not literally in Algeria when writing *BSWM*, but he had been to North Africa as a soldier of the Free French Forces in 1944 and returned as trained psychiatrist to a post in Blida-Joinville in November 1953. For a detailed timeline of Fanon's work and migrations, see Khalfa and Young (2018, 779–783).

10. The question of gender is apparent in Fanon's terminology of the Black *man* and it is one of the problems Spivak has with Fanon: He is—like Freud, Hegel, Adler and everyone Fanon engages—"speaking of the male" (Spivak 2014a, 32). We must acknowledge that as a limitation and work with it. In her chapter on Fanon, Spivak dedicates a section to gender, ironically understated as "Postscript: Gender." Ironic, because the extensive section turns to gender as a "prime mover" (58) for abstraction and capital, even if miscognized as belatedly made possible by emancipatory history (gender presented as achievement of Enlightened modernity, the (sub)titular "postscript"). That section in Spivak's text would require its own, full reading,

but in shorthand and especially in view of its importance for appropriative reading let me state only this: Spivak here turns to Hegel with her own agenda, namely to get to gender as an "instrument of abstractability that is so old that to follow in its tracks is to develop ways of critical intimacy different from rational critique" (59). She takes the tour through Hegel's story of *Bewusstsein*, demonstrating how in its positing of otherness "by bringing it to zero" (60) it hints at simultaneously emergent modes of abstraction in eighteenth-century capitalist, colonial and gendered structures, and social transformations. Beyond Fanon, Spivak points out how in view of gender "Fanon is part of the problem" (63); and yet, noting how Fanon prepared *her* for reading Hegel, she invites us to "[w]atch me" (60) reading Hegel and Fanon with-and-beyond themselves, that is, appropriating their philosophemes for her own project, even if their racist and sexist implications might tempt others to discard them. She turns to the section on life in Hegel's *Phenomenology* preceding the chapter on "Lordship and Bondage." Intimate with Fanon's appropriative claims on Hegel *and* critical of Fanon's gendered and classed bias (38), Spivak veers Hegel with Marx toward a reading of abstraction as the logic that animates life and makes theoretical analyses of the intersections of gender and capital possible in order to reach beyond the narratives of their *historical* emergence (claiming them instead as *conceptual* tools). She performs in a very condensed fashion an "affirmative sabotage" (63) of both Hegel and Fanon.

11. Sylvia Wynter has powerfully drawn critical attention to Fanon's introduction of sociogeny in *BSWM*. Wynter taps into Fanon's concept of sociogeny and develops from there her own project of unfolding being human as a hybrid (bios/mythoi) praxis (see Wynter/McKittrick 2015), as a way to get out of the current biocentric, bourgeois "overrepresentation of Man" (Wynter 2003, 317). For my focus on the intimacies of reading as critical method, I decided to stay with Spivak's explicit dissecting of how Fanon reads. For Wynter's operations of reading Fanon in view of extricating us from the regime of Man2, see Marriott (2011).

12. Much more work is required to think through this proleptic temporality, which is also at work in the process of learning to read literature. Fanon himself notes that "[t]he problem considered here is located in temporality" (2008, 201). For more on temporality and critique, see Thiele in this volume.

13. See also Buck-Morss (2009, 67); Kuykendall (1991); and Diagne (2018) for Adler and Hegel.

14. Hegel was well informed about the Haitian revolution when writing the *Phenomenology* (see Buck-Morss 2009, 40–56). Yet, even if the *philosopheme* is saturated with that historical context (and its onto-epistemological regime that continues as Man2's anti-Blackness until today), Fanon insists on taking theoretical booty out from under the historical. The white masters of history are for Fanon not identical to Hegel's *philosopheme* of the master/slave dialectic. He insists on using the latter against the "racial epidermal schema" (2008, 92) that "legends, stories, history" (92) have congealed, because in the *philosopheme* the "slave turns away from the master and toward the object" (Fanon 2008, 195, note 10). In a similar move, Fanon turns away from Hegel's system of History toward his own question.

BIBLIOGRAPHY

Andrews, Kehine. 2020. "The Other Pandemic." In *The Quarantine Files. Thinkers in Self-Isolation*, curated by Brad Evans for *Los Angeles Review of Books*. April 14, 2020. https://www.lareviewofbooks.org/article/quarantine-files-thinkers-self-isolation/.

Attridge, Derek. 2004a. *J.M. Coetzee and the Ethics of Reading: Literature in the Event*. Chicago: University of Chicago Press.

———. 2004b. *The Singularity of Literature*. New York/London: Routledge.

Buck-Morss, Susan. 2009. *Hegel, Haiti, and Universal History*. Pittsburgh: University of Pittsburgh Press.

Cixous, Hélène. 1986. "Sorties: Out and Out: Attacks/Ways Out/Forays." In *The Newly Born Woman*, edited by Cixous and Catherine Clément and translated by Betsy Wing, 63–132. Minneapolis: University of Minnesota Press.

———. 2009. *So Close*, translated by Peggy Kamuf. Cambridge: Polity Press.

Derrida, Jacques. 1972. "The Ends of Man." In *Margins of Philosophy*, translated by Alan Bass, 111–136. Chicago: University of Chicago Press.

———. 1991. *Acts of Literature*, edited by Derek Attridge. London: Routledge.

Diagne, Souleymane Bachir. 2018. "History and Philosophy, Hegel and Africa." In *Review of Hegel et l"Afrique: histoire et conscience historique africaines*, edited by Alfred Adler (Paris: CNRS Editions, 2017) *The Journal of African History* 59 (3): 485–486.

Fanon, Frantz. 1952. *Peau noire, masques blancs*. Paris: Éditions du Seuil.

———. 1986. *Black Skin, White Masks*, translated by Charles Lam Markmann. London: Pluto Press.

———. 2008. *Black Skin, White Masks*, translated by Richard Philcox. New York: Grove Press.

Hartman, Saidiya. 2020. "The Death Toll." In *The Quarantine Files*: *Thinkers in Self-Isolation*, curated by Brad Evans for *Los Angeles Review of Books*. April 14, 2020. https://www.lareviewofbooks.org/article/quarantine-files-thinkers-self-isolation/.

Hegel, G. W. F. 1966 [1807]. *The Phenomenology of Mind*, translated by J. B. Baillie. London: Allen & Unwin.

Kaiser, Birgit Mara. 2019. "Hélène Cixous"s *So Close*; or, Moving Matters on the Subject." In *New Directions in Philosophy and Literature*, edited by David Rudrum, Ridvan Askin, and Frida Beckman, 102–121. Edinburgh: Edinburgh University Press.

———. 2021. "On the Politics of Diffractive Reading." In *Diffractive Reading: New Materialism, Theory and Critique*, edited by Kai Merten, 31–50. London: Rowman & Littlefield International.

Khalfa, Jean, and Robert Young (eds). 2018. "Key Dates of Fanon"s Chronology." In *Alienation and Freedom*, edited by Frantz Fanon, translated by Seven Corcoran, 779–783. London: Bloomsbury.

Kuykendall, Ronald. 1993. "Hegel and Africa: An Evaluation of the Treatment of Africa in the Philosophy of History." *Journal of Black Studies* 23 (4) (June): 571–581.

Marriott, David. 2011. "Inventions of Existence: Sylvia Wynter, Frantz Fanon, Sociogeny, and "the Damned"." *CR: The New Centennial Review* 11 (3): 45–89.

Ngũgĩ, Wa Thiong"o. 1986. *Decolonizing the Mind: The Politics of Language in African Literature*. Nairobi: James Currey.

Preciado, Paul. 2020. "Learning from the Virus." *Artforum International* 58 (9) (May/ June). https://www.artforum.com/print/202005/paul-b-preciado-82823.

Spivak, Gayatri Chakravorty. 1995. "Afterword." In *Imaginary Maps*, edited by Mahasweta Devi, translated and edited by G. Ch. Spivak, 197–205. New York: Routledge.

———. 2012 [1995]. "Supplementing Marxism." Reprinted in G.Ch. Spivak. *An Aesthetic Education in the Era of Globalization*. Cambridge, MA: Harvard University Press.

———. 2012a. *An Aesthetic Education in the Era of Globalization*. Cambridge, MA: Harvard University Press.

———. 2012b. "What"s Left of Theory?" Reprinted in G.Ch. Spivak. *An Aesthetic Education in the Era of Globalization*, 191–217. Cambridge, MA: Harvard University Press.

———. 2014a. "Fanon Reading Hegel." In *Readings*, edited by G. Ch. Spivak, 28–66. London/New York/Calcutta: Seagull Books.

———. 2014b. *Readings*. London/New York/Calcutta: Seagull Books.

———. 2019. *Ethics and Politics in Tagore, Coetzee and Certain Scenes of Teaching*. Oxford: Oxford University Press.

Thatcher, Margaret. 1987. "No Such Thing as Society." Interview by Douglas Keay. *Woman's Own*. September 23, 1987. https://www.margaretthatcher.org/document /106689.

Wynter, Sylvia. 2001. "Towards the Sociogenic Principle: Fanon, Identity, the Puzzle of Conscious Experience, and What It Is Like to Be 'Black'." In *National Identities and Sociopolitical Changes in Latin America*, edited by Mercedes F. Duran-Cogan and Antonio Gomez-Moriana, 30–66. New York: Routledge.

———. 2003. "Unsettling the Coloniality of Being/Power/Truth/Freedom: Towards the Human, after Man, Its Overrepresentation—An Argument." *CR: The New Centennial Review* 3: 257–337.

Wynter, Sylvia, and Katherine McKittrick. 2015. "Unparalleled Catastrophe for Our Species? Or, to Give Humanness a Different Future. Conversations." In *Sylvia Wynter: On Being Human as Praxis*, edited by Katherine McKittrick, 9–89. Durham: Duke University Press.

7

Critical Vivisection
Transforming Ethical Sensibilities
Timothy O'Leary

In my former home, Hong Kong, voices in the pro-government camp have for a long time wanted to remove the subject called Liberal Studies from the secondary school curriculum. This subject, which encourages critical engagement with social, political, and ethical issues, is now blamed for indoctrinating the young people who took to the streets in huge numbers in 2019 to protest proposed extradition legislation and to defend the promised "high degree of autonomy" of Hong Kong within China. In my new home, Australia, the conservative government recently (October 2020) implemented a new university funding model that would increase student fees in the humanities and social sciences, including, for example, history and environmental studies. This comes at a time when Australia is still grappling with its history of dispossession of Aboriginal peoples, elevated rates of black deaths in custody, and a political refusal to take effective measures to transition to a carbon-neutral economy. At the same time, however, universities around the world promote a sanitized version of "critical thinking" as a unique, employer-friendly graduate attribute that equips young people to "think outside the box" and challenge the status quo. In a world in which there are social and economic forces, from across the political spectrum that strive to silence or co-opt the asking of critical questions, it can be difficult to maintain the belief that the critical-intellectual activities of academics and scholars are worthwhile. For me, this makes the question of the ends, and the methodologies, of critique all the more pressing: what is it that I do when I engage in critique, and to what end?

***

In any society, there will always be forces and interests that are ranged against critique—conceived in the broadest possible sense. Being aware of the nature of those forces, and the form their anxiety takes, can provide a useful clue to the effect critique has. Structures of domination do not like questions, they do not like inconvenient truths, and they do not like creative works that revision and reimagine the world they try to maintain. Using the shorthand devised by the Terra Critica group, one could say that the contemporary CPC formation (capitalism-patriarchy-colonialism) does not like critique. And rightly so. But sometimes, in moments of pessimism, we might also feel that it does not have much to worry about. What effect, really, can reading texts, plunging into archives, engaging with creative works, have on ingrained structures of power and domination?

In this chapter, I propose an account of one of the things that critique can do, one of the things that the CPC formation is, perhaps, right to be anxious about. Critique does many things, there are many ends of critique, and that diversity can itself be described using an equally diverse range of theoretical lenses, from genealogy and deconstruction to schizo-analysis and ideology-critique. Acknowledging the breadth of this diversity and making no pretense to being exhaustive or prescriptive, what I offer here is one way of describing one of the things critique can do. In an earlier paper, published by the Terra Critica group, I characterized critique as a "transformative engagement with the moral sensibilities of our time" (O'Leary 2017, 149). In this chapter, I want to explore some of the ways critique can undertake this kind of transformative engagement, understood now as an engagement with *ethical* sensibilities. This more focused approach to sensibility, I hope, will allow me to highlight those practices (both personal and social) through which individuals come to be ethical subjects. My starting point for this exploration will be the Nietzschean conception of critique as an experimental vivisection that exposes deeply ingrained modes of human engagement with the world and with others. Later in the chapter, I will explore in more detail the notion of ethical sensibility, but my preliminary understanding is that sensibility, in general, is a mode of activity in the world that comprises three capacities: feeling/sensing, perceiving/knowing, and valuing/judging. *Ethical* sensibility comprises that activity in the loosely defined zone of human behaviors that, at any given time and place, are taken to be subject to moral or ethical principles, in particular those activities through which individuals guide their own behavior and attempt to mold their own subjectivities and identities.

In the modern Western tradition, critique has been concerned with the social, economic, and cultural forces—the structural elements—that seek to determine human social and political relations and relations with the natural world. But it has also, necessarily, been concerned with the other end of the spectrum, that is, with the individual relation to self. Critique, therefore, always carries the potential to engage with the domain of ethics, understood in the Foucauldian sense of the relation to self and others, as much as with social structures. In this mode, critique has the potential to transform the very thing it engages with and, hence, it is necessarily connected not only to its own social context but also to the ethical experience of the critic and of their reader. This also means that critique is not primarily a negative intervention that points out shortcomings and flaws. It is an open-ended, positive intervention that has its unpredictable effects through disrupting the well-trodden paths of modes of sensibility. My argument here is that it can disrupt that sensibility in ways that may be both expected and unforeseen; and that one of the ways this is achieved is through critique as vivisection. But it is not just critique, in the narrow sense, that can have these effects. Works of literature can also bring about similar effects of disruption, through practices of vivisection that unravel modes of subjectivity and ethical sensibility.

This chapter makes three suggestions. First, drawing on a theme that runs through Nietzsche's thought in the 1880s, I will show that the work of critique has occasionally been, and still might usefully be, characterized as a form of experimental vivisection. Second, I will suggest that the task of critical vivisection has been undertaken in literary texts as often as in the canonical works of critique. Third, I will propose that the resulting idea of an experimental engagement with ethical sensibility gives us a rich and productive way of understanding one of the ends of critique. In section 2, I will explore some of the wide range of meanings of vivisection in the nineteenth century, both literal and metaphorical. In section 3, I will show how a recent novel, *Milkman* (2018), engages in a critical vivisection of a quite specific mode of ethical sensibility. In section 4, I will consider some of the grounds of possibility and the possible effects of critical, experimental interventions in ethical sensibility, whether they occur in novels or works of academic scholarship.

VIVISECTION, LITERAL AND METAPHORICAL

In the context of this chapter, vivisection works as a metaphor; a metaphor that I believe can help us identify an important feature of critical practice. In the late nineteenth century, however, at the time when Nietzsche, as we will see below, begins to use vivisection as a metaphor for critique, it was also a new and highly controversial method of medical research. Vivisection was the name for the practice of carrying out experiments on living animals; a practice championed by the French physiologist Claude Bernard, whose aim was to establish medical science on the same experimental footing as the other natural sciences. It might seem strange today that Nietzsche chose to use vivisection as a metaphor for critique, but as a metaphor for the self-examination that the modern experience seemed to demand, the term vividly conveyed ideas about hidden depths, courageous explorations, and experimental interventions. It also had an air of danger, and even horror; a potential that H. G. Wells was to fully exploit in his 1896 novel *The Island of Doctor Moreau* (2009), where he takes the idea of live experimentation to its most gruesome conclusion.

Claude Bernard, in his major work from 1865, *Introduction to the Study of Experimental Medicine* (1957), demonstrated for the first time that the experimental method of the natural sciences could also be applied in the field of physiology. One of the practices that made this possible was carrying out experiments on living animals:

> After dissecting cadavers, then, we must necessarily dissect living beings, to uncover the inner or hidden parts of the organisms and see them work; to this sort of operation we give the name of vivisection. (Bernard 1957, 254)

This practice, however, split public opinion to such an extent that, reportedly, even Bernard's own wife Marie Françoise Martin separated from him and joined an anti-vivisection society. In the United Kingdom, a public inquiry was held in 1875 that led to legislation that is the distant ancestor of the animal ethics policies that govern universities and medical researchers around the world today. That inquiry gave a platform to the debate between, on the one hand, proponents of the medical and scientific value of experiments on animals, and on the other hand the anti-vivisectionists who held that no amount of scientific knowledge justified the infliction of pain on animals. The debate was animated by two great opposing ideal images of human progress: the fearless scientist (always male) who wades through blood and suffering to secure scientific advances; and the moral crusader (often female) fighting for an end to cruelty and pain inflicted on the weak and defenseless.

It was in the context of this intense public debate across Europe (Bates 2017) that Nietzsche adopted the use of the term vivisection for his own purposes; purposes which were both polemical and sincere (Dunkle 2018). During the 1880s, vivisection became one of Nietzsche's favorite metaphors for the critical work of philosophy, perhaps because, as one commentator puts it, "vivisection in all of its forms revealed the contingencies that lay behind the innocent necessities of life" (Mitchell 2016, 114). In *Beyond Good and Evil* (2002 [1886]), Nietzsche suggests the time has come to reject the system-building of the moral philosophers and to undertake a much more modest task. What will be necessary for a long time, in the study of morality, he argues, will be "collecting material, formulating concepts, and putting into order the tremendous realm of tender feelings and value distinctions that live, grow, reproduce, and are destroyed" (2002, Section 186). Only then will we be able to sketch "the recurring and more frequent shapes of this living crystallization" (2002, Section 186). Going further, he also describes this work as a kind of vivisection, a slow and careful dissection of the faith in a single, univocal morality: the "examination, dissection, interrogation, vivisection of precisely this article of faith [in one morality]" (2002, Section 186). Nietzsche recommends, therefore, undertaking a dual investigation; one into the dominant forms of moral feelings and value distinctions, the other into the stubborn, naïve belief that "one morality" exists. For Nietzsche, this investigation requires not only patience but also courage, since vivisection evinces an unavoidable horror: "mankind cannot be spared the horrible sight of the psychological operating table, with its knives and forceps" (2004, 2:37).

For Nietzsche, a true philosopher is a person who has this courage, who is skilled at "applying a vivisecting knife to the *virtues of the age*," as much as applying the knife to themselves (2002, Section 212). In this regard, Socrates is exemplary:

> The old physician and man of the rabble who cut brutally into his own flesh like he cut into the flesh and heart of the "noble," with a glance that spoke clearly enough: "Don't act some part in front of me! Here—we are equals!" (2002, Section 212)

The critique of morality that Nietzsche goes on to develop in the course of the 1880s, through successive iterations in *Daybreak* [1881], *Beyond Good and Evil* [1886], and *On the Genealogy of Morality* [1887], consistently develops this idea that the philosopher—especially the philosopher of the future—must exercise a ruthless dissection and examination not only of the historical forms of human morality but also of their own psyche which, necessarily, embodies the same historical forms and structures. For Nietzsche, this incisive opening up is, in one sense, a modest task—more modest, that is, than the philosophical system-building of the past—but it requires courage and persistence, especially when applied to oneself.

Vivisection in nineteenth-century medical science, however, was not just seen as a tool of observation, it also had a potentially significant role in experiment, understood in a different, more creative, sense. This is an aspect of vivisection that H.G. Wells drew on in his portrayal of the grotesque experiments carried out by the protagonist of *The Island of Doctor Moreau* (2009), with the aim of creating a new race of beings. The drive to create a new kind of human being was also shared by Nietzsche, except for him it would not be achieved through medical science, but through critical philosophy and the revaluation of values. Throughout the 1880s, Nietzsche regularly appeals to the notion of the experiment, the test, the attempt (*versuch*) as an essential step in the practice of the philosopher. This is a thread that persists in twentieth-century conceptions of critique, most notably in Foucault's final explorations of the nature of critical philosophy, for example, in his essay "What is Enlightenment?" (1991b, 32–50).

For Nietzsche, however, if vivisection has the capacity to effect these changes in the future, it is because of the long history of human self-inflicted cruelty. In *On the Genealogy of Morality*, Nietzsche uses the metaphor of vivisection to convey the depth of the self-directed incisions that have created the modern human conscience, and not always in a positive way: "We moderns have inherited millennia of conscience-vivisection and animal-torture inflicted on ourselves" (2007, 2:24). According to Nietzsche's genealogy of morality, this first step in the development of the moral subject in early humanity was the turning back of the bad conscience upon the individual psyche, in response to repressive social limitations and demands. This self-torture, occurring over millennia, did indeed create a new kind of human being, but one that embodied a distorted and stunted mode of the will to power. Ultimately, however, at some point in the future, the will to power will be given its positive expression, when slave morality will be replaced with an affirmative morality that is "beyond good and evil." But, as we saw above, in order to carry out this transformation, another form of vivisection is required, the vivisection of contemporary "tender feelings and value distinctions" (2002, Section 186). In Nietzsche's thought, therefore, vivisection is a double-edged sword, both torturer and potential liberator of human beings. And it is also a mark of a fundamental hubris. As a species, humans have displayed a hubris that is, in fact, remarkably similar to that shown by Doctor Moreau:

> *hubris* characterizes our attitude towards *ourselves*,—for we experiment on ourselves in a way we would never allow on animals, we merrily vivisect our souls out of curiosity. (Nietzsche 2007, 3:9)

For Nietzsche, therefore, this cheerful vivisection, as opposed to the cruel conscience-vivisection of early human history, will be an essential technique in the critical moral philosophy of the immediate future.

Given this context, choosing to use vivisection as a metaphor for critique today could be read as a provocation, or worse, a serious error. Is vivisection inherently tied to a nineteenth-century gendered drive to expose hidden truths that ties it to the kind of negative critique that this collection of essays wishes to surpass? Admittedly, as the term suggests, the most vivid and provocative connotation of vivisection is that it is living animals that are dissected; animals that cannot consent to this treatment and for whom it is neither in their own individual or collective interests to be used in this way. Even if these practices are carefully managed by Research Ethics Committees in contemporary universities and laboratories, the fundamental moral questions remain. But critical vivisection, as envisioned by Nietzsche, is in the first place a self-inflicted experimental intervention; it is a practice to which one gives one's consent. And, secondly, vivisection connotes much more than isolated, disinterested acts of dissection and analysis; it also implies an experimental approach to the social world. Critical vivisection, therefore, involves more than an objectivized observation and analysis of the world; it also includes, necessarily, a desire to intervene and modify both oneself and the world as it exists.

It is this concept, of vivisection as an element in an experimental intervention, that is perhaps most appealing for Nietzsche and most evocative for the critical tradition that comes after him. Vivisection, then, is a metaphor that plays on many levels in Nietzsche's thought. It is timely, in the sense that it is very much an issue of the day, but it is untimely in the sense that it designates a brushing against the grain of the present. It is a practice that philosophers have always cultivated, but it is also a practice that must be revived anew in the project of the revaluation of values. It entails cruelty and pain, but it is a necessary step in the experimental pursuit of a higher form of "gay science" (Nietzsche 2001).

A NOVEL EXPERIMENT

The exploratory, vivisective, experimental aspect of the work of critique is not confined to philosophy or critical history. It is also something that can occur in and through works of literature. For some novelists, this connection has been quite explicit. Joyce, for example, in his early unfinished novel *Stephen Hero* (1903–1905), described the modern spirit as being "vivisective" and vivisection itself as "the most modern process one can conceive" (1991, 209). While Zola, who was a near-contemporary of Nietzsche and H. G. Wells, directly aligns the naturalistic novel with the experimental principles of Claude Bernard, the great champion of vivisection. In his 1880 essay on *The Experimental Novel*, Zola (1893) wholly and uncritically adopts the vivisective paradigm directly from Bernard's work, in his attempt to establish the modern naturalistic novel as an experimental human science in which the novelist will "operate on the characters [. . .] as the physiologist operates on living beings" (1893, 18). Vivisection can, however, take place in a novel without the novelist explicitly adopting this term or this methodology. I want to look at Anna Burns's recent novel *Milkman* (2018), with a view to exploring the possibility that a novel can engage in something like a Nietzschean critical vivisection. One of the central elements of Burns's experiment, which I will focus on here, is the removal of almost all names and proper nouns from the discourse of the protagonist and, perhaps, even from the fictional world itself. By introducing this modification into the world of the novel, Burns exposes the mechanisms by which a young woman's splintered subjectivity struggles to shape itself in the face of myriad social and political forces; forces which seem determined to pin down and define her mode of being.

Milkman, which won the Man Booker Prize in 2018, is a multilayered exploration of identity, political violence, gender, power, and growing up female in a broken society. The novel is, in one sense, "set" in Northern Ireland during the Troubles (1968–1998), more specifically in Belfast, perhaps in the Catholic Ardoyne neighborhood, where Burns herself grew up in the 1970s. But one of the most striking features of the novel is that none of these places are actually named. In fact, the novel is almost completely devoid of proper names of any kind; no country, no neighborhood, no political leader is named. How, then, do readers "know" it is set in Northern Ireland? This is a question that would take us on a long tangent, but it seems to be a combination of knowledge that the author grew up in Belfast, an almost perfect "fit" between the world of the novel and the complex political context of Northern Ireland in the 1970s, and a widespread critical consensus that is present in almost every review of the book, including the citation from the Man Booker Prize judges. In addition to the absence of place names, however, the most striking formal innovation of the novel is that none of the characters in the novel are named. That is to say, they are referred to with monikers such as "second brother-in-law," "tablets girl," "maybe-boyfriend," "milkman" (who is not to be confused with "real milkman"), "nuclear boy," "Somebody McSomebody," and so on, but we never learn their given names. One exception, which proves the rule, is the married couple who are ironically and humorously referred to as Nigel and Jason; so named because they are the keepers of the list of unacceptable given names in this community; that is, names that are too closely associated with the unnamed country "over the water"; prime examples being, precisely, the names Nigel and Jason.

This purging of proper names is the most striking formal element of the novel, and one that has a number of far-reaching effects; three of which I will identify here. First, it means that all the cultural and political specificity of that period in Northern Ireland's history can be left to one side. A reader who has no knowledge of that conflict will not be at a loss in reading this novel. As Burns has said, even though the novel is indeed a kind of skewed picture of Belfast in the 1970s, "it's not really Belfast in the 1970s"; rather, she wants it to be "any sort of totalitarian, closed society existing in similarly oppressive conditions" (Allardice 2018). So, it is not surprising that, according to one reviewer (Allardice 2018), many readers with no knowledge of the Troubles have read *Milkman* as being akin to Margaret Attwood's *The Handmaid's Tale* (2018). It can indeed be read as a dystopian novel dealing with, among other things, the noxious effects of male domination in a highly regulated and closely surveilled totalitarian society. Except, in this case, the society existed very recently, and its forms of oppression were not only mediated by the state but were also ruthlessly imposed by the community itself. By choosing to write in terms of "defenders of the state," "renouncers of the state" (22), the "country over the water," and "enemy state-defending paramilitaries from over the way" (13), Burns (2018) makes it possible to universalize the experience of the novel's protagonist. In short, the novel, rather than being "about" Northern Ireland, is, "absolutely and essentially," Burns herself says, about "how power is used, both in a personal and in a societal sense" (Allardice 2018). In this highly fraught context, in which offending the sensibilities of one's own community can lead to one's death, the protagonist tries to thread a way through multiple threats.

The second effect of removing almost all proper names from the novel is that the individual is decoupled from their "proper" indexical in a way that is profoundly unsettling. The protagonist, who is also the first-person narrator of the novel, is an eighteen-year-old woman who is variously referred to by others as "the reading-while-walking person" (3), "maybe-girlfriend" (19), "middle sister" (56), "sister-in-law" (57), "a community beyond-the-pale" (199), and on one occasion, "the pale, adamantine, unyielding girl who walks around with the entrenched, boxed-in thinking" (204). Humor clearly plays a large role in this novel, but this proliferation of non-name names also has an increasingly unsettling effect. At first sight, one might view some elements of this naming practice as positive features of a role-oriented social structure, in which family members are referred to by their relation to the speaker, rather than by a given name. Hence, in the novel, we regularly hear about Ma, Daddy, middle sister, third sister, eldest sister, oldest brother, first brother-in-law, third brother-in-law, sister-in-law, wee sisters, and so on. In the context of this novel, however, and when combined with the other more widespread absence of proper names, what is conveyed here very forcefully is that the protagonist, living as she is in a society that is always on the brink of violence, is struggling to maintain, or even develop, a sense of identity.

When we meet her first, she is literally and metaphorically keeping her head down and trying to avoid attention. But ironically this effort, which is crystallized in her habit of reading nineteenth-century novels while walking (because she does not like the twentieth century), is already drawing negative attention. She is already in danger of becoming one of those community outcasts, a so-called beyond-the-pale. The event that pushes her over this limit is when "the milkman" (who was not a milkman) begins to stalk her in a sexually predatory way. We discover that this milkman, who is twenty-three years older than her and is married, is not the first man to have made unwanted sexual advances to her. Her first brother-in-law, when she was twelve and he was thirty-five (also twenty-three years older), used to make "lewd remarks about me [. . .] and he used words, words sexual, I didn't understand" (1–2). In both cases, her response is muted by her sense that since there was no threat of physical violence, her community, which has been wracked by political violence, would not acknowledge the seriousness of the incidents. As one critic says, "the whole town is engaged in a culturally enforced conspiracy of gaslighting" (Charles 2018). In the case of the milkman, however, the threat is more troubling, as he is a leading member of the paramilitary organization referred to in the novel as the "renouncers-of-the-state."

The third effect of the absence of proper names is that the novel seems to depict a whole society in which nothing is given a proper name. In other words, the no-name convention seems to be not just a narrative choice; it is not just that the narrator chooses not to reveal the names of people and places to the reader. It seems as if this convention also holds sway within the fictional world itself; it seems to be a world without names, or a world in which nobody dares to speak the names of things. Admittedly, it is not completely certain that the people in this society adopt the same naming conventions that the narrator uses (renouncer-of-the-state, the country-over-the-water, etc.), but the all-pervasiveness of the narrator's naming conventions effectively makes it so for the reader. This has, once again, a clearly dystopian and defamiliarizing effect; one that recalls the Newspeak of Orwell and the neologisms of Atwood's *The Handmaid's Tale* (for instance, the convention of naming a handmaid after her "master").

In effect, then, the novel presents the consciousness of a protagonist who is struggling to forge a sense of identity and autonomy in a community in which relations of power, that are interpersonal, social, state-sponsored, and highly gendered, threaten to completely crush her agency. The novel tunes in to the cacophony of voices, both external and internal, that are endlessly telling the protagonist what to do, how to behave, and how to understand the world around her. And it reveals, step by step and in virtual slow-motion, the internal conflict and confusion as she sifts through these voices, challenging them, rejecting them, and occasionally accepting them. As an act of vivisection, the novel opens up the mechanisms through which a society molds and guides the subject-formation of a young woman; along with the corresponding moments of resistance and subterfuge that she cultivates. The narrative technique of dispelling proper names, in favor of unwieldy and slightly absurd monikers, is a defamiliarizing element that helps to expose the interlocking components of a subjectivity that is forming, as all subjectivities do, within a complex web of interpersonal and impersonal relations. The novel's vivisection of the protagonist's subjectivity, therefore, lays bare the intricate workings of this web in vivo, thus opening up the possibility of a critical engagement with the multitude of forces that mold subjects in their relations with self and others.

ENGAGING WITH ETHICAL SENSIBILITY

So far in this chapter, I have suggested that vivisection, understood especially as an experimental intervention, is a helpful metaphor in thinking about the ends of critique today. And I have suggested that, in addition to the canonical works of critique in the Western tradition, works of literature (especially novels) also engage in that critical endeavor. Throughout the discussion, I have referred to "ethical sensibility" as one of the potential targets of critical intervention, but I now need to give a more detailed account of what that term means. My aim is to show that ethical sensibility is a concept that can help us to formulate one of the ends of critique.

In his book on Nietzsche's philosophy, Deleuze draws attention to Nietzsche's appeal in *Daybreak* that we have to learn to "think differently" (Deleuze 2002, 94). The push to think differently is a mainstay of contemporary critique, a principle that Foucault also establishes in his late work, in which the critical attitude is based on the need to "*penser autrement*"—to think otherwise (Foucault 1990a, 9). In Foucault's concept of critique, of course, this moment of thinking needs to be supplemented with a moment of doing that comprises both a refusal and a creative step towards new ways of living. In Nietzsche's formulation, in contrast, the next step after thinking differently is not doing, but *feeling*, differently:

> We have to *learn to think differently*—in order at last, perhaps very late on, to attain even more: *to feel differently*. (Nietzsche 1997, Section 103)

As Deleuze glosses, "the point of critique is not justification but a different way of feeling: another sensibility" (2002, 94). For Nietzsche, then, and maybe also for Deleuze, the end of critique is not to arrive at a correct and complete appraisal of the shortcomings of ourselves and our world; rather, it is to achieve a different sensibility. Or, as Kathrin Thiele (2008) has argued in relation to Deleuze, it is to arrive at a different "poetics of life."

But, how does the concept of sensibility in general, and ethical sensibility in particular, help us to think about the practices and effects of critique? Sensibility is an admittedly complex and amorphous concept. It has a long and somewhat tortuous history, especially in modern Western philosophical approaches to ethics, art, and literature. This might be a good reason to avoid using it, but for me this is part of its attraction: it is a rich and complex concept which, for that very reason, is more likely to be equal to the task of grasping a kaleidoscopic reality. In my understanding, sensibility is a mode of activity in the world, not a passive receptivity: it is a way of actively perceiving, which I take to include both perception (the senses) and knowing, and it is a way of responding to the world, a way of judging ethically and aesthetically. As a concept, therefore, sensibility comprises three interlocked capacities: feeling/sensing, perceiving/knowing, and valuing/judging.

If this is sensibility in the broadest sense, then "ethical sensibility" is the operation of that "whole activity" in the more or less loosely defined zone of human behaviors that, in any given time or place, are taken to be subject to moral or ethical principles. This zone of behavior is constantly changing, as certain acts enter and depart from the field of ethical concern. Likewise, its patterns of intensity, its heatmap, is constantly changing, as elements gain and lose significance due to shifting social mores. And within this zone, there is a constant conflict and struggle underway, between different modes of sensibility. Many social campaigns, I would argue, whether led by governments or activists, can be seen as attempts to sway individuals to adopt a particular mode of ethical sensibility. While an animal rights activist, for example, might want people's ethical sensibility to respond in a certain way to images of battery hens, an anti-abortion activist will likewise want their sensibility to be honed to respond in a certain way to an image of a fetus. There is, in short, an endless battle of ethical sensibilities; a struggle between conflicting sensibilities that plays out in the public sphere, in art, in politics, in culture, and quite often within the individual subject. Understood in this way, specific historically determined modes of ethical sensibility give rise to and guide particular forms of action.

If we search for the philosophical resources to understand and conceptualize this set of phenomena, Foucault's works stands out. From his genealogy of the disciplined body in *Discipline and Punish* (1995) to his painstaking excavation of the desiring, self-caring subject of late antiquity and the early Christian era in volumes 2, 3, and 4 of the *History of Sexuality* (1990a, 1990b, 2018), Foucault's work constitutes a critical excavation of the modern subject of ethics. And his exploration, carried out in a series of late interviews and lectures, of the modes of historical transformation of ethical experience gives us a basis for conceptualizing how an entire apparatus of perception and feeling, a mode of sensibility, can be shifted by a work on the self; a work on the self that might include an engagement with, among other things, critical histories and works of fiction (O'Leary 2009).

William Connolly, however, is one of the few commentators who presents a Nietzscho-Foucauldian ethics under the rubric, precisely, of "ethical sensibility" (1993). He contrasts a Foucauldian ethical sensibility with the kind of philosophical ethics that strives to be transcendentally grounded, whether in norms of reason or human nature. For Connolly, Foucault's core philosophical method, genealogy, actually engages with and transforms sensibilities:

> A new sensibility is *rendered possible* through genealogies [. . .] [genealogies are] a set of artful techniques to modify these contingent installations, these

"feelings." The sensibility that these techniques install functions as a corollary to the cultivation of "virtues" in teleological theories. (Connolly 1993, 373)

Foucault's genealogies, therefore, are effective insofar as they modify an existing sensibility and make possible new ways of thinking/perceiving/feeling. They engage, in my terms, in an experimental vivisection that cuts into a living sensibility, both in order to understand it and to modify it at the same time. This is the same vivisection that we see in play in the novel *Milkman*, in which the protagonist's modes of thinking/perceiving/feeling are carefully probed and examined.

The possibility of reading Foucault's critical histories in these terms exists, I would suggest, in latent form in many engagements with his work. Let me take as one example an essay by Judith Butler (2012) on Foucault, Kant, and critique. Butler presents an analysis of Foucault's work that can be seamlessly supplemented with a concept of sensibility. First, Butler points out that:

> To be critical of an authority that poses as absolute is not just to take a point of view but to elaborate a position for oneself outside the ontological jurisdiction of that authority and so to elaborate a certain possibility of the subject. (2012, 23)

The passage from Nietzsche about the need for a new way of feeling, that I cited above, is set in the context of Nietzsche's rejection of just such an "ontological jurisdiction." Nietzsche says that there are two common grounds on which one might deny morality: either because one believes moral judgments to be hypocritical self-deceptions, or because one denies that they are within the realm of truth. Nietzsche denies morality in the second sense: "I deny morality as I deny alchemy" and of course he similarly denies immorality (1997, section 103). This does not mean, he hastens to add, that he necessarily denies the desirability of actions that have been judged to be good, or that he necessarily denies the undesirability of actions that have been judged to be bad. It is just that if he were to do so, it would be on very different grounds to the dogmatic moralist. Hence the need, in Nietzsche's terms, not just for a new way of *thinking* but also for a new form of moral *feeling*. Now, to supplement Butler on Foucault, we can say that to be critical of an authority is to position oneself outside its ontological jurisdiction and so to elaborate *a new sensibility*, a new way of feeling, which is also of course one aspect of a "certain possibility of the subject" (Butler 2012, 23).

When Butler goes on to point out that "dissent" may entail an "alteration both in and of the subject" and can "challenge and reformulate historically specific modes of rationality" (2012, 23), we can add that this alteration also challenges historically specific modes of ethical sensibility. Likewise, Butler reminds us that Foucault's "no" to power is not purely negative, it also "delineates and animates a new set of positions for the subject; it is inventive" (2012, 24). I would only add that it also calls forth a new mode of sensibility in the subject; in fact, I would suggest that there can be no shift in subjectivity without a corresponding shift in sensibility.

At this stage I want to address a possible concern about my approach so far: given my understanding of ethical sensibility, wouldn't one be justified in assigning it a mere epiphenomenal status? Surely a shift in ethical sensibility is simply a surface-level effect of changes that are more likely to be brought about through argument, evidence, and truth, rather than an intervention in the way we perceive and experience ourselves in the world? In order to address this concern, we need to focus more clearly on the relation between critique and subjectivity. In particular, it is a central claim of my approach here that effective critique will not just change ideas and opinions, but will also change, in however small a way, modes of subjectivity. Critique, as Butler argues, is a practice that necessarily involves a de- and reconstitution of subjectivity. And this is an effect that cannot be brought about exclusively through logic and reason. It requires an intervention that could also be described as somatic, rather than purely intellectual; and as disruptive, rather than incremental. That is, it is an intervention and an engagement that tends to undermine an ingrained mode of subjectivity, rather than simply adding minor modifications to an established pattern. Such a critique can be described as somatic in the sense that it both investigates the somatic elements of the phenomena it studies and in the way that it impacts the reader at the level of feelings and sensations. And it is this impact which, in a multitude of possible ways, contributes to an "alteration in and of the subject" (Butler 2012, 23).

Félix Guattari, in his *Three Ecologies* (2000), suggests a similar move that will help us to grasp these potential alterations in subjectivity. In this work, Guattari lays the groundwork for a new theoretical and practical critique of a world that is rushing toward environmental disaster, thanks at least in part to conditions that have been created by what he calls Integrated World Capitalism (IWC). Guattari proposes a new "ecosophy" that will have three elements: environmental, social, and individual. Underlying all three elements, however, this ecosophical perspective will require a rejection of the modern Western (especially Cartesian, but also Freudian) concept of subjectivity. Guattari suggests that rather than focusing on "the subject," the theorist needs to think in terms of *processes* of subjectivation, or "vectors of subjectification" (2000, 36). Instead of thinking of rigid, stable, isolated subjects, one should rather think in terms of the ways in which subjects are constantly being formed, sustained, deformed, and reformed. Guattari invites his readers, therefore, to reject the modern Western conception of subjects as the ground and center of human experience; and to instead see them as always temporary end points, or as surface phenomena, that emerge from a complex web of forces and processes:

> Vectors of subjectification do not necessarily pass through the individual, which in reality appears to be something like a "terminal" for processes that involve human groups, socio-economic ensembles, data-processing machines, etc. Therefore, interiority establishes itself at the crossroads of multiple components, each relatively autonomous in relation to the other, and, if need be, in open conflict. (2000, 36)

Hence, rather than speaking of "the subject," one should speak of "components of subjectification, each working more or less on its own" (2000, 36). This is a view of subjectivity that is also adopted in *Milkman*, in which the protagonist, positioned at the crossroads of multiple conflicting social and political forces, struggles to establish a stable identity.

If one can speak of vectors and components of subjectivation, then one can go one step further and also speak of vectors and components of *de*-subjectivation; and it is these vectors that, in particular, are of relevance to critique. This shift in focus, from a purportedly substantive individual subject to a process of vectors of subjectivation, also undermines the substance/surface dichotomy that makes possible the epiphenomenal argument mentioned above. Hence, in the account of critique that I propose here, processes that may appear to be merely surface phenomena are in fact the processes that contribute to the formation of the "terminal" illusion of an interior substance.

The claim that the experience of a stable, substantial self is an illusion is central to the idea of critique as an experimental engagement with ethical sensibility. And it is a view that is also shared by Foucault, for whom the subject "is not a substance. It is a form, and this form is not primarily or always identical to itself" (1997, 290). For Foucault, this is one of the core tenets that makes it possible for him to champion a form of critique that aims to untie the knots of subjectivity, thus opening up the possibility of creatively cultivating new practices of liberty. This concept of critique owes a great deal to Foucault's engagement with Nietzsche's philosophy. In his 1971 essay "Nietzsche, Genealogy, History," Foucault explains his understanding of Nietzschean genealogy in this way:

> The analysis of descent [genealogy] permits the dissociation of the self and the proliferation of a thousand lost events on the site of its empty synthesis. (Foucault 1991a, 81 [Translation modified])

This is a description that applies just as well to Nietzsche's concept of genealogy as to Foucault's, and it can also apply to critique more generally. If critique, through an act of vivisection, generates an analysis of the emergence of current modes of speaking, thinking, and doing, then one of its effects would be to dissociate the self as we know it. In place of the fiction of a unified, stable, originary self, there would open up a flood of "a thousand lost events," all those myriad possibilities that had been deselected, for whatever reason, in order to make room for the "empty synthesis" in which, for the most part, life is lived. And out of this unsettling, dissociative experience there would emerge the possibility of a positive, creative work of forming new modes of ethical sensibility, new ways of speaking, thinking, and doing. It is precisely this work of de-subjectivation and re-subjectivation that we see the protagonist of the novel *Milkman* negotiating.

Another way to conceptualize this critical project, which Foucault playfully picks up in his lectures at the Collège de France in 1979–1980, is through the concept of "anarcheology" (Foucault 2014). In the introductory lecture to the annual lecture theme, Foucault tries to distance his approach, which involves a methodological rejection of the necessity of power, from anarchism. He insists that he is not proposing anarchism; but he does want every investigation of power to begin with a methodological assertion of "the non-necessity of all power of whatever kind" (2014, 78). Referring, for example, to his work on the history of the prison, he explains:

> The anarcheological type of study [. . .] consisted in taking the practice of confinement in its historical singularity, that is to say in its contingency, in the sense of its fragility, its essential non-necessity, which obviously does not mean (quite the opposite!) that there was no reason for it and is to be accepted as a brute fact. (2014, 79)

In this case, the "analysis of descent" exposes the fragility of an entire apparatus of power, its "essential non-necessity." This historically oriented, "internal" investigation of contemporary modes of being human, opens up the possibility of an explosive splintering of the self and the exposure of the emptiness at the heart of its synthesis. This fragility of structures and forces that can seem to be so robust is equally conveyed through the experience of the protagonist of *Milkman*, as she makes her way through the minefield of the sociopolitical relations of her society. If one is confronted with the realization that everything in one's mode of subjectivity, in one's ways of living, experiencing, and thinking, is essentially non-necessary, then it is not unreasonable to expect a disruption in the capacity to carry on thoughtlessly in those ways of being.

In developing a concept of ethical sensibility in this chapter, therefore, I have wanted to capture an element of individual subjectivity that exists in the interplay between modes of feeling/sensing, knowing/perceiving, and valuing/judging. This element of subjectivity is particularly caught up in the broadly conceived sphere of ethics: that is, in a person's ways of judging themselves and others and their ways of engaging in reasoning and self-guiding behaviors that bring their actions into conformity with certain general principles. It is an element that is, crucially, open to constant change; both at the level of the individual life and, even more so, at the level of social history. On both of these levels, ethical sensibility is a domain that is a constant target of interventions by a whole range of different influences, from social activism and political movements to mass marketing and public health campaigns. There is clearly a constant conflict *between* differing ethical sensibilities, but there is also a conflict *of* sensibilities, that is, a battle to form, reform, and deform ethical sensibility. And critique, for its part, also intervenes in this conflict, through practices of vivisection that disrupt the smooth operation of habitual ethical sensibilities, thus opening up possibilities for creating new ways of sensing, knowing, and valuing.

THE ENDS OF CRITIQUE

Let me return now to the vignette that opened this chapter. In a world in which even "critical thinking" has been commodified and sanitized by universities, as an employer-friendly graduate attribute, it can be difficult to maintain focus on what it is that makes critique valuable and effective. In this chapter, I have presented one answer to the question of the "ends" of critique and what the value of that end might be. On this view, critique is something that happens in a range of different cultural practices; including volumes such as the one where this chapter is published, works such as Foucault's *Discipline and Punish*, and novels such as *Milkman*. What links these practices is the fact that, in a whole range of different ways, they disrupt the familiar paths of an ingrained sensibility so as to make it possible to question those paths, to undermine their assumed necessity and reveal their essential fragility; and thus, to make it possible to imagine new paths. To conclude, therefore, the practice of critique can be conceived as a meticulous, experimental vivisection that exposes and interrupts habitual modes of sensibility; and its end is to open up those modes of sensibility to a future in which they can be reimagined and reconstructed otherwise.

BIBLIOGRAPHY

Allardice, Lisa. 2018. "Interview with Anna Burns." *The Guardian*, October 17, 2018. https://www.theguardian.com/books/2018/oct/17/anna-burns-booker-prize-winner-life-changing-interview.

Atwood, Margaret. 2018. *The Handmaid's Tale*. London: Vintage Publishing.
Bates, A. W. H. 2017. *Anti-Vivisection and the Profession of Medicine in Britain: A Social History*. London: Palgrave Macmillan.
Bernard, Claude. 1957. *Introduction to the Study of Experimental Medicine*, translated by H. C. Greene. New York: Dover Publications Inc.
Burns, Anna. 2018. *Milkman*. London: Faber & Faber.
Butler, Judith. 2012. "Critique, Dissent, Disciplinarity." In *Conceptions of Critique in Modern and Contemporary Philosophy*, edited by Karin de Boer and Ruth Sonderegger, 10–29. Hampshire: Palgrave Macmillan.
Charles, Ron. 2018. "Milkman—One of the Most Challenging Books of the Year—Is Also One of the Most Rewarding." *The Washington Post*, December 5, 2018. https://www.washingtonpost.com/entertainment/books/milkman--one-of-the-most-challenging-books-of-the-year--is-also-one-of-the-most-rewarding/2018/12/04/c3be904c-f764-11e8-8c9a-860ce2a8148f_story.html.
Connolly, William E. 1993. "Beyond Good and Evil: The Ethical Sensibility of Michel Foucault." *Political Theory* 21 (3): 365–389.
Deleuze, Gilles. 2002. *Nietzsche and Philosophy*, translated by Hugh Tomlinson. London: Continuum.
Dunkle, Ian. 2018. "Moral Physiology and Vivisection of the Soul: Why Does Nietzsche Criticize the Life Sciences?" *Inquiry* 61 (1): 62–81. DOI: 10.1080/0020174X.2017.1371827.
Foucault, Michel. 1990a. *The History of Sexuality, Volume II, the Use of Pleasure*, translated by Robert Hurley. Harmondsworth: Penguin Books.
———. 1990b. *The History of Sexuality, Volume III, the Care of the Self*, translated by Robert Hurley. Harmondsworth: Penguin Books.
———. 1991a. "Nietzsche, Genealogy, History." In *The Foucault Reader*, edited by Paul Rabinow, 76–100. New York: Pantheon Books.
———. 1991b. "What is Enlightenment." In *The Foucault Reader*, edited by Paul Rabinow, 32–50. New York: Pantheon Books.
———. 1995. *Discipline and Punish: The Birth of the Prison*, translated by Alan Sheridan. New York: Vintage Books.
———. 1997. "The Ethics of the Concern for the Self as a Practice of Freedom." In *Ethics, Subjectivity, and Truth: Essential Works of Foucault, 1954–1984*, edited by Paul Rabinow, 281–302. New York: The New Press.
———. 2014. *On the Government of the Living: Lectures at the Collège de France 1979–1980*, edited by M. Snellart, translated by G. Burchell. Hampshire: Palgrave Macmillan.
———. 2018. *Histoire de la Sexualité, tome IV, Les aveux de la chair*. Paris: Gallimard.
Guattari, Felix. 2000. *The Three Ecologies*, translated by Ian Pindar and Paul Sutton. London: The Athlone Press.
Joyce, James. 1991. *Stephen Hero*. London: Paladin.
Mitchell, Benjamin. 2016. "Dancing in Chains: A History of Friedrich Nietzsche's Physiological Relativism." PhD dissertation, York University, Toronto.
Nietzsche, Friedrich. 1997. *Daybreak: Thoughts on the Prejudices of Morality*, translated by R. J. Hollingdale. Cambridge: Cambridge University Press.

———. 2001. *The Gay Science*, translated by Josefine Nauckhoff. Cambridge: Cambridge University Press.

———. 2002. *Beyond Good and Evil: Prelude to a Philosophy of the Future*, translated by Judith Norman. Cambridge: Cambridge University Press.

———. 2004. *Human, All Too Human*, translated by Marion Faber and Stephen Lehmann. London: Penguin Books.

———. 2007. *On the Genealogy of Morality*, translated by Carol Diethe. Cambridge: Cambridge University Press.

O'Leary, Timothy. 2009. *Foucault and Fiction: The Experience Book*. London: Continuum Press.

———. 2017. "Sensibility." In *Symptoms of the Planetary Condition: A Critical Vocabulary*. Lüneburg: Meson Press.

Rabinow, Paul (ed.). 1991. *The Foucault Reader*. London: Penguin Books.

Thiele, Kathrin. 2008. *The Thought of Becoming: Gilles Deleuze's Poetics of Life*. Zurich: Diaphanes.

Wells, H. G. 2009. *The Island of Doctor Moreau*, edited with Appendices by M. Harris. Ontario: Broadview Editions.

Zola, Emile. 1893. *The Experimental Novel and Other Essays*, translated by Belle M. Sherman. New York: Casell Publishing Co.

Part III

INSTITUTIONS AND TECHNOLOGIES

8

Unwinding the Abstraction of Whiteness

Shannon Winnubst

Large pieces of brightly colored material are draped over bars, lying in heaps on the floor, swirling about in the winds of an electric fan. The rhythmic voices of six Latinx performers trading traditional Spanish "trabalenguas" (or "tongue-twisters") in call-and-response. A loosely choreographed movement begins to pulse across the six bodies, even as they are moving in disparate ways: pick up a piece of cloth, move it across the room, drape it over a standing ladder, take it off, move it to another corner, place it on the ground, go look for another piece of cloth or perhaps an electronic cord, pick that up, look around, take it to another piece of cloth, throw the cloth over a high bar, move, pick it up, put it down, change the position of a wooden block, move the laptop computer. And through it all, chant the trabalenguas, with frivolous gusto. Amidst all of this sonic unison and kinetic dispersion, we audience members take our seats and begin to do what we are trained to do, like Pavlovian dogs, as members of an audience: make sense of what is happening.

But we cannot. At first, we may find patterns of movement. Or even cast sub-narratives upon the bodies and objects: "The darker skinned woman keeps moving with the manual labor objects (ladder, block of wood, electric fan) and the lighter skinned woman plays with the laptop, so maybe it is a commentary on racialized capitalism." Our meager brains are rather pathetic in their ridiculous attempts at control. But the confusion is delightful, spurred by the melodic chanting, bright, textured fabrics, and kinetic blending of bodies and objects. It is easy to give in to the pleasure. And, as we do so, we begin to realize something else has been happening: the bodies, these six Latinx performers, have begun removing their clothing. Our comfortable confusion gets a shot of adrenaline.

As the sonic moves from the light-hearted trabalenguas to a disaggregated score of electronic pulses and melodies, we lose the only stable organizing pattern and are immersed in a tantalizing visual tableau of nude bodies, bright swaths of variously textured fabric, and objects of manual labor and technology. We are immersed, one might say, in an abstraction.

***

These are the opening scenes of the 90-minute performance of *This Bridge Called My Ass*, which Miguel Gutierrez and his troupe performed at the Wexner Center for the Arts on the campus of Ohio State University in January 2020. An homage to the 1981 canonical anthology, *This Bridge Called My Back* (coedited by Cherrie Moraga and Gloria Anzaldúa), the performance carries the work of that groundbreaking volume, which was explicitly written "by and for third world women," into Gutierrez's ongoing questions about the parameters and policing of abstraction, particularly in the worlds of dance, performance, and visual arts. As he put it during a panel discussion that preceded the performances at the Wexner Center, he began working on *This Bridge Called My Ass* to think about "abstraction and the particular people who are in the room [. . .] and what it means when artists of color engage abstract ideas together." That quest to engage abstraction explicitly as a racialized and racializing phenomenon has gripped Gutierrez for some time.

In 2018, he wrote a provocative essay, aptly published in *Bomb* magazine, entitled "Does Abstraction Belong to White People?" Located in the messy intersections of dance and performance art, Gutierrez asks a variety of fresh and perennial questions about the universal idiom in which whiteness speaks, lives, and flourishes. He tells a string of short stories from his own experiences with white dancers and choreographers who consistently dodge and avoid the force of race and racism in aesthetic choices: in a Movement Research reading group, "The Afterlives of Slavery: Experimental Performance and the Specters of Race," that discusses the work of Christina Sharpe, Fred Moten, and Thomas DeFrantz, a senior white artist dismisses the subject of race by declaring that "it all starts with motion!"; running a workshop in Nancy, France, Gutierrez divides the dancers by race, placing white dancers on one side and persons of color on the other, only to have a white dancer line up with the persons of color and insist "I am no different than him, gesturing to his best friend in the company who is Black"; responding to a performance that presents a dance from Martha Graham alongside one from Alvin Ailey, a well-known white choreographer insists that "you shouldn't try to interpret [the performance] at all" and yet fails to engage the work of Ailey; visiting an exhibit of William Eggleston at the Museum of Modern Art in New York, while feeling the eyes of other museum-goers on himself and his younger,

Black boyfriend, Gutierrez relays a quotation from Eggleston: "A picture is what it is [. . .] It wouldn't make any sense to explain them." The serial presentation of these stories contracts and intensifies their affective power. When Gutierrez moves from confusion to rage to grief, we are left with the sheer repetition of this endless stream of white choreographers, dancers, critics, and visual artists who never account for their own racialized positionality and refuse the value of interpretation altogether, especially if it invokes race. These white artists and critics move blithely through their careers and lives with the assumption that, as Gutierrez describes it, "their bodies can be signifiers of a universal experience that doesn't need to look at whiteness as an active choice or as the default mechanism of a lazy, non-existent critique." And yet, with this same blithe ignorance, these white choreographers, dancers, critics, and visual artists repeatedly trap people of color in the singular idiom of race.

At the surface, the question of Gutierrez's essay is a bit too easy: yes, as long as white people dominate the industries of aesthetic production, only white people will be given the carte blanche, to pun badly, to explore the aesthetics of pure form. The history of abstract expressionism confirms as much.[1] The more important twist, however, is Gutierrez's complex response to the ongoing reduction of his own work and the work of so many artists of color to the singular issue of race. When white artists move into abstract aesthetics, their work is read on the plane of conceptual interventions and intriguing work in pure form; when artists of color move into abstract aesthetics, their work continues to be read as a commentary on their racialized subject positions.[2] But the former is as racialized as the latter. This disavowal of race is a defining hallmark of whiteness, driven by the recurrent trope of universality that is endemic (although not exclusive) to whiteness, as scholars have diagnosed for over three decades.[3] Gutierrez deftly weaves this persistent disavowal through the essay as a constant thread of his lived experiences with white artists, dancers, choreographers, critics and audiences. But the stress-point for Gutierrez is not only this disavowal by whiteness of a racialized position, but also the doubling of that disavowal with the projection of the trap of race onto people of color. By framing this in the register of abstraction, Gutierrez opens fresh approaches that move us beyond the registers of sociology, economics, ideology, and history that continue to dominate critical diagnoses of whiteness. The focus on abstraction shifts us into the register of epistemology, even if at its most general possible mode. That is, while Gutierrez's essay focuses on the aesthetics of abstraction, especially in dance and performance arts, it opens onto a broader set of concerns and questions about abstraction as an epistemological habit that structures and enables whiteness.

At first glance, the framing of abstraction as an epistemology threatens to evaporate into a set of questions and concerns that is so general as to be meaningless. Taken as an epistemology, abstraction quickly proliferates into endless possibilities to the point of vanishing as a meaningful metric. Consider, for example, this snapshot of the endless list of possible kinds of abstraction-as-epistemology: transcendental critique, eidetic reductions, categorization, metaphysics, representation, analysis, language, generalization itself. Framed as an epistemology, abstraction can describe almost every mental formation and, thereby, begins to lose all definition. My turn to abstraction, therefore, is not an inquiry into abstraction *qua* epistemology, but into abstraction *qua* whiteness. While the more general inquiry into abstraction *qua* epistemology may function as a quintessential fetish of whiteness, I am not exploring that possibility here.

To put this in other terms, my focus in this chapter is on the general economy of whiteness, not of abstraction.[4] Following Gutierrez's lead, I suggest that abstraction is one of the most deeply seated, longest habits of "whiteness." Abstraction enables white institutions, laws, and technologies to hide from and disavow the violence that continues to be done in and through them. It enables a range of habitual modes of living, feeling, and moving through the world, such as liberal sentimentality and pornotroping. Abstraction, as I aim to argue and explore here, functions as both a vehicle of the violence of whiteness and a mechanism that enables white people to distance ourselves from that violence, perpetuating the systems of gross economic imbalance and greed that it feeds.[5] The gravitational pull of abstraction is fierce. In an effort to learn about how it enables and structures whiteness, I restrict my inquiry into abstraction to three specific iterations: the concept of capital; the conceptualization of difference as Other; and the concept of race. The ambition of the entire chapter is to read those three as constitutive parts of a broader habit of whiteness to dwell in the abstract as an enabling technique to disavow the persistent, material violence that perpetuates the social, political, and psychic power of whiteness.

AN ORIGIN STORY

6' × 1'4"
5'10" × 1'4"
5' × 1'2"
4'6" × 1'

I begin with the iconic work of Hortense Spillers's groundbreaking 1987 essay, "Mama's Baby, Papa's Maybe: An American Grammar Book." These are the measurements Spillers takes from the "Brookes Plan," a proposal before the British Parliament "late in the chronicles of the Atlantic Slave Trade" (72) to regulate slave vessels. Based on the investigative reporting of "a Captain Perry" of the slave ship named *The Brookes*, these are the measurements of the space allotted in the holds of slave ships to each "kind" of slave—that is, respectively, to each man, woman, boy or girl. For Spillers and for so much of Black feminist scholarship following her, these measurements are part of her remarkable argument about the systemic ungendering of Black flesh that is the American grammar. The implications of Spillers's work are staggering. For this chapter, I focus directly on the measurements as a concise account that can function as an origin story of the abstraction from violence that upholds whiteness and enables its constitutive disavowals.

The measurements crystallize what we might call the ontologically transformative power of global racialized capitalism. This abstraction of human lives into quantified units of cargo enabled the very early legal and economic systems of insurance and trade to take root and begin to flourish in colonial European countries. Building on a wide range of scholarship, Christina Sharpe explains this clearly in her elaboration of the infamous slave ship named the *Zong* in her latest book, *In the Wake: On Blackness and Being*. Originally based in the Netherlands (it was first named the *Zorg*, which perversely translates as "care" in Dutch), the *Zong* was purchased by a group of Liverpool merchants and became an object of social concern when the 1783 legal case of *Gregson v. Gilbert* was reported in British newspapers. This legal contest between the ship's owners (Gregson) and the insurance underwriters (Gilbert) concerned the economic value of 132 or 140 or 142 (the records are inconsistent) African men, women, and children who were murdered by the ship's captain and crew. Slave ships often attempted to transport more "cargo" than the ships were designed to hold: the *Zong* was designed to hold approximately 220 African men, women, and children, but sailed with 442–470 captive Africans on board. This resulted in what James Walvin calls "a crude human calculus [that] had evolved at the heart of the slave trade and was accepted by all involved: to survive, it was sometimes necessary to kill" (qtd in Sharpe, 36). The legal case between owners and insurers explicitly enacts what Sharpe calls "the lexico-legal transubstantiation" of human bodies into property (Sharpe 2016, 36). This transubstantiation animates the entire transatlantic slave trade and its ongoing afterlives: the immediate violence of physical captures; horrifying months-long transports; meticulously cruel practices of the coffle and the plantation; and the everlasting violence of the legal codes and economic systems of equivalency and fungibility that continue to buoy globalized capitalism. This transubstantiation of the accounting ledgers functions as a founding abstraction of whiteness.

Christina Sharpe brings the perversity of this abstraction fully into view along two paths. The first path is diagnostic. In her work on the *Zong*, Sharpe builds on the scholarship of historians to lay bare the systemic category of property loss, rather than murder, as the vehicle for legal, economic, and public legibility, including the more affective forms of psycho-social legibility such as sentimentality. She joins scholars such as Katherine McKittrick and Simone Browne to demonstrate precisely how this founding epistemology of numerical abstraction continues to enable the subordination of Black and brown bodies through contemporary technologies of power.[6] Alongside that diagnostic, Sharpe turns far greater attention to the second path, which I read as in step with Saidiya Hartman's work of critical fabulation—namely, the sustained labor of bringing forth "the living" of the deceased Africans that disrupts this systemic lexico-legal transubstantiation. In the section on the *Zong*, for example, Sharpe concludes with NourbeSe Philip's poetry, *Zong!*, which literally breathes life into the names of those deceased on the *Zong* through the graphic spacing on the page. Throughout the book, Sharpe elaborates scenes of beauty, joy, and vibrant living inside the ongoing brutalizing violence of "the afterlives of slavery." Sharpe's text thereby enacts, in very broad terms, the writing for survival and flourishing that characterizes so much of the work by Black feminists—and for Black lives.

For this work on whiteness, I argue the first diagnostic path of "the legal-lexico transubstantiation" lays out the labor that we white readers must undertake. More emphatically, I argue that this first diagnostic path should function as an origin story for whiteness: Hortense Spillers's iconic measurements capture both the precise epistemological problem and world-historical power of abstraction. As such, this origin story founds a narrative that is strikingly different from the Marxist narrative of capital. The transformation of African lives into quantified units of cargo subtends the very early stages of capitalism. While Cedric Robinson argued in 1983 for the insufficiency of Marxist analytics to capture the histories and possibilities of radical Black resistance, I argue that the foundational role of this legal-lexico transubstantiation exceeds and reorients the Marxist analytic at its roots. This legal-lexico transubstantiation in the ledgers of the transatlantic slave ships calls for an analysis of the abstraction of capital that is tethered explicitly to whiteness and its defining logic of anti-Blackness.[7]

Consider, for example, Marx's early accounts of alienation in his 1844 manuscripts *The Economic and Philosophic Manuscripts*, where he delineates five forms of alienation that are endemic to capital: nature, labor (product of labor), species, self and others. Marx's general argument is that labor in a capitalist system strips the worker of his (*sic*) essence-being as a human with creative capacities and inherent dignity. That is, capital transforms the worker into an object. But the Spillerian origin story exposes the central postindustrial, Eurocentric assumptions of Marx's account: the foundational transubstantiation of lives into numerical calculations is fundamentally occluded from the Marxist account. Pushing further with the work of Sylvia Wynter (2003), we also grasp how Marx's assumption about the species-being of "the human" is itself already constituted through three centuries of Man1, the colonizing, enslaving figure of whiteness that cloaks itself in the universal idiom of "human." Marx blandly assumes the universal idiom in his accounts of alienation, but only a population that might conceive of themselves as having a claim to the category of "human" can be lamented for losing that humanness. Put differently, the Marxist account is constrained to white subjects; standing outside the economic system as an object of exchange, the slave is already an object and cannot undergo the alienation from subjectivity that Marx describes. The Spillerian origin story exceeds and reorients the Marxist narrative of capital entirely.

My interest in this remarkably truncated account of Marx is, obviously, not with Marx. I am, rather, focused on how this outstripping of the Marxist analytic alters our understandings of whiteness. The intersection between race and class has been a particularly vexed question for scholars working on whiteness.[8] Broadly, this sociological scholarship addresses the need to distinguish class differentials within those who are white; this is also part of a resistance to formulating a strong definition of whiteness as a foundational structure. From a Marxist analytic, the fundamental problems of structural inequality, disenfranchisement and dispossession are explained through capital. The difference of race merely modulates the problem in particular manners, just as other categories of social difference (gender, sexuality, dis/ability, nationality) also modulate the fundamental problem of capitalist exploitation. To follow Spillers, however, is to insist that the specific abstraction of African lives into cargo plays a foundational role in the emergent systems of global capitalism. It is not only or entirely the abstraction of capital, but always and also the abstraction of Black living into numerical calculations that continues to animate the complex psycho-social structure of whiteness. Read through the Spillerian origin story, capital becomes a mode of abstraction from the foundational anti-Black logic that animates global capitalism at its roots. Not only in its function as a globalized mechanism of governmentality, but also as a concept assumed by a great deal of social critique, capital must be rewired both materially and analytically to account for this foundation in anti-Blackness.

AN EARLY TWENTIETH-CENTURY AMERICAN CAUTIONARY TALE

"I don't care what the book say, we don't owe nothing!"

In her most recent, stunning book *Wayward Lives, Beautiful Experiments: Intimate Histories of Social Upheaval*, Saidiya Hartman portrays a lived experience of abstraction that tethers this abstraction of capital to the foundational and ongoing horrors of anti-Black logic that structures the United States (and, *mutatis mutandis*, the globe). As a whole, the book is an astounding feat of sustained critical fabulation. Grounded in archival materials, Hartman excavates endless lives from various archives to portray the rich social life of young Black women who "were in open rebellion" (xiii) at the turn of the twentieth century (1888–1935) in cities along the Atlantic seaboard of the United States. As she tells us, "the aim is to convey the sensory experience of the city and to capture the rich landscape of black social life" (2019, xiii). More specifically, the collection aims "to illuminate the radical imagination and everyday anarchy of ordinary colored girls, which has not only been overlooked, but is nearly unimaginable" (2019, xiv). The stories are mesmerizing. Hartman spins tales that bring figures out of the archives with full-blown psychological interiority, relational nuance, and robust sensory experiences of the city: she "recreates the radical imagination and wayward practices of these young women by describing the world through their eyes" (2019, xiii).

The discourses against which Hartman operates all participate in the epistemology of abstraction. As she enumerates, she draws her knowledge about the lives of these young women from

> the journals of rent collectors; surveys and monographs of sociologists; trial transcripts; slum photographs; reports of vice investigators, social workers, and parole officers; interviews with psychiatrists and psychologists; and prison case files, all of which represent them as a problem. (2019, xiv)

The discourses of capital, sociology, medicine, and the many tentacles of the law frame these lives of young Black women through various forms of abstraction: the accounting ledger; the demographic taxonomy of a different population; the living laboratory ripe for experimentation; and the many lenses upon the pathological and the criminal. Across each of these, we can trace a kind of categorical abstraction that enables the specific abnormality to come to the fore. Out of each of these, Saidiya Hartman wrangles a very different kind of embodied, sensuously detailed, material array of "the insurgent ground of these lives" (2019, xiv).

One example particularly speaks to the questions of abstraction and whiteness I am pursuing here: "A Chronicle of Need and Want." This series of vignettes occur in two apartment buildings on Saint Mary Street in Philadelphia in 1888: "It was a block infamous for gambling, brawling, and whoring. Saint Mary Street was in the ward of the city with the highest death rate and the poorest residents of Philadelphia" (2019, 125). The two buildings are owned and operated by Helen Parrish and Hannah Fox, two women whom Hartman describes as in "a companionate marriage" (2019, xviii). Each of the women carries pristine liberal credentials, especially Miss Parrish, whose family has strong roots in abolitionist and advocacy organizations for "Indian Affairs." Their philanthropic work in the apartment buildings grants them both "a purposeful and meaningful life" (2019, 127) and also a shield against the indictments of "spinster, surplus woman, invert" (2019, 127). As Hartman puts it, "For Helen and Hannah, slum reform provided a remedy for the idleness of the privileged, a channel for the intelligence and ambition of college-educated women, and an exit from the marriage plot and the father's house" (2019, 127). This brief vignette, rooted in astounding historical documentation, offers an incisive and scathing portrait of liberal white femininity: the sentimentality, the narcissism, the feeble will and self-doubt, the moralizing indulgence of white benevolence, and the pornotroping fetish of "the Other" whom she is obligated to save. (We might also shorthand this as white feminine sentimental do-gooder narcissism.) It is an astonishingly concise diagnosis. But even more astonishing is the diagnoses of abstraction as an epistemology that enables and is woven into the affective arsenal of white femininity.

Take, for example, the opening scenes of the vignette: Fanny Fisher is cussing out Helen Parrish to the raucous, laughing delight of other young Black renters. The cause of the dispute is the exemplar of abstraction that grounds whiteness and all its twisted-up, disavowed violence: the accounting book. The scene is almost cartoonish for us twenty-first-century readers, with Helen "raising her voice above the thundering expletives [. . .] [to order] Fanny Fisher to be quiet. 'Don't ever dare speak to me in that manner again! Mrs. Fisher, take hold of yourself' " (2019, 124). This command, of course, only escalates the scene: "Damn Bitch! Katy Clayton doubled over with laughter. Once again they had succeeded in defeating Lady Bountiful and bringing her down to their level" (2019, 124). As Hartman gives us the interior monologue of Fanny following the outburst, "spent and exhausted," we hear the lived experience of the object that has always already been transformed by the accounting ledger. We hear the profound fatigue, the painful shame, the brutal repetition, and the suffocating trap of "the violence required to make life so ugly, or the hate necessary to keep Negroes trapped in the awfulest quarters of the city" (2019, 124). As Hartman expounds:

> No doubt, her dreams were bigger than two small rooms on a block reeking with the stench of human waste and garbage. [. . .] The injustice of having nothing and owing everything made her shout at Miss Parrish [. . .] Fanny objected to the

rent and the book that transformed their lives into columns of credit and debt. [. . .] It was a debt that could never be paid. (2019, 124)

The landlord's accounting ledger carries the slave ship's measurements and the abstraction of capital forward into the quotidian violence of the late nineteenth-century Black ghetto—a space that persists unchanged into the twenty-first century.

With the abstraction of capital fully in play, Hartman moves us swiftly from the accounting ledger to the sentimental interiority of Miss Helen Parrish, this epitome of an elite white liberal woman who conceives herself as a savior—and perhaps even friend—of young Black women. In so doing, the epistemology of abstraction extends beyond the abstraction of capital (personified by the accounting ledger) to the abstraction of the Other. A strong thread of nineteenth- and twentieth-century European philosophy has wrangled mightily with this problem of the Other. From Hegel's Master-Slave dialectic to Levinas's impossible face à face ethics, Lacan's foundational mirror stage and Irigaray's diagnosis of the specular gaze, we who are trained in this tradition are well schooled in this figure of the Other, especially its vexing role in the complex dynamics of recognition that overwhelm the inquiries. In Hartman's work, the abstraction of the Other unravels and fails to play the role of the mirror to the narcissist's unending desire and demand for recognition.

Tangled up in her unabashed narcissism, Miss Helen Parish's obsession with the lives of her renters knows few boundaries: she depends on the porter to spy on her tenants, delivering the delicious morsels that feed Helen's fantasies of what is happening inside her tenants' rooms. But she doesn't know quite how to respond to what she learns: her moralizing high ground proffers only judgment on the licentious sexual practices. Helen falters in her authority, goes to the police, and then regrets doing so. She cares about the women, but cannot find a way to express that care in anything other than judgment. And that voice of judgment is enabled and fueled by the fundamental abstraction of the Other.

Hartman delivers this to us quite clearly: A month prior to being cussed-out by Fanny Fisher, Miss Parrish graciously invited all of her tenants "to the colored lending library for cookies and lemonade" (2019, 128). Despite her disappointment that only the women, who "were a different matter" (2019, 128) from the men, attended, this gathering delivers one of Miss Parrish's fundamental fantasies:

> At the library, Helen and the women spoke freely, as if they were equals. [. . .] For a few hours, Miss Parrish did not threaten anyone with eviction or lecture Negro women about how to live. On a lovely July afternoon with the sun

pouring through the windows, Helen felt satisfied that they were friends. (2019, 129–130)

This confidence of being friends with one's Black inferiors—whether the house-slave, the maid, the tenant, the custodian, the gardener, the repairman, and so on—is a quintessential entanglement of projection and disavowal that structures white femininity and its affective labor. But it remains a fantasy that is fueled and enabled by the basic abstraction of those who are different, especially non-whites, as "Other." For Helen, this fabulous array of young Black women, whom Hartman brings to life with exquisite stories of tenderness, fears, longings, pleasures, dreams, and just pure living, remains "a faceless *them*" (2019, 133).

A mere month after the library lemonade party, Helen recounts her responses to seeing the young Black women "assembled in the yard on a late August afternoon involved in the mundane tasks of hanging clothes, cracking pecans, and tying off buttons" (2019, 133). With lines drawn directly from *The Diaries of Helen Parrish*, Hartman relays the transformation in Helen's perception upon seeing her tenants gathered together in a group: "alone they were amenable, but en masse far from it" (2019, 128). By late August, Helen's fantasies of friendship have morphed to the other side of narcissism's coin: she is paranoid. "Watching them gather in the courtyard, she looked on jealously, believing their intimacy to be a rejection of her" (132). Hartman even casts this in the register of vision that dominates so much of twentieth-century European feminist philosophy: "They were backlit by the late afternoon sun, the flat black shapes like silhouettes against the flank of sheets hanging behind them" (2019, 132). Black silhouettes against white sheets, the women morph quickly into ghoulish threats from deep in the American slavers' psyche. Helen's fragile white feminine ego lives and dies by this sword of the abstraction of young Black women into an Other:

> When they withheld their recognition [. . .] she was unable to find her better self reflected in their eyes [. . .] Helen could only see *treason en masse*, the lines of battle were drawn; she thought, *All are against me*. (2019, 133)

WORSHIPPING "DOG"

From this abstraction of the Other, we can move swiftly to its more specific iteration, the abstraction of the concept of "race." A concept with several lineages, stretching back to fifteenth-century Renaissance humanists and to nineteenth-century theories and practices of scientific racism across the United States and Germany,[9] race carries a complex, albeit quite unified, history of connotations. It is unsurprising, therefore, that it continues to provide a remarkably capacious Rorschach figure for the projection of a range of anxieties and attachments by white culture. In the early twenty-first century, amid the confusion wrought by fifty years of the incursion of neoliberal modes on conceptualizing the world, "race" is largely framed as a matter of ideologies: "Left" institutions celebrate diversity and inclusion, while "Right" institutions insist that they are "colorblind." Across both ideologies, "race" has not been more salient than other modes of social difference, all of which are evacuated of any significant historical or economic force. Just as the robotic list of differences and the infamous etcetera (race, gender, sexuality, age, ability, etc.) indicates, "race" circulates as a fairly meaningless signifier in neoliberal societies.

However, as the truth that belies this neoliberal charade, race is consistently used colloquially by white persons, communities, and institutions as a way to mark non-white bodies, behaviors, views, communities, and populations. Consider the most banal examples of naming Black music or Mexican food or an Indian accent and then indulge the discomfort of naming white music or white food or a white accent: why is the former quite common in white speech and the latter almost nonsensical and even transgressive? As Miguel Gutierrez (2018) illustrates in his essay, a scene is only marked as "raced" or "racialized" when there are non-white bodies involved. "Race" enables the persistent marking of non-whiteness, while hiding—or, perhaps, abstracting from—the hierarchy that it is designed to carry.

This hidden and disavowed hierarchy always carries the same structure: Anglo-Saxons at the pinnacle and Africans at the nadir. This is the explicit schematic that the concept of race is constructed to convey by nineteenth-century theories and practices of scientific racism, as we learn from Stephen Jay Gould's (1981) work on the early nineteenth-century field of craniometry in the United States. Bringing together new practices of anatomy and nascent theories of cognitive science, craniometry isolated the skull as the primary site of intelligence, personality, and behavior. The scientists thereby developed a critical new aspect of the concept of race: they tested their theories on physical bodies. For example, through various forms of "experimentation" and "data analysis," American craniologist Samuel George Morton, who was widely hailed as one of the greatest scientists of his time and who directly influenced eugenic practices of twentieth-century Nazi Germany, collected skulls from all over the world to prove that racial hierarchies were scientifically sound. Through extensive comparisons and meticulous methods of measurement, Morton concluded that the white race is the most superior form of the human species and the Negro race is the most inferior form, with indigenous "Indians" just above them. That is, through a "rational scientific method," Morton produced a scientific hierarchy of the races.

While we readers of the twenty-first century likely reject scientific racism in the name of the dubious concept of progress, we must still recognize that the concept of race develops and gains wide social traction as a mechanism to convey and reenforce this hierarchy. In our contemporary parlance, where scenes and events are "racialized" only when non-white actors are involved, the language of race allows us to avoid naming the hierarchy. Even more strongly, it allows us to avoid naming the centuries-long political-economic structures that uphold white cultures, persons, and institutions as superior to non-white cultures, persons, and institutions. As the work of Sylvia Wynter argues, this nineteenth-century connection of the concept of race to biological differences is not a new concept, but rather a new iteration of an older concept that emerges in the fifteenth century to convey the fundamental structure of white supremacy and its explicit anti-Indigeneity and anti-Blackness.

In "Unsettling the Coloniality of Being/Power/Truth/Freedom," Wynter (2003) follows the work of Aníbal Quijano to argue that the concept of "race" supplants the concept of "god" across the fifteenth to eighteenth centuries in Europe. With the broad strokes typical of early decolonial theory, Wynter provokes us to consider how the theological structure of Renaissance Christianity is carried forward through the concept of race that emerges full-blown in those nineteenth-century epistemologies of scientific racism. Wynter and Quijano reframe traditional readings of the Renaissance period to read the emergence of humanistic secularism alongside the transatlantic slave trade and global systems of colonialism that develop complex mercantile networks across the fifteenth to nineteenth centuries. With this reframing, Wynter argues that the figure of "Man1" emerges through the doubling of secularism and colonialism, including the transatlantic slave trade. This new figure, whom Wynter also calls "the human," is no longer tethered to the concept of God for his ontological placement in the cosmos: he is the nascent figure of the liberated, rational man of the Enlightenment. However, Wynter argues that Man1 does not fully abandon the theological structure of Christianity, but rather replaces the role of God with the concept of race. As she writes in her idiosyncratic prose:

> It was [race] that would enable the now globally expanding West to replace The earlier mortal/immortal, natural/supernatural, human/the ancestors, the gods/ God distinction as the one on whose basis all human groups had millennially "grounded" their descriptive statement/prescriptive statements of what it is to be human, and to reground its secularizing own on a newly projected human/ subhuman distinction instead. (2003, 264)

Wynter specifies the groups who are subordinated to ontologically inferior statuses through this concept of race: "the peoples of Black African descent

[. . .] would be constructed as the ultimate referent of the "racially inferior" Human Other, with the range of other colonized dark-skinned peoples, all classified as "natives," being assimilated to this category" (2003, 266). This is the same hierarchy that the nineteenth-century concept of race also upholds, while writing it in the register of biology and giving rise to Man2. Across Wynter's work, race is the concept that tracks across both figures of the human, fifteenth-century political Man1 and economic, biocentric nineteenth-century Man2.

By rendering the concept of race a descendant of theology, Wynter invites an unwinding of its layered abstractions. At the core of these abstractions is the fundamental structure of white supremacy, anti-Indigeneity, and anti-Blackness that propels the concept of race into existence. The deep connection back to theological structures also invites a Feuerbachian reflection on this transformation from "god" to "race" and the remarkable lasting power that it exerts, despite being debunked over and over as a meaningful biological distinction. The concept of race provides an essential abstraction for the persistent and resilient violence of anti-Blackness and anti-Indigeneity across the modern and contemporary world. It fundamentally occludes and thereby carries forward the ontological transubstantiation of anti-Blackness. Without the concept of race, the modern world would come undone.

FROM "GOD" TO "DOG"

Sylvia Wynter's provocations about the transformation of "god" to "race" brings me back to the final scene of *This Bridge Called My Ass*.

Following the kinetic meditation of nude bodies chanting trabalenguas, the troupe falls into a re-enactment of scenes from popular telenovelas. The melodrama is, of course, high: one man, who is the lover of another man, has had a child with one of the women, who in turn is triangulated with two of the women. The humor is largely lost on us gringos, who are occluded from this distinctly Latinx genre. After a shocking brandishing of a pistol, the handsome, sexy man who is wrongfully accused is shot and a somber turn ensues.

With a funereal air, the concluding scene brings a complete change in lighting, scene, and mood. All props are set to the side as the dancers tie much of the colorful material together into a long cord. They then gather together in a small group on one side of the arena as the spotlight falls to the other side. Touching one another sweetly, the dancers begin slowly pulling the long cord of bright material across the wide floor. As the spotlight brings it into focus, we see a small sculpture tethered to the end of the material cord. Made of random technological artefacts, we come to realize it is the shape of a dog. The entire performance concludes with the actors prostrate in mournful prayer, worshipping the holy of holies, DOG.

This inversion of Christian iconography and theology into the scatological prayers to DOG brings nervous giggles, raucous laughter, and pensive melancholia. The slightly ominous sermon includes such details as the shitting on front yards, providing a gentle and comical skewering of that bastion of whiteness—property. This sweet, melancholic inversion of the lost object of theology, god, into "man's best friend," dog, stimulates further curiosity, questions, and confusion. As a conclusion to this sensorial feast that is Miguel Gutierrez's answer to the whiteness of abstraction and the abstraction of whiteness, the worshipping of DOG leaves us off-balance. There is no routing this back through our dusty conceptual apparati, where whiteness precedes and shapes our interactions in the world so seamlessly that we do not see it. We leave the performance highly stimulated and rather joyfully confused. We can dismiss the confusion as the fault of an incoherent performance or some other long habit of aesthetic derision. Or we can open ourselves to the invitation, extended ever so provocatively, to carry the energy of this Latinx collective out into a world that may no longer mirror the abstracted narcissism of whiteness so clearly.

If we are to empower critique in the twenty-first century, I suggest this sort of decentering of white narcissism, affects, and epistemologies—grounded as they all are in an unexamined habit of abstraction—should be an essential point of departure.

NOTES

1. To follow out the precise contours of "abstraction" across various aesthetic fields exceeds the scope of this chapter. But abstract expressionism is a simple place to show the white domination of "the abstract," particularly as Black artists, such as Norman Lewis, were consistently framed as painting "about race."

2. For further discussion of this dynamic, see Uri McMillan's analysis of Adrian Piper's development as an artist who is interested in pure form and forever vexed by the constant demand to engage Blackness.

3. This is a dominant theme in scholarship from the 1990s on whiteness; see especially Dyer and Frankenberg.

4. I draw this term "general economy" from the three volumes of *The Accursed Share* by Georges Bataille. For Bataille, the framework of "general economy" affords a perspective that, while not pretending to be transcendental (or abstract), grasps connections that are not readily legible. See also *Queering Freedom* and *Reading Bataille Now* for elaborations.

5. To turn to the unraveling of whiteness as abstraction, I offer the following definition of whiteness: the legal, economic, and cultural formation that emerges through

settler and imperial colonialism, which are coterminous with the transatlantic slave trade, in colonizing and enslaving cultures across the sixteenth, seventeenth, and eighteenth centuries and persists into the twenty-first century, where it functions as a hegemonic, globalized psycho-cultural structure. Physiological demarcations, especially the "hair, skin and bones" that DuBois called out long ago, continue to guide this long-standing mapping of power, which can be seen all too easily at both local and global scales.

6. Katherine McKittrick's work extends Sharpe's analysis into the systems of surveillance and accounting that dominate contemporary living in the twenty-first century and draws on Simone Browne's work on facial recognition and the "arithmetics of skin."

7. The analytic ought also to be tethered to anti-indigeneity, but the specificity required for that joint-analysis is beyond the focus of this chapter. For excellent accounts of this dual analytic, see Day and King.

8. Canonical works in this area include Lipsitz, Omi and Winant, and Roediger.

9. See Gould and McWhorter for two meticulous accounts of how scientific racism is grounded in the assumption that there is a "natural" hierarchy between different races, with Anglo-Saxon at the pinnacle and Africans at the nadir.

BIBLIOGRAPHY

Anzaldúa, Gloria, and Cherríe Moraga (eds). 1981. *This Bridge Called My Back: Writings by Radical Women of Color*. Bloomsbury, London: Persephone Press.

Bataille, Georges. 1991. *The Accursed Share: An Essay on General Economy, Volume 1: Consumption*, translated by Robert Hurley. New York: Zone Books.

———. 1993. *The Accursed Share: Volumes 2 and 3: The History of Eroticism and Sovereignty*, translated by Robert Hurley. New York: Zone Books.

Browne, Simone. 2015. *Dark Matters: On the Surveillance of Blackness*. Durham and London: Duke University Press.

Day, Iyko. 2015. "Being or Nothingness: Indigeniety, Antiblackness, and Settler Colonial Critique." *Critical Ethnic Studies*, 1, no. 2 (Fall): 102–121.

Dyer, Richard. 1997. *White: Essays on Race and Culture*. New York and London: Routledge.

Frankenberg, Ruth (ed.). 1997. *Displacing Whiteness: Essays in Social and Cultural Criticism*. Durham and London: Duke University Press.

Gould, Stephen Jay. 1981. *The Mismeasure of Man*. New York and London: W. W. Norton Company, Ltd.

Gutierrez, Miguel. 2018. "Does Abstraction Belong to White People?" *Bomb Magazine*, November 7, 2018.

Hartman, Saidiya. 2019. *Wayward Lives, Beautiful Experiments: Intimate Histories of Social Upheaval*. New York and London: W. W. Norton Company, Ltd.

King, Tiffany Lethabo. 2019. *The Black Shoals: Offshore Formations of Black and Native Studies*. Durham and London: Duke University Press.

Lipsitz, George. 1998. *The Possessive Investment in Whiteness: How White People Profit from Identity Politics*. Philadelphia: Temple University Press.

Marx, Karl. 1978. "The Economic and Philosophical Manuscripts of 1844." In *Marx/Engels Reader*, edited by Robert C. Tucker. New York and London: W. W. Norton Company, Ltd.

McKittrick, Katherine. 2015. "Mathematics of Black Life." *The Black Scholar* 44, no. 2: 16–28.

McMillan, Uri. 2015. *Embodied Avatars: Genealogies of Black Feminist Art and Performance*. New York and London: New York University Press.

McWhorter, Ladelle. 2009. *Racism and Sexual Oppression in Anglo-America*. Bloomington: Indiana University Press.

Omi, Michael, and Howard Winant. 1986. *Racial Formation in the United States: From the 1960s to the 1990s*. New York and London: Routledge.

Philip, M. Nourbese. 2008. *Zong! As Told to the Author by Setaey Adamu Boateng*. Middletown, CT: Wesleyan University Press.

Robinson, Cedric. 1983. *Black Marxism: The Making of the Black Radical Tradition*. Chapel Hill, NC: University of North Carolina Press.

Roediger, David R. 1991. *The Wages of Whiteness: Race and the Making of the American Working Class*. New York and London: Verso.

Sharpe, Christina. 2015. *In the Wake: On Blackness and Being*. Durham: Duke University Press.

Spillers, Hortense. 1987. "Mama's Baby, Papa's Maybe: An American Grammar Book." *Diacritics* 17, no. 2 (Summer): 64–81.

Wilderson, Frank III. 2010. *Red, White and Black: Cinema and the Structure of Antagonisms*. Durham and London: Duke University Press.

Winnubst, Shannon. 2006. *Queering Freedom*. Bloomington: Indiana University Press.

———, ed. 2007. *Reading Bataille Now*. Bloomington: Indiana University Press.

———. 2020. "Race: The Ontological Crisis of the 'Human.'" In *Philosophy for Girls: An Invitation to the Life of Thought*, edited by Kimberly Garchar and Melissa Shew, 179–191. Oxford: Oxford University Press.

Wynter, Sylvia. 2003. "Unsettling the Coloniality of Being/Power/Truth/Freedom: Towards the Human, After Man, Its Overrepresentation—An Argument." *CR: The New Centennial Review*, 3, no. 3: 257–337.

9

How Not to Be Governed Like That by Our Digital Technologies

Mercedes Bunz

Studying my email inbox at the time when whistleblower Edward Snowden revealed the existence of U.S. mass surveillance by the NSA, I noticed something was wrong. My inbox was populated by my 2,401 email contacts, who were mostly outraged Europeans. But only one of them, my uncle Axel, who had worked for the European Commission for half of his life, sent me an email to let me know his new details using an email service secured against state eavesdropping. This fascinated me. There was explicit outrage that we did not want to be governed like this by our digital technologies, but without consequences—we were concerned but kept on using them. And I was a part of this problem one could describe as a lack of resistance. I had not changed my email addresses either. The problem stayed with me, until a few years later things got computationally more intense. By then, digital technologies had started to enter the next level, not just distributing information but calculating meaning: Deep neural networks had advanced machine learning systems to create algorithms that calculated the meaning of language and images better than ever before; tasks of "Artificial Intelligence" with which computer science had before struggled with for decades. And by calculating meaning they were entering our technical realities even further. I knew it was time to finally face the gap that had emerged between critique and technology and had become visible in that lack of resistance, time to sit down at my keyboard and ask "how not to be governed like that" by our digital technologies.

***

Digital technologies demand from us to return to Foucault's text "What Is Critique?," in which he famously posed the question "how not to be governed *like that"* (Foucault 1978, 44). Now that digital technologies and computation shape the realities of the overdeveloped world, what does it mean to ask "How not to be governed like that"? How are we being governed? Are we being governed *with* digital technology, that is, has this technology become an instrument of power? Or are we governed *by* that technology, is that technology a power of its own right? And if so, how does its power operate differently? After all, politics *counts* (Rancière 1995, 6) while the algorithms running our digital technologies *calculate*. Asking these questions, this chapter seeks to explore how digital technologies shift the power mechanism by returning to Foucault's inquiry into power and critique to show that the process of digital calculation obscures the power exercised on the individual and the individual's subjugation. Now there can be power, but that does not automatically mean anymore that there also can be individual resistance. Faced with this problem, the second part of this text searches for a different way of critiquing digital technologies, turning to Deleuze for philosophical support and to computer scientist Philip E. Agre for techno-theoretical assistance. Can Agre's concept of a "critical technical practice," which evolves from a *situation* instead of from a *subject*, become a way to insist "not to be governed like that" in the technical realities we live in today? To follow our desire "not to be governed like that" by our digital technologies, however, one first needs to return to the conceptual beginnings of this quest.

"LIKE THAT AND AT THAT COST"

Foucault's thinking of critique is profoundly inspired by Immanuel Kant's contribution to the question in his 1784 essay "What is *Aufklärung* [enlightenment]?" Foucault relates strongly to that text letting us know in "What Is Critique?" that his understanding of it is "not very different from the one Kant provided" and "not very far off in fact from the definition he was giving of the Aufklärung" (Foucault 1978, 47). This link to Kant's text is important. Kant's approach toward *"Aufklärung"* revolves around a specific unit that will also be the one Foucault is looking at—that of the individual: "Enlightenment is man's release from his self-incurred tutelage," is the famous opening sentence of "What Is Enlightenment?" (Kant 1784, 29). Similar to Kant's "release," Foucault approaches "critique" as a technology of the self, a practice involving the subject.[1] In his "very first definition of critique," Foucault (1978) characterizes it as "a way of thinking [. . .] I would very simply call the art of not being governed or better, the art of not being governed like that and at that cost" (45). The text then goes on to specify this "way of thinking" further as a "critical practice" which lies in the "desubjugation" of the subject itself and is directed against the "movement through which individuals are subjugated in the reality of a social practice through mechanisms of power" (47). Here, Foucault understands the subject not as a substance, but as "a form which is constituted through practices that are always specific to particular social and historical contexts," as Timothy O'Leary (2002, 110) specifies. Following Foucault along those lines to the contemporary historical context of neoliberalism, Shannon Winnubst (2020, 109) has delivered a trenchant analysis of the most recent form of a constituted "subject." That is, the rise of a subjectivity conceived as a market with distinct characteristics, leading to the effect that the subject is becoming "fungible" and is following a "calculating rationality." This chapter is taking up Winnubst's analysis while it is at the same time moving it from the reality of a social practice to the reality of a technical practice, two realms that overlap. The particular "reality of a social practice" has in some parts become the "reality of a technical practice," and this technical reality will be the focus of this text.

Let us sketch the expansion of technical practices to show their power to "subjugate" individuals. Digital technologies have become a resource of social life leading to technology and sociality becoming tightly interwoven, at times inseparable (Marres 2017, 7–44). Ever since digital technology spread widely into our everyday lives, device by device, service by service, and data point by data point, it has played a substantial part in the everyday actions of our overdeveloped world. This is the first line of inquiry that comes into view, when moving closer to our object of study: the omnipresence of digital technologies, which informs their mechanisms of power. This omnipresence led to digital technologies taking on more and more important roles on different levels from the social to the political: digital technologies transformed the *micro-level* of everyday life as users delegated "a vast swath of everyday activities to highly packaged and curated software" (Morris and Murray 2018, 8) waking us up in the morning, connecting us to our loved ones far away, while at the same time disturbing our work/life balance by seducing us with notifications to work on weekends. They also transformed the *macro-level* of whole populations: computational infrastructures and digital devices are being used for mass surveillance (Snowden 2019; Zuboff 2019) and enact new modes of racial profiling (Benjamin 2019), while they also spread messages of political resistance (Tufekci 2017).

Let us stay with this last paragraph for a moment, as it is worthy of further inquiry. The examples from the list above, covering both the micro and macro-level of technical practices, demonstrate how widespread digital technologies are. This, as Jef Huysmans (2016; also Bratton 2015) pointed out, is leading to new ways for power as it is now being more and more prevalent beyond institutions. Huysmans refers to this as "extitutional," in opposition to "institutional," noting that "the relations and practices of governance in various areas of life, including education, medical practice, mental health, and security [. . .] are dispersing beyond the physical and spatial confines of the institutions that exercise them" (2016, 78). The shift toward power being exercised in an extitutional manner is important. Digital technologies are media that disperse governance beyond institutions, thereby opening up "extitutional worlds," "sites" and "moments," and this has resulted in digital technologies becoming closely interwoven with "power" in a new and different way.

At the same time and running somewhat contrary to the above observation of technology's link to power, the examples listing how digital technologies have transformed the micro- and macro-level of our everyday world also demonstrate how open-ended and many-sided those technologies are. When it comes to power and resistance, digital technologies can be used to enhance power as well as to resist power, thereby showing that they are inhabited by a critical paradox that confirms Foucault's remark that "power is not something that is acquired" once and for all (1976, 94). Power exercised through technology is *situated*: one and the same technology can be used to *sustain* as well as to *resist* political power, meaning that digital technologies are often at the same time emancipatory *and* suppressive, democratic *and* dictatorial. So, technology is not of a specific power, because of its potential of taking part in both: power and resistance. This paradox characterizes digital technologies, which are being used to govern us; at the same time, we use them to resist being governed "like that." Now, for readers of Foucault this critical paradox is not at all unexpected. In a brief passage, consisting of five pages regarding "power" in *The History of Sexuality, volume 1*, Foucault (1976, 92–97) links power closely to "resistance" which is "never in a position of exteriority in relation to power" (95).

More interesting regarding an understanding of the governance of digital technology is, however, that in this passage he also points to a third element next to "power" and "resistance": "force" or "force relations"—and it might be here where one can learn that technology is not a power but that it operates a new and different power mechanism. Foucault's positioning of "force" as "the first instance" of power is unusual, as Deleuze (1986, 112–115) has noticed. Foucault (1994) uses the term (in French also *force*) eleven times over the five pages exclusively concerned with power (*pouvoir*), whereby "force" is never addressed as an activity and also does not appear as a verb. Throughout Foucault's argument "force" remains an attribute linked to relations, a word that is always used in its plural form: "force relations" translated from the French expression *rapports de force*, an expression usually used to describe a still developing "power relationship" or a "balance of power" that is still evolving. According to Foucault, "power must be understood in the first instance as the multiplicity of force relations immanent in the sphere in which they operate, and which constitute their own organization" (92).

Described as a "multiplicity" or as "manifold," Foucault uses "force" as a way to open up power and to position it as a sphere made up of still-evolving force relations that are about to become specific connections; connections either of resistance to the manifesting powers or of power itself. It is here that Foucault's remarks resonate directly with observations that have been made about digital technologies, such as Donna Haraway's remark: "We're living in a world of connections—and it matters which ones get made and unmade" (cited in Kunzru 1997). But as digital technologies make up a field that operates fundamentally different to politics—not counting but calculating—we will need to ask ourselves which connections are being made as well as how those connections function. The question this text follows is therefore: How do the multiplicities of force relations take effect in digital technologies?

Critical technology studies began to investigate the relations and connections being made by digital technology early on. For example, Kittler (1993), Agre (1997), Chun (2006), Suchman (2007), Mackenzie (2006, 2017), or Rieder (2020) explored the functionalities of digital technologies as mechanisms of power in fine detail, thereby contributing to new scholarly fields such as critical media theory and critical technology studies. At the same time, other scholars used computational aesthetic interventions to critically map the borders of computational logic (Fuller 2003; Goriunova and Shulgin 2005; Andersen and Pold 2011) or studied relevant technical interventions in computational counterculture such as hacking (Coleman 2012). Over time and as digital technology became more and more part of everyday life, a third approach started to evolve, looking at algorithms sorting information and communication for the new masses now being called "users" (Bratton 2015, 254–292). Computational toolkits for cultural and sociological research such as digital methods (Rogers 2013) emerged, leading to the approach of digital sociology (Marres 2017). Those seminal critical studies of digital technology analyzed their force relations in great detail by working through and critiquing algorithmic features and their properties. This soon showed that digital technologies should not be simply understood as an "instrument" used to operate our existing social realities. Rather, digital technologies have to be understood as transforming the mechanisms of governance itself. For in their calculated socio-technical realities, "to be governed" means something profoundly different.

"TO BE GOVERNED"

Foucauldian studies of governance have become a field of their own ever since Foucault introduced the neologism "governmentality" in his late work to explore the mediation between power and subjectivity (Lemke

2016, 3). Apart from a few exceptions such as Winnubst (2015, 2019), this dimension of Foucault's work has long been discussed in the context of biopolitics and questions of security, before an increasing impact of digital technologies led to a range of studies exploring algorithms as their own unique technique of governmentality (among others Amoore 2009; Rouvroy 2011, 2013; Cheney-Lippold 2011; Mackenzie 2017, 51–74; Rieder 2017, 2020; Aradau/Blanke 2017, 2018; Bucher 2018, 32–38; Benjamin 2019). And next to these excellent studies advancing our knowledge of algorithms being used by power, there were very soon also studies on how the usage of algorithms transformed the power mechanism itself (Rouvroy 2013; Goriunova 2019a); a transformation so profound that it created the need to rethink critique.

Linking worries about a more general crisis of critique (Latour 2004; Drucker 2015) with the power mechanisms of data analysis, Antoinette Rouvroy declared even "The end(s) of critique" (2013). Or was it that critique simply needed to be thought anew? Could it be that this was the end of a specific power mechanism and its force relations, and the start of another? Rouvroy's groundbreaking text "The end(s) of critique: data behaviorism versus due process" describes in detail how algorithmic practices profoundly transform the mechanisms of critique as we know it, key point by key point—regarding knowledge, subject and with it power relations. The text investigates the way in which knowledge of algorithmic governmentality is set up profoundly differently to the knowledge gained in political governmentality. In the algorithmic realm, Rouvroy writes, "reality—that knowledge appearing to hold—is always already there, immanent to the databases, waiting to be discovered by statistical algorithmic processes" (2013, 147). The effect is that "knowledge is not produced *about* the world anymore, but *from* the digital world" (147, emphasis added). By reducing its operation to digital data "from the digital world" only, the new power mechanism manages to sideline the role of the subject. Power "operates with infra-individual data and supra-individual patterns without, at any moment, calling the subject to account" (Rouvroy 2013, 144–145).

This new power mechanism of algorithmic governmentality as "without subject" is an observation that has also been explored in-depth by Olga Goriunova (2019a). The transformation of the subject in the digital realm, which Goriunova's text brings fully to the fore, plays a key point in the context of the question "how not to be governed like that," because Foucault's and also Kant's critiques evolve from the subject, the individual. And due to a repositioning of subjectivity in our digital technologies, the case of critique has become more difficult. In "The Digital Subject: People as Data as Persons," Goriunova analyses step by step the "new form of subject construction that arise out of computational procedures" (2019a, 3). Referencing earlier research into data (Gitelman and Jackson 2013, 8–9), she starts by pointing out that concepts of "data double" or a "data shadow" are misleading when referring to digital subjects. What matters more than linking specific data decisions back to one individual subject is the availability of a wide range of decision patterns. The individual subjectivities behind those decisions do not matter, fragmentary aspects and "shreds" are sufficient, there is no need to prove them authentic. On the contrary, the decisions are rooted in the calculation of thousands of fragments taken from thousands of individuals from which "supra-individual patterns" evolve. In Goriunova's words:

> Digital subjects are values, dynamically re-instantiated correlations, rules, and models, shreds of actions, identities, interests, and engagements, which are put into relation with each other, disaggregated, categorized, classified, clustered, modelled, projected onto, speculated upon, and made predictions about. (2019a, 9)

When creating a digital subject, data is always interlinked and processed, a technical aspect that is essential: digital traces of one individual subject alone are algorithmically not relevant. While from the point of view of a human subject moving through the digital world, there is a direct relation to her or his data, this is different from the point of view of the algorithm. When calculating, the human subject and its individual data are linked up by the algorithm with other data points in order to find supra-individual patterns. Only when several data points can be calculated can the data "make sense" from the algorithm's point of view. The plurality of data is of much greater importance to the calculation of the digital subject than the scarce input by one individual.

Through foregrounding the calculation, algorithmic governmentality avoids direct force relations to individual entities or subjects. Earlier forms of governmentality used disciplinary, instrumental, or neoliberal reasoning to shape the subjectivities of human individuals they ruled over, aiming for direct impact: disciplining, reasoning with, addressing the subject. The operation of algorithmic governmentality, however, is grounded in calculation which is fundamentally "opposed to relation," as Goriunova writes (2019a, 4). The new power mechanism operates by setting up a non-relation, by establishing "distance." "Distance" is the mechanism through which algorithmic governance rules: "a digital subject is neither a human being nor its representation but a *distance* between the two" (Goriunova 2019a, 4), and this distance can be "interrupted, recruited, intersliced" (6). The effects on the power mechanism of algorithmic governance and its force relations are profound. With the emergence of the digital subject, "to be governed" has changed. The reciprocal relation that was typical for the power mechanism described by Foucault: "Where there is power, there is resistance, and yet, or rather consequently, resistance is never in an exteriority to power" (1976, 95). This relation has been interrupted. The fact that there is power no longer means that there will be resistance because the relationship is no longer reciprocal. There is a relation from the individual subject to the data input which sets off the calculation of the digital subject, but the same direct relation is not the case anymore the other way around. The data of the individual initiates a calculation that does not lead to "its" digital subject, because the digital subject is always already part of a much broader calculation. In other words, the digital subject is always more characterized by the data set than by the individual who initiated the calculation and, as a mere prompt, finds itself now exterior to power.

Being calculated through data mining and analytics, the digital subject is linked to an infra-personal pattern for which the individual subject does not count. That infra-personal pattern is found through data mining calculations that are not representative—they exceed conventional statistics, as Adrian Mackenzie writes: "[C]onventional statistical regression models typically worked with 10 different variables (such as gender, age, income, occupation, education level, income) and perhaps sample sizes of thousands" (2015, 434). While ten variables remain representative, the data mining calculation that creates the digital subject depends on many more variables, or as Mackenzie puts it: "data mining and predictive analytics today typically work with hundreds and in some cases tens of thousands of variables and sample sizes of millions or billions" (434). Using "tens of thousands of variables" and "sample sizes of millions or billions" to create a digital subject obscures any link to the individual's sample that initiated a calculation. By calculating and mixing the individual's sample with millions of other data bits, the individual has been successfully distanced from its input. Instead of a direct relation between individual and digital subject, the millions of other samples used for the calculation of the digital subject have deflected any direct relation. The computational power mechanism operates by keeping the individual at a distance, by denying a certain relation. Through distancing the individual from the digital subject, the force relations have changed. The reciprocal relation of power/resistance described by Foucault (1976, 95–96) is annulled. The construct of a digital subject, through which algorithmic governance operates, cannot be negated anymore directly by the individual, because its individual input has become irrelevant through calculation, through mixing the individual's data with thousands of other data points. Now there can be power, but that does not automatically mean that there also can be individual resistance—unless a different way of resisting can be found.

"BY OUR DIGITAL TECHNOLOGIES"

Finding this new method of resistance is not straightforward. When algorithmic practices transformed the reciprocal relationship of power/resistance thereby shifting the power mechanism, they also outmaneuvered the power of "negativity" that had been intimately linked to critique (Coole 2006). Critique "*not* to be governed like this" was fueled by the reciprocal relationship between resistance and power, or in Foucault's words: "Resistances [. . .] are inscribed in the latter [power] as an irreducible opposite" (1976, 96). In the case of algorithmic governmentality and its digital subject, however, power shapes the digital subject (a construct that does have power and produces an effect on the individual); at the same time, the calculation of the digital subject has been linked to millions of other samples and obscured by a calculation, thus making the action of one individual who resists that algorithmic power irrelevant.[2] The individual cannot inscribe itself as an opposite to the algorithm, or as Rouvroy states: "Algorithmic governmentality is a mode of governmentality without negativity" (159). And exactly this aspect—the helplessness demonstrating the loss of the power of negation—can be seen in contemporary sociological observations as the following three examples show: the concern about privacy disclosures on Facebook, the mapping and acquiring of public space by Google, and the mass surveillance by U.S. security services. In all three cases, there is critique as well as extant alternatives that could lead to a negation of the status quo, but no action is taken by the subjects.

First, platforms and the disclosure of personal information: It is a well-known issue that the power of platforms and their reign over personal information has led to privacy issues, for which one of the most successful platforms at the beginning of the twenty-first century, Facebook, is a good example. Over a longer period of time, research studies have shown again and again that "users" are worried about their data. A 2014 survey found that 91 percent of Americans "agree" or "strongly agree" that people have lost control over how personal information is collected (Madden 2014), and that a substantial percentage of Facebook's users are worried (Wilson et al. 2012). Interestingly, while this concern has been articulated in these studies, the same users behaved differently when online, and several reports noticed this discrepancy between reported privacy concerns and actual privacy behavior online (Wilson et al. 2012, 212 quoting Acquisti and Gross 2006; Stutzman and Kramer-Duffield 2010; Tufekci 2008). From the perspective of the user, there seems to be a non-relation between their individual concern and their online profile. They are concerned, but their concern does not lead them to delete their Facebook accounts.

Second, the monopolistic power of specific services: A second case showing the same paradox of personal concern not leading to personal action is the discrepancy between the critique in Germany being uttered against the corporation Google and the usage of the same service. German digital culture is known for being extremely sensitive about data privacy. Consequently, German citizens are highly critical of big technology corporations collecting users' data, and especially critical toward Google (Schomakers et al. 2019; Sauerbrey 2014). This might be expected to manifest itself in Google's services being left in favor of a more independent search engine, for example, DuckDuckGo. The actual usage of the search engine Google in Germany, however, is paradoxically among the highest worldwide with a market penetration of 95 percent; compared with a lower market share of 88 percent among its far less concerned U.S. users (Kunst 2019).

Third, the surveillance of digital communication: An example can be found in the minimal reaction to whistleblower Edward Snowden's disclosures of global U.S. surveillance. Top secret documents leaked by ex-NSA contractor Snowden were made public in June 2013. They proved the collection of internet communications facilitated by U.S. internet companies such Microsoft, Facebook, Apple, or Google. Those U.S. companies were legally obliged to hand over email, video and voice chat, file transfers, videos, photos sent to or from specific selectors as well as their social networking details, information that was then stored on government databases. After the disclosures, U.S. citizens expressed discomfort with this activity. In a survey conducted by the Pew Research Centre (Madden 2014), 61 percent of respondents assumed that the government is monitoring their personal communications and said they have become less confident that surveillance efforts serve the public interest. This criticism, however, stands in contrast to people's actual behavior: only 18 percent say they have changed the way they use email "a great deal" or "somewhat" (2014, 4) leading the Pew Research Centre to remark that "a notable numbers of citizens say they have not adopted or even considered some of the more commonly available tools that can be used to make online communications and activities more private" (5).

If we take a step back from these examples, what is it that comes into view? The link between power and resistance appears to be interrupted. We find individuals who do "not want to be governed like that" but at the same time continue as if nothing had happened—they could withdraw but they do not resist the very powers which they see as oppressive. As digital consumers, we all continue to comply with our digital services, even though we feel threatened and do not like the way we are treated. The belief that direct resistance is possible, or that in direct resistance there is a counter-power, seems to be absent in times of algorithmic governmentalities and of "platform sovereignty" (Bratton 2015, 51, 374). In the examples above, resisting—negating the technical practice by withdrawing from it—does not seem to be seen as having an effect on the technical practice, or as having an effect on the power of a technical service. From the point of view of the individual in front of the screen, from *our* point of view, a turn to a different digital tool is merely a change of interfaces. Choosing a new tool does not affect the way power is enforced on us. On screen and through data mining, we have become part of a technical practice that through calculation always already exceeds our own individuality and that of any other individual. Even though the calculation has been triggered by our data, the fact that it is then further processed and calculated means that our data has been effectively positioned out of direct reach. The contemporary operation of digital technology transforms the data of an individual into a pattern. The pattern affects the subject but does not represent it—there is no direct link. This "non-relation" with which the digital subject operates is a very effective power mechanism. Negating a non-relation is not an option. Different ways to criticize digital technology and its calculations need to be found. Ways that center the efforts of critique less on a direct link between power and the subject. These ways emerge when we approach the concept of critique from a different angle: That of problematization leading to affirmation, a possibility frequently discussed by Deleuze which has been brought forward productively by, for example, Grosz (2003) and Thiele (2008). In the following, Deleuze's concept of critique will be read in view of our desire "not to be governed like that" by our digital technologies, to be then linked to observations about a critical technical practice by computer scientist Philip E. Agre.

"NOT"

While the option of resistance through direct negation has been deflected, our desire remains: we still do "not" want "to be governed like that." The task is now to find other ways to bring about the "not" in order to resist. To explore this task, this section will turn for assistance from Foucault to his comrade Deleuze while still being guided by Foucault's iconic motto that he himself called "the eternal question" (1978, 44): How not to be governed like that. In exploring alternative ways of "not" doing something, Deleuze's work on the production of theoretical concepts, including his problematization of negation, is helpful (Braidotti 2017, 291–292). While Foucault's main interest lies in analyses of power through detailed genealogies, Deleuze's work in the 1960s tends toward more conceptual and theoretical thinking that aims to leave the concept of direct negation behind, turning toward a radical version of "affirmation"—radical as it needs to be a different path for resistance. However, Deleuze and Foucault share a common philosophical gesture. As others have shown (Koopman 2016), both were critical of the reception of programs of negative dialectics dominant in their country and time, and both shared a debt to a certain aspect of Kantian philosophy. This results in a general appreciation for each other's work in interviews and reviews, leading Foucault to embrace the concept of affirmation that Deleuze had developed in *Difference and Repetition*, on which he commented in his review of Deleuze's book:

> The freeing of difference requires thought without contradiction, without dialectics, without negation; thought that accepts divergence; affirmative thought whose instrument is disjunction; thought of the multiple [. . .] We must think problematically rather than question and answer dialectically. [. . .] And now, it is necessary to free ourselves from Hegel—from the opposition of predicates, from contradiction and negation, from all of dialectics. (Foucault 1970, 358–359)

Turning with Foucault to the Deleuzian concept of radical affirmation, the first thing to note is that this kind of affirmation is not straightforward—it is not simply affirming something, as Thiele (2017) has pointed out. Just switching from a negative to a positive attitude is not deemed radical enough. According to Deleuze, such a move would still remain within the framework of practicing dialectics. To generate radical difference, a difference that is at the same time "different in itself" (Deleuze 1968, 55) is needed.

Deleuze enrolls, therefore, a carefully constructed neglect of the negative step by step and without negation; work that started in his writings on Nietzsche's *Bejahung* [affirmation] in *Nietzsche and Philosophy* (1962), which was then developed further in *Difference and Repetition* (1968). This is the book in which Deleuze leaves Nietzsche further behind by making his suspicion of the negative fully explicit: "One can always mediate, pass over into the antithesis, combine the synthesis, but the thesis does not follow" (Deleuze 1968, 51). For: "difference in itself [. . .] cannot be reduced or traced back to contradiction" (51). "It is not the negative which is the motor" (55). Having found that affirmation cannot be the "other" of negativity, Deleuze maneuvers around the concept of negation thereby changing the view: "Negation is difference but difference seen from its underside, seen from below. Seen the right way up, from top to bottom, difference is affirmation" (55). By changing perspectives, the concept appears anew. Indeed, everything looks radically different as Deleuze notes: "This proposition, however,"—the proposition to see difference from top to bottom—"means many things" (55); and he starts to list them: "that difference is an object of affirmation; that affirmation itself is multiple; that it is creation but also that it must be created, as affirming difference, as being difference in itself" (55).

Deleuze's take on affirmation places it as unrelated to negation. None of its features (being multiple, being a creation, which must be created, being different in itself) is related to an oppositional negative. To Deleuze, "difference is the object of affirmation or affirmation itself" (52). So how could this affirmation, whose motor is radical difference, work to criticize digital technologies?

Turning again to the text, one sees that Deleuze describes affirmation not as a simple relation, that is, it is not the affirmation *of* something one is for—a move that can be useful as the power mechanism of technology also operates with a "non-relation" as Goriunova (2019a) pointed out. Instead, Deleuze explicitly connects difference with affirmation describing it as "multiple" and as "a creation which must be created" (1968, 55). Here, affirmation is *a process* that is creative, and is producing something. To describe this process, Deleuze makes use of a somewhat obscure image he steals from Nietzsche; after all, "theft is primary in thought" (200). The image of a game of dice is taken from Nietzsche's *Thus Spoke Zarathustra*. This image figures prominently in Deleuze's *Nietzsche and Philosophy* as well as in *Difference and Repetition* and *Logic of Sense* (1969)—an image that Deleuze scholars (e.g., Thiele 2008, 183–184) turn to often. Adapting two paragraphs of *Thus Spoke Zarathustra*, Deleuze links the throw of dice to chance and addresses chance as "an object of affirmation" (1968, 198). Deleuze describes the force relations at play further as constituting a new structure, one that forms a new problem: "The throw of the dice carries out the calculation of problems, the determination of differential elements or the distribution of singular points which constitute a structure." And "the disparates which emanate from a throw begin to resonate, thereby forming a problem" (198). This forming of a problem is the core work of Deleuze's radical affirmation. It unfolds through the creation of a problem, a problem that has not been set up intentionally but that happens through chance which needs to be affirmed, to allow it to constitute its own structure.

Interestingly, Foucault saw his own work related to this approach remarking: "The notion common to all the work that I have done [. . .] is that of problematization, though it must be said that I never isolated this notion sufficiently" (Foucault 1984 cited in Koopman 2016, 106). Could this notion of problematization, which Foucault and Deleuze embrace, and which recently also gained attention in sociology (Savransky 2020), help to find a way of critiquing digital technology? Can Deleuze's slightly cryptic and obscure concept become a way to approach the calculations of our digital technologies critically? At first this seems unlikely, the more as it is known that Western discourse usually addresses digital technologies not at all as the "forming" of "a problem" but rather uncritically as a "solution" as Morozov (2013) showed. But what if we instead understand the calculations performed by our data mining digital technologies not as a solution but as a process of creation? The next section will explore this with the help of observations that computer scientist Philip E. Agre (1997) made in his text "Towards a Critical Technical Practice."

"HOW"

Agre's text "Towards a Critical Technical Practice: Lessons Learned in Trying to Reform AI" lends itself well to Deleuze's and Foucault's approach of "thinking problematically" instead of "answering dialectically" (Foucault 1970, 358). As a computer scientist informed by post-structuralist theory, in particular Foucault (Agre 1997, 148, see also Dieter 2014), the text can be read as an example of criticizing digital technologies through problematizations, which is described by Agre as a move "Towards a Critical Technical Practice"; a move that happens on two intertwined levels. On the level of *critical* practice, the text repositions and opens up technical practice via problems toward a constructive collective engagement. On the level of *technical* practice, to which the next section will turn, the text recalls Agre's struggle in pushing a paradigm change in Artificial Intelligence against a rule-based symbolic approach that reduced the world to a rule-following model mirrored by an artificial mind (143).

Agre and his collaborating colleagues did not want to approach AI as an artificial mind that simply follows rules. They were trying to divert from this mentalist notion of AI adopted by the established community of AI researchers at the time. They wanted to think of AI instead as a calculation that could acknowledge the complexity and uncertainty of the world and its messiness—a world in which even "routine interactions" would be inhabited by "chance" (1997, 149). Incorporating that chance into programming, they believed that AI needed to open up to interaction and improvisation. To support his research problematizing the planning approach followed by others in the field and in order to find a different computational approach, Agre started studying things and situations that did not go according to plan in his own everyday activities.

> I became interested in what I called "hassles," which are small bits of trouble that recur frequently in routine patterns of activity. Having noticed a hassle (e.g., an episode in which silverware tried to jump into the garbage disposal while washing dishes), I would write out in some detail both the episode itself and the larger pattern's attributes as a hassle. (146)

Agre recorded those "hassles," the "mundane mechanics of his daily life" (146) as he also called them, exploring them in depth. Describing this with a Deleuzian vocabulary, one could say: when distributing singular points through writing up a hassle in detail, disparates start to emanate from this "throw." Soon, Agre started to notice an effect of his problematizations: "writing out the full details of an actual episode of being hassled would raise an endless series of additional questions, often unrelated to what I was looking for" (146). Agre remarks that this activity pushed him further away from the concepts that he had been taught. Agre's practice of problematization was "forming a problem":

> In broad outline, my central intuition was that AI's whole mentalist foundation is mistaken, and the organizing metaphors of the field should begin with routine interaction with a familiar world, not problem solving inside one's mind. In taking this approach, everything starts to change, including all of the field's most basic ideas about representation, action, perception, and learning. (149)

Far beyond just correcting the calculations of mentalist AI, Agre's approach was soon questioning the field's "most basic ideas"—and it is here that Agre's technical struggle resonates with Deleuze's concept of radical affirmation. This resonance starts with finding a problem through writing up the hassles from which new and additional questions emanate; it then leads Agre to a profound reorientation in which "everything starts to change" including the field's basic ideas, making Agre's approach toward AI "different in itself" (Deleuze 1968, 55). This results in Agre's approach being one of "affirmative difference" because Agre is not positioning his approach as an alternative to or negation of the prevailing mentalist notion of AI as a mind. On the contrary, as he states, "the very concept of alternatives is misleading" (150).

By refuting alternatives, Agre deviates profoundly from (still existing) approaches toward digital technologies and their strong focus on solutions. A focus that often tempts computer scientists, as Agre writes, to assume that "the only legitimate form of critical argument is that 'my system performs better than your system on problem X' " (150). Agre's approach leaves behind this technical rationale and its goal "to write programs that solve problems better than anybody else's" (149). His reorientation from planning to being explicitly open to "hassles" (or "problems") directs him instead toward a different technical practice when addressing computational problems. But while Agre's description of finding and developing such a different technical practice resonates as shown above with Deleuze, one piece is still missing. In what way is Agre's approach more than just a new technical practice? What is it exactly that makes it a *critical* technical practice? And which aspects of his critical practice can be used for our quest "not to be governed like that" by our digital technologies?

Agre does not want to deliver a solution but aims to find and follow technical problems. As we will see in this section, the critical part of Agre's technical practice starts with introducing this very different approach toward technology: "to think problematically" (Foucault 1970, 358). Certainly, this is the suggestion one finds at the end of Agre's own text—to pay attention to finding and diagnosing technical difficulties and problems:

> Faced with a technical difficulty, perhaps we can learn to diagnose it as deeply as possible. Some difficulties, of course, will be superficial and transient. But others can serve as symptoms of deep and systematic confusions in the field. (1997, 154)

It is the technical difficulties which lead to the critical part of a technical practice, because only through those difficulties and problems does "critical engagement" (153) with the "deep and systematic confusions" emerge. And this "engagement" is to Agre a concept so important that it becomes the heading of the last section of his text. Much like Deleuze, Agre does not believe in simply negating the "confusions" of others. His experience was that it is "actually impossible to achieve a radical break with the existing methods of the field," which is why "the goal of this [critical technical] practice should be complex engagement, not a clean break" (151). Therefore, "critical engagement" (153) is the point at which Agre's move "Towards a Critical Technical Practice" culminates: "maintaining constructive engagement" (154). And that, according to Agre, is not easy:

> As I worked my way toward a critical technical practice, this was the part that I found hardest: maintaining constructive engagement with researchers whose substantive commitments I found wildly mistaken. It is tempting to start explaining the problems with these commitments in an alien disciplinary voice, invoking phenomenology or dialectics as an exogenous authority, but it is essentially destructive. (154)

Turning away from this destruction and instead focusing on technical practice as a "constructive engagement" (and not as a solution delivered by an equation, algorithm, service, or device) results in opening up those technologies to a creative as well as a more collective process. It means to enter the power mechanism not in the moment of its execution (the creation of the digital subject) but earlier, at a time when force relations are still multiple as the calculation (data/model) is being developed and negotiated. And where could such an engagement be more effective as in digital technical practice, in which force relations remain always open, because the next version of a technology is always emerging leaving room for engagement. As Agre writes, a critical technical practice is a technical production that is spanning "borderlands, bridging the disparate sites of practice that computer work brings uncomfortably together" (155). For computer engineers, "uncomfortably" would mean that those nontechnical voices are not just used for "testing" to optimize the design solutions at the very end of a computational production.

What would engaging with the force relations of a digital practice in that manner mean for scholars in digital humanities or media and technology studies? Most certainly "maintaining constructive engagement" (154) comes with the need to embrace some "uncomfortable" (155) technical understanding and to acquire some expertise in the inner workings of computation to link up technological with intellectual infrastructure, an approach that can be seen in the work of Olga Goriunova (2019b), Leif Weatherby (2020), or Bernhard Rieder (2020). This approach, which Alan Liu (2012) already called for a decade ago, deeply intertwines theory with the inner mechanics of digital technologies instead of projecting well-established critical questions upon it. A work that is important: Digital technologies have become an extitutional place for power, and the force relations of this power need multiple engagements as well as to be opened up and shared. Agre's *critical* technical practice could be read as a call for a *collectively* produced technology that is constantly evolving; an algorithmic practice that is always generating new additional questions to which engineers, media and technology scholars, and the communities they work in, with or for need to turn, in order to critically explore the force relations and adjust the algorithmic practice version by version.

UNCOMFORTABLE CONCLUSION

As we have seen, the power mechanisms at work in digital technologies are structured in profoundly different ways from older forms of power. Despite this, far too often we still seek orientation in the Hegelian metaphor of "master and servant," a metaphor which deeply informed the power mechanisms of politics and its force relations; a mechanism we are deeply familiar with. One can easily see that the concept of a political subject with its strong individual agency is seductive. It promises more than a distributed agency which would be typical for a constructive engagement as Agre envisioned it; an engagement that would be very differently set up as "a matter of intra-acting" (Barad 2007, 214), offering "semi-agency" as Kaiser (2012, 2017) conceptualized it. However, despite being seductive when it comes to our digital technologies, the construct of a political subject is nothing but a confusion. Digital technologies are not masters and users are not their servants. The power mechanism of digital technologies and their force relations function differently—digital technologies calculate and do not count—and because of that a form of resistance informed by politics will come to nothing. Once we are willing to leave behind the idea of digital technology as an "instrument" that functions and is supposed to serve us, and we are willing to adopt a more collaborative approach that includes a more profound engagement with it, then different urgently needed forms of critical practice will come into view.

Algorithmic governance has introduced a "distance" between the individual and the digital subject, which is always already part of a much broader calculation. Absorbing the individual in this calculation has dissolved the reciprocal relation of power and resistance. However, the eternal question of "how not to be governed like that" by our digital technologies remains. Agre's move toward a critical technical practice allows us to turn the power mechanism of algorithmic governance upside down to enter into the middle of algorithmic calculation asking "uncomfortable" questions such as: How is this calculation configured? What are the technical reasons for configuring it like this? What situations are produced by this configuration? Which ones have been forgotten and ignored, which ones cannot be addressed by the calculation? But also: Who controls the distance in which the digital subject is produced? Who can break this distance down? When should it be broken down? These are critical questions that do not negate, but critically *and* constructively *engage* with the technology and the situation it produces, thereby mirroring a remark Joanna Drucker (2015) once made: "We need to formulate a modernism of engagement founded in a recognition of complicity—ours and its—with the machinations and values according to which we live."

Having arrived at the end, let us return to our beginning. When Kant wrote "Was ist Aufklärung?," he assigned the work of emancipation not to the powerful who might be asked to share their power and give us a say. Rather, by asking *everyone* to use their own reason to free themselves from their self-incurred tutelage, he distributed that emancipating work that is the power "not to be governed like that." According to "Was ist Aufklärung?," every citizen was capable of and self-responsible for utilizing their capacity for reason. Today, the contemporary way of knowing or using reason is more often than not a knowing or reasoning with algorithms—and so it is important we remain involved in their technical practice. Digital technologies have become the means by which we find and distribute knowledge, through which we make decisions about each other and calculate our way in the world. And when using our digital reason, we need again to free ourselves from our self-incurred tutelage. Accepting a responsibility toward the technical practices we use, and engaging critically in their adjustments, does not mean that everyone needs to learn how to code. It does mean, however, that we have to leave behind our idea of technology as an instrument that merely serves us and do our homework: to understand its technical practice. As we find the old form of subjugation put aside, our task is now to critically engage in the new form, the calculation, and in the shaping of the situations the calculations around us create in order to "not be governed like that" by our digital technologies.

NOTES

1. This is worth noting—after all, the point for initiating critique is not necessarily the subject; it can also be a class, a movement, or an event. At the very end of his lecture on critique, Foucault does link critique not just to an "individual" but also to a "collective attitude" (67).

2. Interestingly, Winnubst (2015, 184) has likewise observed the evaporation of the force of negativity through differences becoming superficial and fungible.

BIBLIOGRAPHY

Agre, Philip E. 1997. "Toward a Critical Technical Practice: Lessons Learned in Trying to Reform AI." In *Social Science, Technical Systems, and Cooperative Work: Beyond the Great Divide*, edited by Geoffrey C. Bowker, Susan Leigh Star, William Turner, and Less Gasser, 131–157. New York: Psychology Press.

Amoore, Louise. 2009. "Algorithmic War: Everyday Geographies of the War on Terror." *Antipode* 41 (1): 49–69.

Andersen, Christian Ulrik, and Søren Bro Pold. 2011. *Interface Criticism: Aesthetics Beyond Buttons*. Aarhus: Aarhus University Press.

Aradau, Claudia, and Tobias Blanke. 2017. "Politics of Prediction: Security and the Time/Space of Governmentality in the Age of Big Data." *European Journal of Social Theory* 20 (3): 373–391. https://doi.org/10.1177/136843101666762.

———. 2018. "Governing Others: Anomaly and the Algorithmic Subject of Security." *European Journal of International Security* 3 (1): 1–21. https://doi.org/10.1017/eis.2017.14.

Barad, Karen. 2007. *Meeting the Universe Halfway. Quantum Physics and the Entanglement of Matter and Meaning*. Durham/London: Durham University Press.

Benjamin, Ruha. 2019. *Race After Technology: Abolitionist Tools for the New Jim Code*. Cambridge: Polity.

Braidotti, Rosi. 2017. "Generative Futures. On Affirmative Ethics." In *Critical and Clinical Cartographies. Architecture, Robotics, Medicine, Philosophy*, edited by Andrej Ratman, and Heidi Sohn, 288–308. Edinburgh: Edinburgh University Press.

Bratton, Benjamin. 2015. *The Stack: On Software and Sovereignty*. Cambridge, MA: MIT Press.

Bucher, Taina. 2018. *If . . . Then: Algorithmic Power and Politics*. Oxford: Oxford University Press.

Cheney-Lippold, John. 2011. "A New Algorithmic Identity: Soft Biopolitics and the Modulation of Control." *Theory, Culture & Society* 28 (6): 164–181.

Chun, Wendy Hui Kyong. 2006. *Control and Freedom: Power and Paranoia in the Age of Fiber Optics*. Cambridge, MA: MIT Press.
Coleman, E. Gabriella. 2012. *Coding Freedom: The Ethics and Aesthetics of Hacking*. Princeton: Princeton University Press.
Coole, Diana. 2006. *Negativity and Politics: Dionysus and Dialectics from Kant to Poststructuralism*. London: Routledge.
Deleuze, Gilles. [1962] 2006. *Nietzsche and Philosophy*. Translated by Hugh Tomlinson. New York: Columbia University Press.
———. [1968] 1994. *Difference and Repetition*. Translated by Paul Patton. New York: Columbia University Press.
———. [1969] 1990. *The Logic of Sense*. Translated by Mark Lester and Charles Stivale. New York: Columbia University Press.
Dieter, Michael. 2014. "The Virtues of Critical Technical Practice." *Differences* 25 (1): 216–230.
Drucker, Johanna. 2015, May 3. "Recognizing Complicity." *LA Review of Books*. https://lareviewofbooks.org/article/ recognizingcomplicity.
Foucault, Michel. [1969] 2002. *Archaeology of Knowledge*. Translated by A. M. Sheridan Smith. New York: Routledge.
———. [1970] 1998. "Theatrum Philosophicum." Translated by Donald F. Brouchard and Sherry Simo. In *Foucault, Essential Works, Volume 2: Aesthetics, Method, and Epistemology*, edited by James Faubion and Paul Rabinow, 343–367. New York: New Press.
———. [1976] 1978. *The History of Sexuality. Volume I: An Introduction*. Translated by Robert Hurley. New York: Pantheon.
———. [1978] 2007 "What is Critique?" Translated by Lysa Hochroth. In *Michel Foucault: Politics of Truth*, edited by Sylvère Lotringer, 41–81. Los Angeles: Semiotext(e).
———. 1994. *Histoire de la sexualité, tome I: La volonté de savoir*. Gallimard.
Fuller, Matthew. 2003. *Behind the Blip: Essays on the Culture of Software*. New York: Autonomedia.
Gitelman, Lisa, and Virginia Jackson. 2013. "Introduction." In *Raw Data' Is an Oxymoron*, edited by Lisa Gitelman, 1–14. Cambridge, MA: MIT Press.
Goriunova, Olga. 2019a. "The Digital Subject: People as Data as Persons." *Theory, Culture & Society* 36 (6): 125–145. https://doi.org/10.1177/0263276419840409.
———. 2019b. "Face Abstraction! Biometric Identities and Authentic Subjectivities in the Truth Practices of Data." *Subjectivity* 12: 12–26. https://doi.org/10.1057/s 41286-018-00066-1.
Goriunova, Olga, and Alexei Shulgin. 2005. *Software Art & Cultures*. Aarhus: Aarhus University Press.
Grosz, Elizabeth. 2003."Deleuze, Theory, and Space." *Log*, Fall No. 1: 77–86. https://www.jstor.org/stable/41764951.
Huysmans, Jef. 2016. "Democratic Curiosity in Times of Surveillance." *European Journal of International Security* 1 (1): 73–93.
Kaiser, Birgit Mara. 2012. "To Experiment and Critique with Kleist's Käthchen" Position Paper for *Terra Critica: Re-visioning the Critical Task of the Humanities*

in a Globalized World, Utrecht University, December 7/8. http://terracritica.net/w
p-content/uploads/Kaiser_positionpaper.pdf.
———. 2017. "Semi-Agency." In *Symptoms of the Planetary Condition: A Critical Vocabulary*, edited by Mercedes Bunz, Birgit Mara Kaiser, and Kathrin Thiele, 143–148. Lüneburg: Meson Press. https://doi.org/10.25969/mediarep/1893.
Kant, Immanuel. [1784] 2007. "Was ist Aufklärung?" Translated by Lewis White Beck. In *Michel Foucault: Politics of Truth*, edited by Sylvère Lotringer, 29–37. Los Angeles: Semiotext(e).
Kittler, Friedrich. 1993. *Draculas Vermächtnis: Technische Schriften*. Leipzig: Reclam.
Koopman, Colin. 2016. "Critical Problematization in Foucault and Deleuze: The Force of Critique Without Judgment." In *Between Deleuze and Foucault*, edited by Nicolae Morar, Thomas Nail, and Daniel W. Smith, 87–119. Edinburgh: Edinburgh University Press.
Kunst, Alexander. 2019. "Search Engine Usage by Brand in Germany 2019." *Statista*, June 18, 2019. https://www.statista.com/forecasts/998761/search-engine-usage-by-brand-in-germany.
Kunzru, Hari. 1997. "You Are Borg: For Donna Haraway, We Are Already Assimilated." *Wired 5*. https://www.wired.com/1997/02/ffharaway/.
Latour, Bruno. 2004. "Why Has Critique Run out of Steam? From Matters of Fact to Matters of Concern." *Critical Inquiry* 30 (2): 225–248.
Lemke, Thomas. 2016. *Foucault, Governmentality, and Critique*. New York: Routledge.
Liu, Alan. 2012. "Where is Cultural Criticism in the Digital Humanities?" In *Debates in the Digital Humanities*, edited by Matthew K. Gold, 490–509. Minneapolis: University of Minnesota Press.
MacKenzie, Adrian. 2006. *Cutting Code: Software and Sociality*. New York: Peter Lang.
———. 2015. "The Production of Prediction: What Does Machine Learning Want?" *European Journal of Cultural Studies* 18 (4–5): 429–445.
———. 2017. *Machine Learners: Archaeology of a Data Practice*. Cambridge, MA: MIT Press.
Madden, Mary. 2014. "Public Perceptions of Privacy and Security in the Post-Snowden Era. Few see core communications channels as "very secure" places to share private information" [report]. *Pew Research Center*, November 12, 2017. https://www.pewresearch.org/internet/2014/11/12/public-privacy-perceptions/.
Marres, Noortje. 2017. *Digital Sociology: The Reinvention of Social Research*. Cambridge: Polity.
Morozov, Evgueny. 2013. *To Save Everything, Click Here: Technology Solutionism and the Urge to Fix Problems that Don't Exist*. London: Allen Lane.
Morris, Jeremy W., and Sarah Murray. 2018. *Appified: Culture in the Age of Apps*. Ann Arbor: University of Michigan Press.
O'Leary, Timothy. 2002. *Foucault and the Art of Ethics*. New York: Continuum.
Rancière, Jacques. [1995] 1999. *Disagreement: Politics and Philosophy*. Translated by Julie Rose. Minneapolis: University of Minnesota Press.
Rieder, Bernhard. 2017. "Beyond Surveillance: How Do Markets and Algorithms 'Think'?" *Le foucaldien* 3 (1) 8: 1–20. https://doi.org/10.16995/lefou.30.

———. 2020. *Engines of Order: A Mechanology of Algorithmic Techniques*. Amsterdam: Amsterdam University Press.
Rogers, Richard. 2013. *Digital Methods*. Cambridge, MA: MIT Press.
Rouvroy, Antoinette. 2011. "Governmentality in an Age of Autonomic Computing: Technology, Virtuality and Utopia." In *Law, Human Agency and Autonomic Computing*, edited by Mireille Hildebrandt and Antoinette Rouvroy, 119–139. London: Routledge.
———. 2013. "The End (s) of Critique: Data Behaviourism Versus Due Process." In *Privacy, Due Process and the Computational Turn: The Philosophy of Law Meets the Philosophy of Fechnology*, edited by Mireille Hildebrandt and Katja de Vries, 157–182. London: Routledge.
Sauerbrey, Anna. 2014. "Why Germans Are Afraid of Google." *The New York Times*, October 11, 2014. https://www.nytimes.com/2014/10/11/opinion/sunday/why-germans-are-afraid-of-google.html.
Savransky, Martin, ed. 2020. "Special Issue: Problematizing the Problematic." *Theory, Culture and Society*, November. https://doi.org/10.1177/0263276420966389Schomakers.
Schomakers, Eva-Maria, Chantal Lidynia, Dirk Müllmann, and Martina Ziefle. 2019. "Internet Users' Perceptions of Information Sensitivity—Insights from Germany." *International Journal of Information Management* 46 (6): 142–150. https://doi.org/10.1016/j.ijinfomgt.2018.11.018.
Snowden, Edward. 2019. *Permanent Record*. New York: Henry Holt.
Stutzman, Fred, and Jacob Kramer-Duffield. 2010. "Friends Only: Examining a Privacy-Enhancing Behavior in Facebook." *Proceedings of the SIGCHI Conference on Human Factors in Computing Systems*, 1553–1562.
Suchman, Lucy A. 2007. *Human-Machine Reconfigurations: Plans and Situated Actions*. Cambridge: Cambridge University Press.
Thiele, Kathrin. 2008. *The Thought of Becoming. Gilles Deleuze's Poetics of Life*. Berlin: Diaphanes.
———. 2017. "Affirmation." In *Symptoms of the Planetary Condition: A Critical Vocabulary*, edited by Mercedes Bunz, Birgit Mara Kaiser, and Kathrin Thiele, 25–29. Lüneburg: Meson Press. https://doi.org/10.25969/mediarep/1893.
Tufekci, Zeynep. 2008. "Can You See Me Now? Audience and Disclosure Regulation in Online Social Network Sites." *Bulletin of Science, Technology & Society* 28 (1): 20–36.
———. 2017. *Twitter and Tear Gas: The Power and Fragility of Networked Protest*. New Haven: Yale University Press.
Weatherby, Leif. 2020. "Critical Response I. Prolegomena to a Theory of Data: On the Most Recent Confrontation of Data and Literature." *Critical Inquiry* 46 (4): 891–899.
Wilson, Robert E., Samuel D. Gosling, and Lindsay T. Graham. 2012. "A Review of Facebook Research in the Social Sciences." *Perspectives on Psychological Science* 7 (3): 203–220. https://doi.org/10.1177/1745691612442904.
Winnubst, Shannon. 2015. *Way Too Cool: Selling Out Race and Ethics*. New York: Columbia University Press.
———. 2020. "The Many Lives of Fungibility: Anti-Blackness in Neoliberal Times." *Journal of Gender Studies* 29 (1): 102–112.
Zuboff, Shoshana. 2019. *The Age of Surveillance Capitalism: The Fight for a Human Future at the New Frontier of Power*. London: Profile Books.

10
Defective Institutions
or, Critique
Jacques Lezra

Contubernio. *It's the word—the strange, ugly word—that would eventually be used to explain officially why my father's family was forced into exile in 1938 by Franco's forces:* el contubernio judeo-masónico-comunista-internacional, sometimes el contubernio judeo-masónico-marxista-internacional, even el contubernio judeo-masónico-comunista.[1] *By the time the word* contubernio—*which the historian Paul Preston translates, wonderfully, as "filthy concubinage"—started to interest me, the immediate wounds to my father, uncle and grandparents were some forty years cold (Preston 2012, 59; 132). The wounds gave my childhood and adolescence a scarred, lumpy shape. We lived in what the regime called "democracia orgánica," a form of governance that subordinated the principle of representation to the principle of identity and to the logical figure of tautology—identity constituted in, and expressed by, what were called "authentic living truths" or "authentic life-truths,"* auténticas realidades vitales. *The 1933 "Puntos iniciales" of* Falange Española *lay out just what this "democracia orgánica" consists in: a "total," "totalitarian" state unified by a reawakened and hegemonic belief ("creencia" rather than "fe") in the "historical reality" of the "unity of destiny"* (unidad de destino; *almost better: the "unifiedness of destiny") bearing historically the name "Spain" (Primo de Rivera 1949, 132–133; translations throughout mine). This hegemonic and hegemonizing belief "unifies" the state administratively as well as ideologically; it is what every element of it must share with every other. Every element, person or administrative unit, participates in the "unity" or the "oneness" of the state, and that is why it is an "element" in the first place: we are in the world of a vulgarized Platonism. Three authentic life-truths form the tripod on which the State stands; three institutions.*

> *Un Estado verdadero, como el que quiere Falange Española, no estará asentado sobre la falsedad de los partidos políticos, ni sobre el Parlamento que ellos engendran. Estará asentado sobre las auténticas realidades vitales: la familia; el municipio; el gremio o sindicato. (133)*
>
> A true State, such as Falange Española desires, will not be built upon the falsehood of political parties, or upon the Parliament they engender. It will be built on the authentic life-truths: the family; the municipality; the guild or syndicate.

Insidious, spectral, the contubernio judeo-masónico-comunista-internacional—*the low alliance of Jews, Masons, Communists, and Internationalists*—threatened *"organic democracy." It threatened the hegemonizing belief that individuals might have in the unity of "Spain," and it offered an alternate form of association, even of institution.* Contubernium *was the unsanctioned marriage pact between slaves, or between a slave and an owner, in the Roman republic which only recognized, legally, the* conubium, *the institution of marriage between free Romans.* Contubernium *was also the lowest, smallest unit of accommodation in the Roman legions, the group of six or eight soldiers to a tent.* Contubernium *was (by the eighteenth century) the name for illicit, extra-marital living arrangements. By 1925, the relative lowness, commonness, or servility of its protagonists typically bubbled upward to characterize moral dispositions. For the hoary* Diccionario de la Real Academia de la lengua *published that year it means, figuratively, "Alianza o liga vituperable," a despicable, condemnation-worth league or alliance (DRAE 1925). The connubial, unitary state seeks to build its ghostly adversary in its image—as a "vituperable" alliance or league of elements (protagonists, parties, ethnicities, dispositions—levels are crossed, differences erased) united in insidious opposition to "organic democracy." One organism against another. Built in the organic state's image, the contubernial alliance can be eliminated justly by the state—through extermination or through exile. The familiar register of biopolitical determination is at hand: extermination, exile, expulsion, immunity.*

It is 1938, perhaps. I imagine the frantic packing, the car-ride out of Melilla (my sick uncle in the back seat), my family's arrival at last in Tangier, the international city in the International Zone where legal, civil, procedural, institutional regimes multiplied and jostled chaotically against each other: French, Spanish, British, Portuguese, Italian, Belgian, Dutch—even the United States had a legation and collaborated in the administration of the zone. From where I write, imagining and remembering, I can also see that the fantasy of the unitary, immanently, and transcendentally "unified" State against which the zone stood has survived the end of Tangier's peculiar status, in 1956; it has survived the end of Franco's regime in 1975 (and of his direct allies'—*the list is long*), *and I expect that it will survive the end of* explicitly *totalitarian forms of governance.*

***

FROM CRITICAL *ACT* TO POLITICAL *SUBSTANCE?*

I am writing these words at a moment when the failure of governance in the United States shockingly, clamorously stands forth. I hear calls for strengthening institutions, for defending liberties ostensibly protected by such institutions.

Let us set out, as the first moment of a new critical project, to rescue *contubernium* and all that we can make it stand for, all the minimal forms of *apparently* extra-institutional association, the illicit, the non-connubial, let us set out to rescue it from its specular capture by the connubial State. Otherwise, *conubium* and *contubernium* and the institutions for which they serve as metonyms will just muddle on fraternally, to this day and as far as we can imagine, wherever hegemony takes the shape of belief in unitary, immanently or transcendentally coherent institutions, and wherever identities bear a relation of shared participation in, or of universal mediation with regard to, those institutions.

In what follows, I offer a more or less formalized concept of "Defective Institution" that will serve small-r republican governance. A few assertions, first off. To step away from the fratricidal, specular struggle that the unitary State and its doubles offer, I will have to step (for a moment at least) outside the walls that protect our thought: The walls where hegemonic ideas, as such, are set into traditions of thought, procedures of conceptual verification, testing, and discipline—the sheltering walls of institutions like the university. Political philosophy today should be nonacademic in a specific sense: it should abandon the critique of *acts* of institution or of the *substance* of actually existing institutions or political concepts. Those tasks are familiar and congenial to the University frame, to the think-tank frame, and to the more or less smooth transition between the institution of the university and the institutions of political governance. They are tasks undertaken with a view to establishing the fundamental continuity *between* acts of institution and the substance of actually existing institutions or political concepts, or out of a desire to strengthen actually existing institutions and to clarify their relation to subtending political concepts, thereby producing new and stronger institutions or new and stronger, more coherent political concepts.

The task of critique in political philosophy today is other. "Continuity" is the domain of markets and of the universal and universally translatable standard of economic value that we now call global capital. Institutions imagined to stand on the continuity between the act of institution and the substance instituted are, indeed, the form that value-standard takes *as* the domain of the political.

Today, in the very heat of the crisis of global institutions and of national ones in the United States, in Spain, in Bolivia, in Chile, in Venezuela, in the United Kingdom, in Hong Kong, the task is different: To produce and put into discursive play defective narratives, defective political concepts, and defective institutions. ("Defective" will mean: discontinuous, dis-organized, open, untellable, effectual as well as effective, possibly rhythmic.) A fully and radically differentiated democratic society stands not only on decentering and disorganizing its political subjects, but on reimagining the concept of its institutions. The sovereignty of such reimagined, defective institutions is always divisible; the time and conditions of their emergence and persistence are never given in the axioms of their own or other institutions; the narratives they install are generically both over- and underdetermined; the logical shape required of statements about them is unfamiliar. Defective institutions and the wild republics they organize persist and decline according to discontinuous logics and times. They entail regimes of representation, narratives, police forces, pedagogies, rhetorics, and lexicons that do ephemeral work, with often reversible results, transparently. They are an-organic without being, exactly, machinic. And a further definition. Republicanism in its most radical form, in its wildest shape, in a shape fundamentally incompatible with the logical forms of global capital and of "organic democracy," is the intractable governance of defective institutions.

I am aware that worlds are at stake in the ambiguous grammar of that sentence, the subjective-objective genitive expression "The intractable governance *of* defective institutions." Coming up with and setting in practice modes of governance that retain and radicalize this ambiguity—that is the task of this wild republicanism. How do we approach this cluster of affirmations today? Today, when the streets of Portland, Los Angeles, Chicago, Charlottesville, and Washington, DC, are alight with the radicalizing claim that Black Lives Matter? How, from within the university-institution today, do we do as Sylvia Wynter did in 1992, and ask after the specifically, even practically, political outcomes of critique today, and in particular of the field of what could be called *radical* institutional critique? In May 1992, in the immediate wake of the Rodney King judgment and the subsequent repression and riots in LA (April 29 and the days following), Sylvia Wynter called for her colleagues at Stanford and across the university-institution to "undo" the "narratively condemned status" of "all the Rodney Kings," of the "starving *'fellah*,' (or the jobless inner city N.H.I. [No Humans Involved], [of] the global new poor, or *les damnés*)" (Wynter 1992, 16). The gesture is not new for Wynter, though the occasion is perhaps more terrible. As early as 1987, in her "On Disenchanting Discourse," Wynter holds that the task of the pedagogical elites who have "institute[d] the 'truth' " of social abjection as the "truth" of capital should be to produce "rhetorical motivation systems" serving to "decenter the human subjects whose behaviors enable the stable replication of their own autopoesis as systems" (Wynter 1987, 243). Pedagogical elites would be tasked with "put[ting] into discursive play [. . .] the [human subjects'] own intentionality and autonomy as autopoetic systems [. . .] [which] whilst largely compatible with, are not reducible to that of their individual subjects" (243). In 1987, as in 1992, then, those who had wittingly or not "institute[d] the 'truth' " of social abjection as the "truth" of capital were now meant to produce and to institute alternative narratives. This, via critique and by means of critical pedagogies carried out in a rethought university-institution more habitable and welcoming both to (eventually) decentered subjects and to the "largely compatible" but distinctly nonidentical forms of "intentionality and autonomy" that decentered subjects bear as "autopoetic systems." Other regimes of truth; other ceremonies.

Today, I approach these questions and Wynter's injunctions lopsidedly. Here is a characteristically provocative excerpt from Wynter's late (2015) essay "The Ceremony Found: Towards the Autopoetic Turn/Overturn, Its Autonomy of Human Agency and Extraterritoriality of (Self-)Cognition." These sentences close the introductory section of "The Ceremony Found":

> [O]n the basis of a proposed new and now meta-biocentric order of knowledge/episteme and its correlated emancipatory view of who-we-are as humans (themselves as ones that will together now make possible our collective *turn* towards what I shall define as our *Second Emergence*), we can become, for the first time in our species' existence, now fully conscious agents in the autopoetic institution and reproduction of a *new* kind of planetarily extended cum "intercommunal" community (Huey Newton via Erikson 1973). And this new kind of community would be one, therefore, that secures the "ends" no longer of biocentric (neo)Liberal-monohumanist ethno-class *Man*(2), nor indeed that of the religio-secular counter-ends of the contemporary westernized imperialist and/or fundamentalist forms of the three Abrahamic monotheisms, but instead superseding them all, *inter alia*, by that of the We-the-ecumenically-Human. (Wynter 2015, 194)

Just what "autopoetic institution" means is not yet clear. Wynter is responding, in 2015, to her own call, in 1984, to seek, in "a science of human systems [. . .] which makes use of multiple frames of reference and of [. . .] rhetorical techne," to "attain to the position of an external observer, at once inside/outside the figural domain of our order" from which to "find" ceremony (Wynter 1984, 56). "[W]e are governed," she says in 1984, in the way we know the world by the templates of identity or modes of self-troping speciation, about which each human system auto-institutes itself, effecting the dynamics of an autopoetics, whose imperative of stable reproduction has hitherto transcended the imperatives of the human subjects who collectively put it into dynamic play. The proposed science of human systems decenters the systemic subject. Instead, it takes as the object of its inquiry the modes of symbolic self-representation about which each human system auto-institutes itself, the modes of self-troping rhetoricity through which the Subject (individual/collective) actualizes its mode of being as a living entity. (44)

Decentering, then, the systemic, we might say the *institutional* subject. How to do so? In the course of the 2015 essay "The Ceremony Found," Wynter distinguishes between the verbal and the nominal senses of "institution"—between that which an agent does, the act of *instituting*; and that material and subsisting effect of the act, the *institution*—and she clarifies that her interest lies with the first of these. Both aspects of "institution"—the concept's verbal and substantive aspects, if you will—are subject to sociogenic codes "or *Masks*." Wynter says, these are "the indispensable condition of our being able autopoetically to institute ourselves as *genre*-specific, fictive modes of eusocial, inter-altruistic, kin-recognizing kind" (2015, 201). "[T]he terms of our eusocial co-identification as humans," she maintains, "can never pre-exist each society's specific mode of autopoetic institution, together with its complex of origin-narratively encoded socio-technologies" (2015, 201). Autopoetic institution is then an agent's generically determined act (of institution); because it is co-occurrent and coterminous with "each society's specific mode of autopoetic institution," it tends to make agents co-occurrent and coterminous as a class—We-the-ecumenically-Human—while *also* instituting them as the retroactive effects *of* the class of "We-the-ecumenically-Human." The ancient problem at the core of the concept of institution is seemingly solved: for an act to found an institution—for an act to "institute"—it must work in the context of a lexicon and set of protocols governing its interpretation; establishing the conditions for its felicity; guaranteeing its repeatability or the repeatability of subsequent acts it permits; and so on. Every act of instituting requires an existing institution, *just as* every institution derives its legitimacy and its coherence from a primary act of institution. Here the formula "just as" expresses the logical-causal impasse that Wynter's term "autopoetic institution" seeks to solve. The solid, almost tautologous architecture of specular acts of institution can become a new "fundament," to use Wynter's term: specular acts of autopoetic institution can become a new fundament for the *second*, substantive sense of "institution," the persistent social device or system instituted to define, collect, guard, classify, and distribute resources among "We-the-ecumenically-Human" in what

Wynter calls a "lawlikely" manner. What the "institutions" instituted upon this autopoetic institution would look like is left unexamined—the question is not her concern; "We-the-ecumenically-Human" system may well *be* such an institution, the first, the necessary one, prior even to that other "first" institution identified by anthropologists, the family. Other institutions may follow, founded on We-the-ecumenically-Human's fundament: that is not her essay's brief.

I am skeptical that one can move in thought from the critical *act* to the political *substance* outside a globalizing neoliberal frame that was not yet, in 1984, fully consolidated, its incoherence not yet fully reinscribed and monetized as "risk," its violence as correlative to individualism, freedom, property, and other unassailable values. At least not without a wholesale rethinking of both the *act* and *substance* of (an) institution. Wynter herself is not starry-eyed about the possibility of moving either from the act of instituting to the institution, or genealogically and deductively backward, from actually existing institutions to the field of instituting acts on which they stand. The devices and lexicon that make this movement possible in her work are explicit and remain largely untouched between 1984 and the later essays—on one level, the language of "ceremony" itself; on another, related level, a Girardian account of the "sacrificial" relation at work where the "individual" and the "genre" face each other, as Don Quijote faces the genre of romances of chivalry, and as Alonso Quijano "the Good" faces the confessional conventions of early seventeenth-century La Mancha; on another level still, a conception of the university-institution as comprising collectives of "colleagues" who serve as "institutors" of the confining regime of truth and abjecting social narratives of capital. Finally, for Wynter, moving either from the act of instituting to the institution, or genealogically and deductively backward, from actually existing institutions to the hypothesis of a primal act of instituting, means replacing the concept of "hegemony" by what Wynter calls "[r]hetorical motivation systems whose function is to bring differing modalities of 'human being' into being, by means of enculturating discourses generated from the grounding premise of an environmentally 'fit' conception of life/death" (1987, 243).

What does my skepticism about moving between act of institution and instituted substance get me? Well, it gets me "Defective Institutions"; it gets me devices for guarding and extending, rather than seeking to reduce or render "largely compatible," the radical difference between human autonomy and intentionality, and subjects' "own intentionality and autonomy as autopoetic systems" (Wynter 1987, 243). It gets me a definition of the domain of politics as the domain in which that radical difference is negotiated, administered, instituted, and derogated. It may get me sets of devices for coordinating critical acts and institutions that have not been assimilated into, and possibly may not be assimilable to, either "organic democracy" and its avatars, or the genres of thought offered by the neoliberal globalizing frame. I will eventually get around to an example—the example of a terrifically defective institution, the university.

A BRIEF FOR FALSIFICATION

> We owe it to each other to falsify the institution, to make politics incorrect, to give the lie to our own determination.
>
> Harney and Moten, *The Undercommons* (2013, 20)

A remark.

"Defective Institutions" is a coinage manifestly intended to excite the imagination in the mode of what is called in psychological literature the "White bear" or the "polar bear" problem. "Try to pose for yourself this task," wrote Dostoevsky in 1863 in a little travelogue called *Winter Notes on Summer Impressions*, "[try] not to think of a polar bear, and you will see that the cursed thing will come to mind every minute" (Dostoevsky 1997, 49). Hence the "white bear" problem. Pose for yourself this task: try not to think of a "defective institution," and the cursed thing will come to mind—a raft of them, every institution you have had the chance or the mishap to encounter. Electoral colleges, judiciaries, families, universities. Today, especially today, especially in the context of the response to COVID-19, of the last presidential election in the United States, of the Senate confirmation hearings that followed Donald Trump's inauguration, and of the impeachment inquiry in the U.S. House of Representatives, and eventual trial in the Senate; in the context of Brexit, of the crisis of the project of the European Union; in the context of a university-institution in crisis also: today the "curse" of institutional defectivity is glaringly with us. Indeed, it is hard to think of an "institution" that is not gravely defective, or weak, or misformed. The inverse exercise—offering for you, say, the provocation of the title or the concept "Effective institutions," or "Strong institutions," or "Working institutions" or even "charismatic institutions"—is likely to produce few examples. Few will "come to mind," to use Dostoevsky's phrase. Whether in fact what we generally call "institutions" are more subject to defect today than they were (for instance) in 1984; or more subject to defect *here*, more defective here, for instance, in the United States or in Bolivia or in Chile, than elsewhere, for example, in France or the Netherlands. We will agree, maybe, that today institutions are *represented* as being more defective than at many other times and places. Take this remarkable proposal by the political theorist Corey Robin, recently published in the journals *Jacobin* and the *Guardian*:

[T]he worst, most terrible things that the United States has done have almost never happened through an assault on American institutions; they've always happened through American institutions and practices. These are the elements of the American polity that have offered especially potent tools and instruments of intimidation and coercion: federalism, the separation of powers, social pluralism and the rule of law. (Robin 2020)

Thus Corey Robin. He does not say so, but we may infer that a commitment to the *converse* of this proposition has enabled "the worst, most terrible things that the United States has done" historically, and that this commitment will enable the United States to do further terrible thing in the next years. The strong "American institutions" serving to make concrete political concepts like federalism or the separation of powers will always and as a matter of course resist the assault of skewed, partial, or totalitarian agendas or personalities *because* of their strength—a commitment to this notion *has enabled, and will enable,* the worst. Because institutions are believed to be strong, because these institutions suffer only minor defects of execution rather than disabling defects of structure, they have historically "offered especially potent tools and instruments of intimidation."

What counts as a "defective" institution? We make judgments regarding the value, coherence, strength, and utility of devices and institutions in different ways historically—ways conditioned by what "making judgements" means socially, for whom, and under what conditions. Today, for instance, I buy a car or a blender. I have in mind something I want it for: I want my car for getting to work, my blender for making soup. If one or the other does not work to that end I will say it is "defective," a lemon, broken. I trade it in for another that will do the trick. An intentional structure is presumed; I have in mind this end for that device. We can be more or less loose with this conception, but its structure seems irreducible. Let us say, to be a little looser in my "making judgments," I buy a car and I have in mind more than one end. The car gets me to work, but alas it does not serve the other end I intended, openly or perhaps even secretly, secretly even for myself. I wanted a car that would help me do what the advertising campaign for this car also promises, to find a glamorous partner and breeze down coastal highways romantically. My Volkswagen Jetta is perfectly good at one thing, but perfectly useless at the other. I will not say it is "defective," since it gets me to work; I'll say it is disappointing, since it does not also get me a glamorous romantic partner. And now let us say that my therapist gets me, hours into expensive analysis, to disclose to myself why it is that my car, while not defective, still disappoints me. I had another unacknowledged end in mind for the device, and it is not working to that end. An *intentional structure*, even if my intention is or has been secret, still shapes my judgment. Our judgments about cars and blenders are, to use Kant's lexicon, *teleological*.

Are institutions to be understood in that way today? For not *all* judgments are of this sort, and not all objects of judgment are like blenders or cars: Some, for instance, are like polar bears or white bears, or the color yellow, or a sunset. But institutions, today, are much more like blenders or cars than they are like bears or sunsets or poems. They have ends and they have use-values. For Corey Robin, political institutions in the United States have two sorts of ends and use-values. Political institutions serve to give shape to the political concepts or fantasies at the heart of the modern secular state—federalism, the separation of powers, social pluralism, and the rule of law; they *also*, as he says, "offer [. . .] especially potent tools and instruments of intimidation and coercion" (Robin 2020). This latter may not be an explicit *end* of these institutions, any more than my desire for hooking a romantic partner is when I buy a useful car. But for some it can become so, and in any event when the astute therapist or philosophical diagnostician of current political disappointments reveals the secret, my secret, the institutions' secret, then political institutions can be held to the implicit end of producing coercion and intimidation, and found to be disappointingly wanting or excitingly effective. We might say that institutions today are the political form of use-value, and our judgments regarding the effectiveness, strength, utility and so on of institutions are not just teleological and technical, they are nakedly expressed in the language of political economy, of efficiencies, of excellences, of outcomes, customer-relations, and so on.

Is there an alternative? Are there ways of conceiving institutions that do not subject their concept, and judgments about their structure, value, effectiveness, to the logics of the intentional structure, the teleological judgment, or the technical a priori? For Kant one answer lies in aesthetic judgments. These judgments are purposive without having purposes, and we form them with regard to natural objects (a towering cliff, a beautiful sunset, a polar bear) and (slightly differently) with regard to manufactured objects that we agree to call aesthetic because they have no technical function—works of art, the dome of St. Peter's (which has a function, of course, but which we do not admire *for* its function), or even something like a mathematical proof. That is not the direction I am going to take here, though my alternative does bear comparison to moments in Kant's Third *Critique*. I want instead to make an argument for conceiving institutions as *contingent* objects—and for making judgments about them in those terms, taking account of contingency not only as it pertains to future states or outcomes, but more strangely as it pertains to present states (objects may or may not be thus and so, institutions are and are not this or that) and, most counterintuitively, as pertains to past states.

Judgments regarding these special objects called "institutions" will then depend, for their truth-value and coherence (and, importantly, with Harney and Moten, for their effectiveness in *falsifying* and in rendering incoherent and an-organic judgments legitimated *by* such special objects-institutions), on what has not-yet-occurred; on what is and is not in the present; and on what, having occurred, is nonetheless to be thought as radically contingent, that is, as possibly-having-occurred-otherwise or not at all. Whatever such special objects, institutions, are, they are not themselves in any way I easily recognize: they are not necessarily what they are now, or will be, or even what they were. They subject tautology to the solvent of contingency. Defective institutions are heterologous, and judgments concerning them are heterological.

Let me approach the matter hand in hand with the work of the Jesuit philosopher and theologian Stanislas Breton, a thinker a generation younger than Walter Benjamin. Breton's extraordinarily rich essay, "Dieu est Dieu: Sur la violence des propositions tautologiques," of 1989, shows that the proposition "Dieu est Dieu" on which monotheism stands is inhabited by violence (Breton 1989, 2017). As are, Breton marvelously suggests, three of the great principles of Western logic, subtending the "proper sphere of 'understanding,' language" (to lean on Benjamin's words)—the primary mode of articulation of reason, *logos*, or speech/thought, the principles of identity; of noncontradiction; and of sufficient reason (Benjamin 2004, 245). Breton's brief essay is provoking. It argues that the *form* of the proposition "Dieu est Dieu" on which monotheism stands is violent (as are, in a general sense, *any* tautologies, including the propositions "violence is violence," "The University-institution is the University-institution," "It is what it is"). "Violence" here, for Breton, means: tautology installs and depends upon a regime of the identical. (The self-identical; that which can be represented, inasmuch as what represents it will be self-same *and* will stand for something self-same: just what Harney and Moten's view of the undercommons targets: "We cannot represent ourselves. We can't be represented" [Harney and Moten 2013, 20].)

A BRIEF FOR FAILURES

"The University-institution is the University-institution." The claim could be made less broadly, but by using the university-institution I hope to offer something of the order of a meta-example. For the university-institution is not just *any* case. The university has historically been the institution in which the passage from, or between, the *act* of instituting and the *substance* of institution or the instituted substance becomes an object for thought. It is where "liberty" and "autonomy" are defined by, in, and as the domain of thought; and it is the institution concerned with establishing the exemplarity of examples—that is, with establishing what, in an instance, a case, or an element, makes the example representative of more than itself. What makes the example exemplary, in short. (Historically as well as conceptually, the struggle over the limits separating the university, the law, and the church is fought on just this terrain: who will be sovereign in determining not just the representativity of the example, but what indeed counts *as* representative in an example. Schmitt: Sovereign is he who determines the example.) The university writes knowledge—and this is why disciplines that it protects and organizes can be charged, as Wynter does in 1984, with "rewriting knowledge." "It is we who institute this 'truth'," Wynter writes in 1992 to her colleagues at Stanford and beyond—and this is why "we" can be charged with "undoing" the "narratively condemned status" of the " 'fellah,' (or the jobless inner city N.H.I., the global new poor, or *les damnés*)." "Critique" is the name that we, yes "we," give to the practices that arrest, disorganize, denaturalize, de-hegemonize, the passages that the university-institution builds between an act of instituting and the institution; between the instance and the manifold it represents; between example and exemplarity.

Academic disciplines rest, tendentially, on tautological propositions: a truth in the discipline of history is true according to the protocols of the discipline of history (but not, perhaps, according to those of physics, philosophy, or business). In principle, this assertion could be shown to be true for any corporate entity and of any coherent set of protocols, that is, for any discipline destined to produce an object, of any sort, from which it takes its value. The rhythm of a discipline's identity is measured in reference to these tautological propositions. The techniques and the subject-matter that we teach, what students learn, the things we and they handle and the objects of knowledge we and they produce—inasmuch as these things and objects are identifiably the effects of our discipline, they also affirm our discipline's identity, and its value as a mechanism for producing such things and objects. Philosophy is philosophy, our tautological disciplinary proposition runs, inasmuch as it produces for inspection subjects and objects that are deemed to be, and can be consumed as, examples of a philosophical formation. In the academy, we thus remark an uneasy reciprocity between the circulation and the processes of valuation and relating of academic things (of things, object, and matter in the academic context), and what the British researchers Roger Brown and Helen Carasso recently called "the Marketisation" of higher education (Brown and Carasso 2013). The thing-as-datum provides *homo academicus* and his (!) brethren with value tradable across markets and languages, and transforms the university-institution into a cloistered, autopoetic factory for the production of globally tradable, translatable information-commodities.

Defective Institutions 213

But this is not entirely what Wynter means by "autopoetic," or by an autopoetic system. She insists, as we saw, on the goal of "put[ting] into discursive play [. . .] the [human subjects'] own intentionality and autonomy as autopoetic systems [. . .] [which] whilst largely compatible with, are not reducible to that of their individual subjects" (1987, 243). Against the tautology of disciplinarity, then, her task, the task she calls on her colleagues to take on, is to make use critically of the non-reducibility of system and individual subjects. The university-institution is the critical frame for this use and should be assessed and thought as such; indeed, providing this frame is—beyond the technical goals of the contemporary STEM university system—the end itself of the classical, liberal-arts university-institution. And by saying this, of course, I am reinstalling the logic of teleological judgments at the university-institution's core, since critique, or critical thinking, or the critical use of the non-reducibility of system and individual subjects, or "freedom," become the products, at the second level, of the autopoetic university-institution.

This recursive trap is particularly hard to avoid. Brown and Carasso's study focuses on the United Kingdom; the comparable work reflecting on the development of the modern university-institution in the United States (and globally) is Bill Readings's *The University in Ruins*. Readings tracks the effects of the use of the vacuous criterion of "excellence" in assessing research and teaching outcomes. Here is how he describes the state of affairs:

> [E]xcellence serves as the unit of currency within a closed field [. . .] a purely internal unit of value that effectively brackets all questions of reference or function, thus creating an internal market. Henceforth, [. . .] the question of the University-institution is only a question of relative value-for-money, the question posed to a student who is situated entirely as a consumer, rather than as someone who wants to think. (1996 [1999], 16)

"As an integrating principle," he maintains, "excellence has the singular advantage of being entirely meaningless, or to put it more precisely, non-referential" (22). Disciplines, especially those that took shape in funding regimes inspired in one version of the Cold War (Title VI programs, comparativist disciplines imagined as attending to cosmopolitan rather than narrowly national concerns, the modern humanities), find their standing in the university-institution in question when they appear to fail the test of non-referentiality. This failure might take one of two shapes, and each would be violent in its way. A discipline might fail to satisfy the conditions of "excellence" by seeking to link the free-floating commodity-form of the university-institution to some object or state of affairs outside of it (i.e., by producing an object of knowledge that "refers" to an actually existing object or state of affairs outside the closure of the discipline). Let us call this the *transcendent* failure of the university-institution-institution. The value of the "discipline" is then dependent on something it does not produce; the closure of the university-institution is threatened, but only to the degree that this "outside" cannot be reincorporated within the closure of the university-institution—cannot become the object-of-study for a future, notional discipline. And this inflation of disciplines is just what we see occurring, around the globe. The university-institution-machine is a capturing device, a translating device, I said—so a *transcendent* failure, a *transcendent* critique of the reflexive university-institution value-form will not do the trick.

But a discipline might fail the test of non-referentiality in a second way. A discipline might produce, *within* the strangely self-referential value system that Readings imagines the university-institution to have become, excesses or lacks of reference—spots where the closure of the university-institution discourse is threatened from within. (In this case, we would say that the discipline produces "objects" which cannot, and could not, be valued in the terms given by other disciplines. It is an object analytically excessive or defective with respect to them, or both.) We will call this a sort of *immanent* failure of the disciplinary machine.[2]

Let us try to understand a little more clearly what it might take to produce this double failure, immanent as well as transcendent, transcendent because immanent and vice versa, within the university-institution, by submitting disciplines built on tautological bases to "translation" and "relation's" absolutization of the not-one; to the *heterologization* of foundational propositions regarding the university-institution. A university-institution is a university-institution, except that the objects of study the university-institution produces, its most intimate result and the condition of its self-intelligibility and of its market value, no longer fall either within the scope of the university-institution, or without it. They are, in sum, tautological propositions in a sense unlike the sort to which we are accustomed; im-pastoral glosses obeying what Breton calls "a new imperative: 'Stop nowhere!', for He gives you movement in order 'always to go beyond.'"

> The essential thing here is not to condemn images: rather, to multiply them to infinity, so none of them, fascinating us, succeeds in seducing us. The person of faith resembles a sort of Don Juan, on the search for the eternal feminine. Searching for the eternal divine, he reads in this tautology a new imperative: "Stop nowhere!", for He gives you movement in order "always to go beyond." "One has to stop somewhere," we often say: this is, though, an *axiom of laziness*, as every cliché [*évidence*] is. (139)

This imperative, Breton says, describes the form of thinking that he would like to choose—never to allow one function of the tautology of propositions to seduce him, thus allowing him to choose mercy over violence, Pauline humanism over the fundamentalism of the Unique Law. This, he says, is what he *would like*: to retell the story of the Enlightened University-institution, which passes from the theologico-political violence of tautological propositions to the softer violence of instrumental or ancillary pedagogy, always leading-beyond-itself, as the Augustinian sign always leads beyond itself toward an ultimate, grounding, and transcendent sign.

This is one dimension in which the radical critique of institutions unfolds today. Like Wynter's, it is susceptible of capture—it can be inscribed in a sacrificial structure, even the fideistic, Christic structure that she, and Breton, and Girard, and the long legacy of the confessional university share. This dimension of the critique of institutions is theoretical, even spatial: Wynter, for instance, calls on the pedagogical elites to "attain to" and install or institute, as the model of subjectivity that will uninstall the "truth" of capital's abject subject-positions, "the position of an external observer, at once inside/outside the figural domain of our order" (1984, 56). For this reason, Wynter's "external observer" of institutions is positioned "at once inside/outside the figural domain of [the] order" (1984, 56). Thus, the critical anthropologist, to be sure, but also the university itself—theoretical observers *of* society, but also *parts of* that society. They are religious figures that fall inside the order of human representation, incarnate, and also stand outside, divine. These are paradoxes of position, and they are violently paradoxical *necessarily*, if and only if, either the "external observer" or the "figural domain" is *one*, one *being* at one time positioned in more than one spot; or one being at one time in a spot or position which is itself *not one*. Like the rational impasse to which Breton is led, the decentering of subjectivity we find in Wynter has as its ceremonial outcome the re-centering of the subject-structure relation upon a symmetrical and sacrificial figure, in a lawlikely domain: The *one* is maintained, as subject *or* as institution, but each only at the cost of the other. In this higher-order, ceremonial, "figural domain," the "decentered subject" and the institution face-off like squabbling twin brothers according to a sacrificial narrative and according to a necessary logic that converts the violence of tautological propositions, the violence that is critique, into the administrative, lawlikely form of noncontradiction. The state so conceived, conceived as the ceremonial figurative-administrative domain in which the One of the decentered subject and the One of the institution face-off and exchange the quality of being One, or in which the One of a particular institution like the family exchanges with the aggregate of similarly Unitary institutions the quality of being One—the State so conceived is *in one sense* Hegelian through and through—it appears purged in the last instance of all defect and all contradiction; it is Christological, Universitary, immaculate, teleological.

Breton for his part offers a pedagogical, pastoral alternative emerging, one might say, from a different Hegelianism, from an unpurged Hegel. "Dieu est Dieu" closes on Breton's remark that he has no rational way of choosing between formally identical tautologies (and hence that he rests, or rather that he remains caught, *in* the contradiction, in the defect, in what is not-One), which is a way of saying that he locates in thought itself, in critique, the violence of the choice between tautologies: There is no sphere of thought, as thought, of thought-as-thought and of thought-as-thought-about-objects-of-thought, that is untouched by violence. No paradox of position this. There is no outside to thinking, no inside; or rather, the relation between thinking and its object, like the relation between the act of instituting and the institution, does not fall, for thinking, on one or the other side, on the side of the act or on the side of the substance or the object. Whatever, wherever, and whenever it is, the critical, patient remaining-caught or forbearing that Breton offers his readers *as thought*, the "as thought" of the language of the defective university-institution, the "as thought" that the defective institution turns on in order to understand, to express, to translate, and also to guard the violence of its theologico-political foundation: This critical "as thought" opens the human animal, for Breton, to the explosive truth of theologico-political foundation, while *also* "falsifying" and "making incorrect" (Harney/Moten) its invariably institutional form.

THE OPERATOR OF DEFECTION

Without quite achieving the rousing power I had hoped to summon, I have tried to offer an alternative view to the twin Hegelianisms I have attributed to Wynter and Breton. I have sought to argue for defective subjectivities acting, not necessarily in concert and not necessarily intentionally, to constitute defective institutions in a field in which the figure of the domain—the figure of domination by whatever forces bound and order the field—is inconstant, discontinuous, *un*lawlikely, and defective; and to which correspond contingent judgments I have called heterological.

This trebly defective concept of institution defuses the symmetries, substitutions, and mimetisms of the "figurative domain" of the State. Like a car that does not work, it will not take me where I wish to go; and like the unacknowledged symbolic car that figures my market-driven desires, it goes where it wishes for me—that is, it leads me to what it puts on offer, it builds and hews to the map of my desires. It yields an unfamiliar narrative time; it yields acts whose substantive effects are not immanently, or transcendentally, derivable from those acts, and substances for which no determining act of institution can be simply derived. It yields substantial institutions the performative authority of whose instituting acts cannot be established—that authority is not unitary; it derives, paradoxically, from a divided sovereignty.

I have imagined a University. Now imagine, heterologically, a family, the hoariest, most primitive institution; perhaps the first. *Conubium.* All families are subject to fortune—death, birth, estrangement, violence, exile. Yes. And now add to that the factic, defective quality of "family's" concept: the family is not one—the family is not the family, and it is never necessarily one; it is not a multiple of individuals related by blood or bond or custom; it can be no model for the organic state's governance. If it can be said to have any substantive value, the family will be ephemeral, elective; depositional rather than positional; irreconcilable with classic forms of possession; possibly productive, but if at all, autoheteropoietic. No act institutes it immediately; nor does a multiplicity of acts aggregated according to a common wish, a social desire or need, the ceremony of reproduction, say. In this "family," genital logic, blood logic, the logic of possession and entailment, the logic of speciation, the figural realm in which ontogeny and phylogeny stand in solid continuity, even the logic of election that would allow me, sovereign over my decisions, to choose my bond unsanctioned by any ceremony—all these stand deposed. The operator of defection subjects these logics to the divided sovereignty of the heterologics of contingency. Can I count these? Not without some violence. *What* counts (under certain circumstances, for now, for you, for me, for her, here) as being-together, *what* counts as "a relation," as well as who, what, when, under what conditions, for what purposes, for whom, and so on—the mobile, ephemeral aspectuality of differential and *differantial* negotiation and translation.

I offered at the beginning of this chapter the suggestion that republicanism in its most radical form is the intractable governance of defective institutions, and that coming up with a conception of sovereignty or governance that retains and radicalizes the phrase's ambiguity is a precondition of the republic. That *constructive* project must be the practical goal of critique *today.*

NOTES

1. For a review of the term *contubernio*'s genealogy and uses, see J. A. Benimeli Ferrer, *El Contubernio Judeo-Masónico-Comunista* (1982).

2. For reenvisionings of the University-institution in the wake of Readings, Brown and Carasso, see the collection of essays edited by Willy Thayer, *La Universidad (im)posible* (2018).

BIBLIOGRAPHY

Benimeli Ferrer, J. A. 1982. *El Contubernio Judeo-Masónico-Comunista: Del Satanismo Al Escándalo De La P-2*. Madrid: ISTMO.

Benjamin, Walter. 2004. *Selected Writings I*, edited by Marcus Bullock and Michael W. Jennings. Cambridge, MA: Harvard University Press.

Breton, Stanislas. [1989] 2017. "'Dieu est Dieu': Essai sur la violence des propositions tautologiques." In *Philosophie buissonnière*, edited by Stanislas Breton. Grenoble: Millon, 1989, 133–140. Translation by Jacques Lezra, "'God is God': Essay on the Violence of Tautological Propositions." In "Allegory and Political Representation." *Yearbook of Comparative Literature* (2017), 203–211.

Brown, Roger, and Helen Carasso. 2013. *Everything for Sale? The Marketisation of UK Higher Education*. Abingdon: Routledge.

Dostoevsky, Fyodor. 1997. *Winter Notes on Summer Impressions*, translated by David Patterson. Evanston, IL: Northwestern University Place, 1997.

Harney, Stefano, and Fred Moten. 2013. *The Undercommons: Fugitive Planning & Black Study*. New York: Minor Compositions.

Preston, Paul. 2012. *The Spanish Holocaust: Inquisition and Extermination in Twentieth-Century Spain*. New York: Norton.

Primo de Rivera, José Antonio. 1949. *Revolución nacional: Puntos de Falange*. Madrid: Ediciones Prensa del Movimiento.

Readings, Bill. [1996] 1999. *The University in Ruins*. Cambridge, MA: Harvard University Press.

Robin, Corey. 2017. "American Institutions Won't Keep Us Safe from Donald Trump's Excesses." *The Guardian*, 2 February 2017. https://www.theguardian.com/commentisfree/2017/feb/02/american-institutions-wont-keep-you-safe-trumps-excesses. Accessed March 23, 2020.

Thayer, Willy, Elizabeth Collingwood-Selby, Mary Luz Estupin, and Ral Rodrguez Freire (eds.). 2018. *La Universidad (im)posible*. Santiago: Ediciones Macul.

Wynter, Sylvia. 1984. "The Ceremony Must be Found: After Humanism." *Boundary 2* 12 (3): 19–70.

———. 1987. "On Disenchanting Discourse: 'Minority' Literary Criticism and Beyond." *Cultural Critique* 7 (II): 207–244.

———. 1992. "*No Humans Involved:* An Open Letter to My Colleagues." *Voices of the African Diaspora* 8 (2): 13–16.

———. 2015. "The Ceremony Found: Towards the Autopoetic Turn/Overturn, Its Autonomy of Human Agency and Extraterritoriality of (Self-)Cognition." In *Black Knowledges/Black Struggles: Essays in Critical Epistemology*, edited by Jason R. Ambroise and Sabine Broeck. Liverpool: Liverpool University Press, 184–252.

Index

abstraction, 12–13, 79, 122, 134–35; abstraction-as-epistemology, 164; of capital, 166–70; of the Other, 170–71; of whiteness, 161–66
Adorno, Theodor W., 11, 58, 61–62, 70
aesthetic education, 12, 78, 119–24; as training of the imagination, 121, 123
Agre, Philip E., 13, 180, 183, 189, 192–96. *See also* practices, critical practise; technical practise
Ailey, Alvin, 162
algorithm, 13, 179–80, 195–96; algorithmic governmentality, 184–85, 187, 196; machine-learning, 13, 179
alienation effect [*Verfremdungseffeckte*], 65; V-effect, 65, 67, 74. *See also* Brecht, Bertolt
Anthropocene, 78
anti-Blackness, 166–67, 173–74
Attridge, Derek, 120–21
Atwood, Margaret, 21, 146, 148
Autopoiesis: autopoetic institution, 205–7; autopoetic systems, 112, 205, 213; Autopoetic Turn/Overturn, 23–29, 101, 112, 205

Barad, Karen, 26–28, 31–32, 196
Barthes, Roland, 65–66, 82–84
Benjamin, Walter, 181, 184, 211
Bernard, Claude, 141–42, 145

Best, Stephen, 102–5, 107, 110, 113
Bloch, Ernst, 11, 29–30, 58–62, 70, 86–87. *See also* Utopia
Bourdieu, Pierre, 99
Brecht, Bertolt, 11, 57–58, 62–72. *See also* pedagogium, pedagogy
Breton, Stanislas, 211, 214–16
Brewster, Ben, 64, 68
Brooks, Cleanth, 102, 103
Browne, Simone, 166
Butler, Judith, 12, 151–52
Butler, Octavia, 32

Camus, Albert, 44, 51–53
capitalism, 58, 81, 140, 165–66; capitalism-patriarchy-colonialism (CPC), 8, 118, 124, 140; Integrated World Capitalism (IWC), 152; racialized capitalism, 161, 165
Castiglia, Chris, 78, 81
Césaire, Aimé, 25, 112, 129
change, 24–25, 29, 87, 104, 189; changeability [*Veränderbarkeit*], 57, 71. *See also* Brecht, Bertolt; changing methods, 31, 66–67, 133, 152; climate, 5, 11, 98–101, 105–6, 113–14, 123; social, 20–21, 152, 155, 170. *See also* differentiation; Heidegger, Martin; transformation
Coetzee, J. M., 120

coloniality of Being, 10, 22–28, 31, 173
Connolly, William, 150–51
constructive engagement, 194–95
contubernium, 202–3; conubium, 202, 217
COVID-19, 2, 9, 19, 77, 90, 97–98, 113, 117–18, 133, 208
critique: critical intimacy, 12, 117, 119, 124–35; critiquiness, 78, 81; Crrritique, 3, 104; ends of, 7–12, 21, 42, 53, 133, 140–41, 149; postcritique, 3–4, 6, 22, 80–81; situated critique, 6, 98. *See also* *epicritique*; Foucault, Michel

DeFrantz, Thomas, 162
Deleuze, Gilles, 13, 15, 149, 180, 182, 189–94
Derrida, Jacques, 10–11, 19–20, 41–54, 82, 101–3, 108–13, 119; "The Ends of Man", 1, 10, 101, 108–9; *Given Time*, 10, 44–52; *Theory & Practice*, 19–20
differentiation, 6–7, 88. *See also* transdifferentiation
diffraction, 26–28, 32; diffractive approach, 9
digital subject, 184–87, 194, 196; digital technology, 13, 180–89, 196
Drucker, Joanna, 184, 196

ecologies, 7, 9, 29, 100; *The Three Ecologies*, 10, 152. *See also* Guattari, Félix; *Un/Limited Ecologies*, 27, 28. *See also* Kirby, Vicki
Enlightenment, 13, 118, 122, 124, 173, 180; European, 4, 8. *See also* Foucault, Michel
entanglement, 7–8, 30–31, 107; colonial, 9; as planetary condition, 5
epicritique, 11, 78, 80, 87, 90–91. *See also* critique
epigenesis, 11, 78–79, 85–87
ethics, 43, 140–42, 149–50, 155, 170; ethical sensibility, 12, 140–41, 149–55; ethics of reading, 110, 119–21

Fanon, Frantz, 12, 25, 28, 113, 117–19, 122; *Black Skin, White Masks*, 12, 25, 124–25; "Fanon Reading Hegel", 124–26, 129–31
Felski, Rita, 80–81, 89, 104–5, 107
Ferreira da Silva, Denise, 23–24, 28, 31
force relations, 182–86, 191, 194–95. *See also* Foucault, Michel; *rapports de force*, 183
Foucault, Michel, 10, 13, 82, 186–92, 194; critique of Man, 23; genealogy, 150–53, 189. *See also* Nietzsche; governmentality, 183–84. *See also* governance; "What is Aufklärung [enlightenment]?", 143, 180–81;"What is critique?", 179–84. *See also* critique

Gallop, Jane, 81–82
Glissant, Édouard, 31–32
god-trick, 81–83
Goriunova, Olga, 183–85, 191, 195
governance, 6, 181–82, 201, 204, 217; algorithmic governmentality, 184–87, 196; neoliberal governance, 9, 117; small-r republican governance, 13, 203. *See also* Foucault, Michel; institution, defective
Grosz, Elizabeth, 70, 189
Guattari, Félix, 10, 12, 152
Gutierrez, Miguel, 12, 162–64. *See also* abstraction, of whiteness

Haraway, Donna, 15, 98, 183; *Staying With the Trouble*, 104, 107–8. *See also* god-trick
Hartman, Saidiya, 117, 166–72
Hegel, G. W. F., 12, 90, 108–9, 119, 190, 195; *The Future of Hegel*, 87–88; Hegelian tradition, 6, 215–16. *See also* Fanon, Frantz
Heidegger, Martin, 90, 108–10; *The Heidegger Change*, 79, 85–86
hermeneutics of suspicion, 3–4. *See also* Ricoeur, Paul

humanism, 1, 25–27, 32, 108–10, 113; after humanism, 10, 22–27, 101; liberal humanism, 6; monohumanism, 23–24; posthumanism, 10; Western humanism, 10–11, 23–24

innocence, 7, 49; non-innocence, 15; *White Innocence*, 15. *See also* Derrida, Jacques
institution, 1, 4–5, 7–9, 11, 63–64, 66, 68, 97, 201, 206; autopoetic institution. *See* autopoiesis, autopoetic institution; defective institution, 13, 203–4, 207–8, 211, 216–17; university as, 8–9, 205, 211–16; whiteness as, 127, 130, 164, 172–73

Jameson, Fredric, 81, 103

Kant, Immanuel, 13, 85, 90, 151, 180, 184, 210; Kantian liberal tradition, 6; Kantian philosophy, 190; "Was ist Aufklärung?", 196. *See also* Foucault, Michel
Keeling, Kara, 31–32
Kirby, Vicki, 27–28, 32
kritische Haltung, 57, 67. *See also* Brecht, Bertolt

Latour, Bruno, 2–5, 98–107, 112–13, 184; Latourian redescription, 107–8; matters of concern, 105

Mackenzie, Adrien, 183–84, 186
Malabou, Catherine, 11, 78–80, 82–88. *See also* Hegel, G.W.F., *The Future of Hegel*
"Man", 11, 22–26, 33, 100–101, 108–9, 167, 173; "Man 2", 23, 98, 101, 111, 128, 174, 205; *homo oeconomicus*, 23, 101; modern Man, 11, 100–101. *See also* Wynter, Sylvia
Marcus, Sharon, 102–5, 107, 110, 113
Marin, Louis, 61–62

Maturana, Humberto, 24
Mauss, Marcel, 49
McKittrick, Katherine, 23, 26, 28, 166
Meyssan, Thierry, 99
Milkman, 141, 145–48, 151, 153–55
Moretti, Franco, 102
Morozov, Evgueny, 191
Moten, Fred, 30–32, 208, 211, 216
Muñoz, José Esteban, 29–32

necropolitics, 117
Nietzsche, Friedrich, 12, 149–51, 153, 190–92. *See also* vivisection

pedagogium, 11, 61, 64–71; pedagogy, 25, 66, 68–69, 215
pharmakon, 45
plasticity, 11, 78, 82–83, 85–86, 88–90; destructive plasticity, 79–80. *See also* transdifferentiation
play-acting [*Theaterspielen*], 66, 69–71
practices: critical practice, 61, 65, 70–71, 118, 141, 180–81, 192, 196; micro-practice, 122–23; reading as a practice, 110, 119–20, 123, 132; shock-practice, 65–66; technical practice, 187–89, 192–96. *See also* vivisection
Prévieux, Julien, 71
psychoanalysis, 126, 128

race, 5, 13, 23, 143, 162–64, 167–68, 171–74, 221
reading: reading, ethics of, 110, 119–21; reading as unlearning appropriation, 121–22; rereading, 108–11; suspicion, 111. *See also* suspicion; symptomatic reading, 98, 101–5, 107–11, 113–14. *See also* practices
Readings, Bill, 213–14
redescription, 11, 101, 105, 107–8
Ricoeur, Paul, 3, 59–60, 69
Rieder, Bernard, 183–84, 195
Robin, Corey, 208–10
Robinson, Cedric, 166

Robinson, Kim Stanley, 77–79, 90–91
Rooney, Ellen, 103
Rouvroy, Antoinette, 184, 187

Sharpe, Christina, 162, 165–66
spacetimemattering, 26–28, 33. *See also* Barad, Karen
Spillers, Hortense, 164–67
Spivak, Gayatri, 12, 80, 89, 108, 119–26, 128, 130–32; untranslatability, 120. *See also* practices, critical practise; reading
suspicion, 2–4, 98, 103–5, 110–14, 190. *See also* hermeneutics of suspicion
Symptoms of the Planetary Condition, 3

tautology, 201, 211, 213–14
teleological judgment, 210, 213
temporality, 1, 27, 29, 32, 91; affective temporality, 22; critical temporality, 22, 81; prolepsis, 128
Terra Critica, 1–10, 19, 140, 220
theatre of instruction [*Lehrtheater*], 68
time, 22, 29–32, 46, 85, 100, 107, 216; plasticity of, 79, 83; "today-ness", 8. *See also* Derrida, Jacques; spacetimemattering
transdifferentiation, 83; transdifferentiation, plasticity of, 84. *See also* differentiation

transformation, 11–13, 24, 27–32, 58, 83–84, 86, 89, 121, 135, 174; change difference, 85. *See also* Malabou, Catherine; critique and, 20–21, 32, 78, 118–19, 125, 184. *See also* vivisection

Utopia, 58–62, 123; *Cruising Utopia*, 29–30; *Lectures on Ideology and Utopia*, 59; utopian discourses, 11; utopian vision, 121; *Utopics: Spatial Play*, 60

violence, 13, 23–24, 27, 50–53, 86, 88–89, 130, 207, 211, 215–17; racialized, 146–48, 164–66, 169–70, 174; transcendental, 10, 42–46, 49. *See also* Derrida, Jacques
vivisection, 140–45. *See also* Nietzsche, Friedrich

Weatherby, Leif, 195
whiteness, 13, 127, 162–72, 175. *See* abstraction
Wynter, Sylvia, 101–11, 130, 167, 174, 204–7, 212–13, 215–16; sociogeny, 28, 126–28; thought-practice, 10, 22, 28, 33. *See also* Autopoetic Turn/Overturn; "Man"; spacetimemattering; violence

About the Contributors

Mercedes Bunz is Deputy Head of the Department of Digital Humanities, King's College London. She studied philosophy, art history and media studies at the Free University Berlin and the Bauhaus University Weimar, and wrote her thesis on the history of the internet driven by a deep curiosity about digital technology. Until today, she has not been disappointed by the transforming field that is digital technology, which reliably provides her with new aspects to constantly think about. At the moment, that is artificial intelligence and "machine learning." Mercedes Bunz is heading a research project into "Creative AI" with an AHRC grant and co-leads the Creative AI Lab, a collaboration with the Serpentine Gallery, London. Her last publications are "The Internet of Things" (2018) with Graham Meikle and "The calculation of meaning: on the misunderstanding of new artificial intelligence as culture" published in the journal *Culture, Theory and Critique* (2019).

Birgit Mara Kaiser is Associate Professor of Comparative Literature and Transcultural Aesthetics at Utrecht University in the Netherlands. Her research spans literatures in English, French, and German from the late eighteenth to the twenty-first century, with special interest in aesthetics, affect, and subject-formation. She also publishes in the fields of postcolonial literary studies, critical cultural studies, and feminist new materialism. Book publications include *Figures of Simplicity. Sensation and Thinking in Kleist and Melville* (SUNY 2011), *Singularity and Transnational Poetics* (ed. Routledge 2015) and *Symptoms of the Planetary Condition: A Critical Vocabulary* (Meson Press 2017, with K. Thiele and M. Bunz). She has recently contributed to *Comparative Literature, Interventions, Parallax, Textual Practice* and *PhiloSOPHIA: A Journal of Continental Feminism*. With K. Thiele, she is founding coordinator of *Terra Critica: Interdisciplinary Network for the Critical Humanities* (www.terracritica.net).

Leonard Lawlor is Edwin Erle Sparks Professor of Philosophy and Director of Graduate Studies at Penn State University. Before joining Penn State, he held the chair of Faudree-Hardin University Professor of Philosophy at the University of Memphis (2004–2008). His research interest focuses on nineteenth- and twentieth-century continental philosophy, and his expertise on the tradition of contemporary critical theory (developed in the 1990s especially in the United States) is highly relevant to the network, as is his work on immanence and life. His book publications include *The Implications of Immanence: Towards a New Concept of Life* (which now exists in Italian translation), Fordham University Press, 2006; *Thinking Through French Philosophy: The Being of the Question*, Indiana University Press, 2003; *The Challenge of Bergsonism: Phenomenology, Ontology, Ethics*, Continuum, 2003; *Early Twentieth-Century Continental Philosophy*, Indiana University Press, 2011; as well as *From Violence to Speaking Out*, Edinburgh University Press, 2016. Lawlor is currently working on a book on Bergson and another book on violence.

Jacques Lezra is a Professor of Spanish at the University of California—Riverside, where he teaches classes on Spanish and Latin American literature, culture, and philosophy. His most recent books are *República salvaje: De la naturaleza de las cosas* (2019), *On the Nature of Marx's Things* (2018), and *Untranslating Machines: A Genealogy for the Ends of Global Thought* (2017). He is author of works on Cervantes, and of *Wild Materialism: The Ethic of Terror and the Modern Republic* (2010). With Emily Apter and Michael Wood, he is the coeditor of *Dictionary of Untranslatables* (2014).

Sam McAuliffe is Lecturer in Visual Cultures at Goldsmiths, University of London, where he works in the fields of modern European philosophy and critical theory, with particular emphasis on questions of image, language, and the politics of aesthetic experience. Recent publications have focused on the fiction of Raymond Queneau and René Daumal, and he is currently writing a monograph on the culture of *ressentiment* in modernist literary practice, organized around the motif of self-accusation and the "turn against oneself."

Timothy O'Leary is Professor of Philosophy and Head of the School of Humanities and Languages at UNSW Sydney. He previously spent many years at the University of Hong Kong. His research has been largely in the field of Foucault, ethics, and literature. His work includes the books *Foucault and the Art of Ethics* (2002), *Foucault and Fiction: The Experience Book*

(2009), and the coedited collections *Foucault and Philosophy* (2010), *Ethics in Early China* (2011), and *The Blackwell Companion to Foucault* (2013). His current research focuses on literature and the critique of ethical sensibility.

Esther Peeren is Professor of Cultural Analysis at the University Amsterdam and academic director of the Amsterdam School for Cultural Analysis (ASCA). She directs the ERC-funded project "Imagining the Rural in a Globalizing World" (2018–2023). Recent publications include *The Spectral Metaphor: Living Ghosts and the Agency of Invisibility* (Palgrave, 2014) and the edited volumes *Peripheral Visions in the Globalizing Present* (Brill, 2016, with Hanneke Stuit and Astrid Van Weyenberg), *Global Cultures of Contestation* (Palgrave, 2018, with Robin Celikates, Jeroen de Kloet, and Thomas Poell) and *Other Globes: Past and Peripheral Imaginations of Globalization* (Palgrave, 2019, with Simon Ferdinand and Irene Villaescusa-Illán).

Kathrin Thiele is Associate Professor of Gender Studies and Critical Theory at Utrecht University. Her research intervenes into contemporary debates around systemic in/equalities, de/coloniality, feminist (new) materialism, and critical (post)humanisms. She has published widely on these questions. Her most recent publications include the coedited volume *Biopolitics, Necropolitics, Cosmopolitics: Feminist and Queer Interventions* (Routledge 2021) and a coedited special issue for *Feminist Theory* on "Materiality-Critique-Transformation" (2020). Together with Birgit M. Kaiser, she coordinates *Terra Critica: Interdisciplinary Network of the Critical Humanities* (www.terracritica.net).

Jennifer Wagner-Lawlor is Professor of Women's, Gender, and Sexuality Studies at Penn State University. She has published extensively on utopian literature and feminism. Her most recent work has focused on plastic pollution as an environmental crisis, the concept of plasticity, and the use of art as science communication.

Shannon Winnubst is Chair and Professor of Women's, Gender and Sexuality Studies at Ohio State University. She has written two books, *Way Too Cool: Selling Out Race and Ethics* (Columbia, 2015) and *Queering Freedom* (Indiana, 2006), as well as many essays spanning feminist theory, queer studies, philosophy of race, and twentieth-century French philosophy. She is currently working on the figures of non/personhood, white death, and the transhistorical force of the Door of No Return.

Made in United States
North Haven, CT
27 September 2022